The Church on the World's Turf

Recent titles in
RELIGION IN AMERICA SERIES
Harry S. Stout, General Editor

Saints in Exile
The Holiness-Pentecostal Experience in
    African American Religion and Culture
Cheryl J. Sanders

Democratic Religion
Freedom, Authority, and Church Discipline
    in the Baptist South, 1785–1900
Gregory A. Willis

The Soul of Development
Biblical Christianity and Economic
    Transformation in Guatemala
Amy L. Sherman

The Viper on the Hearth
Mormons, Myths, and the
    Construction of Heresy
Terryl L. Givens

Sacred Companies
Organzational Aspects of Religion and
    Religious Aspects of Organizations
Edited by N. J. Demerath III,
    Peter Dobkin Hall, Terry Schmitt,
    and Rhys H. Williams

*Mary Lyon and the Mount Holyoke
    Missionaries*
Amanda Porterfield

Being There
Culture and Formation in Two
    Theological Schools
Jackson W. Carroll, Barbara G. Wheeler,
    Daniel O. Aleshire, and
    Penny Long Marler

The Character of God
Recovering the Lost Literary Power of
    American Protestantism
Thomas E. Jenkins

The Revival of 1857–58
Interpreting an American
    Religious Awakening
Kathryn Teresa Long

American Madonna
Images of the Divine Woman in
    Literary Culture
John Gatta

Our Lady of the Exile
Diasporic Religion at a Cuban Catholic
    Shrine in Miami
Thomas A. Tweed

Taking Heaven by Storm
Methodism and the Rise of Popular
    Christianity in America
John H. Wigger

Encounters with God
An Approach to the Theology of
    Jonathan Edwards
Michael J. McClymond

*Evangelicals and Science in
    Historical Perspective*
Edited by David N. Livingstone,
    D. G. Hart and Mark A. Noll

*Methodism and the Southern Mind,
    1770–1810*
Cynthia Lynn Lyerly

Princeton in the Nation's Service
Religious Ideals and Educational Practice,
    1868–1928
P. C. Kemeny

Church People in the Struggle
The National Council of Churches and the
    Black Freedom Movement, 1950–1970
James F. Findlay Jr.

Tenacious of their Liberties
The Congregationalists in
    Colonial Massachusetts
James F. Cooper Jr.

Nothing but Christ
Rufus Anderson and the Ideology of
    Protestant Foreign Missions
Paul William Harris

The Church on the World's Turf

*An Evangelical Christian Group
at a Secular University*

Paul A. Bramadat

OXFORD
UNIVERSITY PRESS
2000

OXFORD
UNIVERSITY PRESS

Oxford   New York
Athens   Auckland   Bangkok   Bogotá   Buenos Aires   Calcutta
Cape Town   Chennai   Dar es Salaam   Delhi   Florence   Hong Kong   Istanbul
Karachi   Kuala Lumpur   Madrid   Melbourne   Mexico City   Mumbai
Nairobi   Paris   São Paulo   Singapore   Taipei   Tokyo   Toronto   Warsaw

and associated companies in
Berlin   Ibadan

Copyright © 2000 by Paul A. Bramadat

Published by Oxford University Press, Inc.
198 Madison Avenue, New York, New York 10016

Oxford is a registered trademark of Oxford University Press

Library of Congress Cataloging-in-Publication Data
Bramadat, Paul A.
The church on the world's turf : an evangelical Christian group at
a secular university / Paul A. Bramadat.
p.   cm. — (Religion in America series)
Includes bibliographical references and index.
ISBN 0-19-513499-0
1. Inter-Varsity Christian Fellowship.   2. Christian college
students — Religious life — Ontario — Hamilton.   3. Christianity and
culture — Ontario — Hamilton.   4. McMaster University — Students —
Religious life.   I. Title.   II. Series: Religion in America series
(Oxford University Press)
BV970.I6B73   2000
306.6'6761'0971352 — dc21   99-16827

1 3 5 7 9 8 6 4 2
Printed in the United States of America
on acid-free paper

For Karen

Preface

As we enter this new century, it seems more and more likely that two of the most significant changes we see in North America[1] are intimately and perhaps dialectically related: the increasing levels of economic and cultural globalization and, in response, the genesis of new forms of tribalism. In the religious sphere, or more specifically, in the interaction between religion and culture, one witnesses a related dialectical process. Over the past century (but especially in the past thirty-five years), many of our main institutions have been re-created along either fully secular (largely post-Christian) or at least religiously pluralistic lines. And in response to these processes in North America, we have seen the rise of a form of conservative Protestantism which seeks (creatively and effectively, as we shall see) to protect its heritage and the putative Christian foundations of Western civilization, both of which are, they tell us, under siege.

As far as many of these Protestants are concerned, they are foot soldiers in nothing less than the battle for both the soul of North America and the souls of North Americans. But there is a limit to the usefulness of this kind of generalization. True, we may be witnessing a struggle between worldviews or ideologies. However, I am more and more convinced that if we want to make any progress in our understanding of the tension between what we might (vaguely, I admit) call modernism-secularism-pluralism on the one hand and various kinds of religious exclusivism on the other hand, we need to analyze specific sites of this struggle through a more finely calibrated lens. Discussions of secularization, differentiation, and other general explanations of current trends will remain strictly academic unless these debates are embedded in the actual experience of individuals and groups.

As a means of exploring crucial issues in the relationship between contemporary culture and traditional religion, I conducted extensive fieldwork with the Inter-Varsity Christian Fellowship chapter at McMaster University in southern Ontario. Throughout my fieldwork, I benefited from the grace and generosity of many people. Buff Cox, the chapter's competent and indefatigable staff worker, was remarkably open to and supportive of my research. Her compassion, intelligence, and respectful comprehension of my project were indispensable. On several occasions when I has having a difficult time understanding an individual member or a group process, she provided sage and timely insights which greatly facilitated my analysis.

Because I have agreed to protect the anonymity of the group's student members as much as I can, I cannot thank the majority of other people whose cooperation made this project possible and enjoyable. However, I trust that the group's president and the members of the executive committee, the Lithuania team, the How to Give Your Faith Away Small Group, the Large Group Worship Band, and many others who shared their lives with me know that I am extremely grateful. These young Christians—especially the president and the Lithuania team—"stretched" and "discipled" me more than they can know.

A few months after I left Ontario, one of the senior members of the group conveyed her qualified approbation of an early draft of this book. She wrote that she felt I had done an excellent job of understanding the group, its language, customs, symbolic substructure, members, and relationship with the non-Christian world. However, she felt I had missed something important during my research because, to use evangelical rhetoric, I had not been drawn closer to Christ. I know that this criticism of my project (and, in truth, of me) was not hers alone. I am unsure how to respond to these critics except by saying that I tried throughout this project to remain both intellectually and emotionally open to their Lord, but in the end I did not feel drawn into a relationship with Jesus. I do feel, however, that I now have a much better and more sympathetic understanding of what such a relationship means to them. For now—for me—that is enough.

During my research at McMaster University, I was very fortunate to receive encouragement, friendship, and constructive criticism from several extremely capable scholars. Louis Greenspan and Richard Preston from McMaster and John Simpson from the University of Toronto provided penetrating analyses and read early drafts of this book. John Robertson from McMaster helped to focus some of my reflections during many edifying bicycle excursions around the spectacular rural regions of southern Ontario. Finally, I can hardly overstate the influence of McMaster's Ellen Badone on both this book and my intellectual development. I was especially fortunate that her superb and painstaking scholarly abilities are complemented by her tireless and sensitive mentorship. Although I take full responsibility for this book and its weaknesses, my debt to these other scholars is immense.

I would also like to thank executive editor Cynthia Read and production editor MaryBeth Branigan at Oxford University Press. Their confidence in this project is greatly appreciated. My wife, Karen Palmer, has been an inexhaustible source of reassurance and perceptive critical feedback. In many ways, she has been the midwife of this project.

University of Winnipeg   P. B.
Winnipeg, Manitoba
12 March 1999

Contents

ONE   Introduction   3

TWO   Four Life Histories   26

THREE   IVCF Rhetoric   53

FOUR   Otherness   70

FIVE   The Role of Women   90

SIX   Satan and the Spiritual Realm   102

SEVEN   Witnessing at McMaster and Abroad   119

EIGHT   Conclusion   139

Notes   151

Bibliography   183

Index   201

The Church on the World's Turf

ONE

Introduction

One warm Sunday evening in September 1993, I found myself walking aimlessly around the McMaster University campus. Earlier the same week, I had seen a poster advertising "Church at the John," an event organized by the McMaster chapter of the Inter-Varsity Christian Fellowship (IVCF). Since I was academically interested in conservative Protestantism, and since at that point I knew no one in the city, I decided, for lack of other options, to attend this meeting. What I found there fell completely outside my expectations, prompted an elaborate series of questions, and ultimately resulted in the present book.

Since I assumed that the meeting would be small, I worried that being ten minutes late might draw unwanted attention to my presence. As I descended the stairs of the Downstairs John (or simply "the John"), McMaster's largest student bar, I could hear the noises of a large group of people. I thought I might have misread the poster a few days earlier; when I entered the bustling room, I was virtually certain I had.

Except for the well-lit stage at one end of the room, the John was dark, and almost six hundred people were crowded into a space designed for no more than four hundred and fifty. The room was narrow and long, with a low stage at one end, pool tables at the opposite end, and a bar along the side of the room. People were standing and sitting in the aisles, on the bar, and against the walls beneath the bikini-clad models and slogans that festooned the neon beer signs. I discreetly asked one person who was standing against the wall if this was the right room for the IVCF meeting, and he replied that it was. I looked at him more intently to determine if he was joking, but he just smiled at me politely and bowed his head. After a few confusing moments, I realized he was praying. I turned away from him and noticed that all the other people in the room had bowed their heads in a prayer being led by a demure young woman on the stage.

I had to proceed slowly and sideways to make my way through the throngs of people filling the minimal standing room. After the prayer was over, the "worship band" mounted the stage and led the audience in singing several upbeat folk-rock worship songs, the lyrics of which were projected onto three white bedsheets hung from the ceiling throughout the room. Everyone sang heartily, and some people swayed, closed their eyes, and raised their hands as they sang. Standing in the middle of a large group of other latecomers, I was struck by my neighbours' fervor. For the next three hours, I was absorbed in this event, which also included announcements, skits, and a forty-five minute sermon.

I had attended four Canadian universities during the course of my undergraduate and graduate education and had never experienced any event (including sporting events) at which so many students displayed so much of what the French sociologist Émile Durkheim would have called "collective effervescence" (1973:181), the solidarity-producing enthusiasm which is sometimes generated during large gatherings. I experienced an unsettling moment of cognitive dissonance (Festinger 1962) when I remembered I was standing in a campus bar, its floors still sticky from the previous night's revelry, singing, "As the deer panteth for the water, so my soul longs after you." I am not a Christian, so the words of these songs (in this case, from Psalm 42) probably meant something quite different for me than they did for my neighbors. But still, somehow the act of singing and being with so many spirited believers drew me closer to the uneasy lives of the members of McMaster's Inter-Varsity Christian Fellowship. Since this initial exposure to the IVCF, I have entered more fully into the social and religious lives of these Christians. The official context of this immersion was the ethnographic research I conducted between 1994 and 1996 within this student-led, nondenominational evangelical group.

Context and Methodology

The IVCF group at McMaster is the largest and most active chapter in Canada, with a total membership of more than two hundred students[1] of a campus population of approximately fourteen thousand. Although the following seven chapters of this book provide the descriptive texture essential for understanding this diverse group, some preliminary generalizations will provide a rough sense of the group's composition. The participants are almost exclusively white and approximately 70 percent female. Most of them were raised in conservative evangelical families. Based on the interviews and observations I conducted, McMaster IVCF members belong mainly to the middle and upper-middle classes. The IVCF includes evangelical Christians from a wide variety of denominations: from Mennonites to Baptists to Pentecostals to Brethren to Presbyterians. The Canadian IVCF has chapters in well over fifty universities, forty colleges, three hundred high schools (through Inter-

School Christian Fellowship), and forty nursing programs (Stackhouse 1993). Its activities in the United States are equally extensive; there are chapters on nearly every postsecondary campus.[2]

Like many other chapters in Canada, the McMaster group has a "staff worker" who raises her own salary through direct appeals to students, parents, and community leaders, as well as through fund-raising events. The McMaster chapter's staff worker is Elizabeth "Buff" Cox,[3] a forty-year-old ordained Baptist woman with deep roots in the Hamilton community. Cox pays special attention to the composition and direction of the chapter's "executive committee," comprised of eight students,[4] who, with Cox, set the tone of the group's activities, oversee the larger mission of the chapter, and try to strike a balance between the various tendencies within the evangelical tradition. Although the IVCF is officially student-led, with Cox serving technically only as a trained advisor, most of the executive committee members admire and rarely contradict her. Nevertheless, group members do not slavishly obey Cox. As we shall see, the group is too complicated to be characterized as a simple hierarchy or an example of charismatic domination.

I conducted participant-observation fieldwork with the McMaster IVCF chapter from January to April 1994 and from September 1995 to June 1996 and was in regular contact with the group before and after these periods. The 1994 period of the research was focused solely on the Church at the John, the event I describe at the beginning of this chapter, and was intended in part to determine whether a larger study would be welcomed by the group's leaders and members. The warm reception I received during this preliminary project convinced me that I would not encounter any serious obstacles from either the group's "gatekeepers" or the general membership.

The fieldwork I conducted entailed attending all of the weekly "large group" worship meetings, "Friday lunch" discussion groups, "small group" Bible studies, monthly Church at the John praise events like the one I described, a weekend retreat in January 1996, and several prayer meetings. As well, I attended and participated in a variety of special events and business meetings, including end-of-term banquets, executive committee and nominating committee meetings, parties, and fund-raisers such as car washes, clothing drives, and all-you-can-eat dessert events. The final and most intensive section of my fieldwork involved joining a group of seven IVCF missionaries on their 1996 mission trip to Lithuania, where the Canadian "team" supported the nascent evangelical groups that have emerged on Lithuanian campuses. This final stage of fieldwork entailed participating in fund-raising, pretrip meetings, a full-day posttrip debriefing session, and posttrip social events. After spending three weeks in Lithuania with the mission team, I accompanied them as they enjoyed a five-day holiday in Saint Petersburg, Russia.

During my fieldwork, I conducted sixty open-ended interviews with members of the chapter. About three-quarters of the participants in these interviews were drawn from a sign-up sheet I circulated after I formally introduced myself to the participants at one of the first large group meetings in September 1995. I personally invited other members to participate in interviews because they seemed to be key members of the group, represented an interesting position on some issue, or were absent when the original sign-up sheet was passed around. During interviews, I collected information on each member concerning his or her present age, age and context of conversion, denominational background,[5] parents' denominational background, academic discipline, and other factors. We spent most of our interview time discussing a loosely structured series of questions I had prepared in advance.[6] Their answers determined the pace and essential content of these conversations, which lasted an average of one and a half hours. In addition to conducting formal interviews with these sixty students, in the two years I spent with the group, I had the opportunity to interact in a variety of ways with dozens of students I never officially interviewed. As the information in Table 1 indicates, the sixty students in the official data set represent a wide variety of evangelical beliefs and backgrounds.

Only about half of those I interviewed appeared to have strong attachments to a particular church or denomination, probably because many of these students were living away from their homes. For example, many of the twenty-four students in the Fellowship Baptist category attend the same church, largely because of its charismatic pastor and proximity to the McMaster campus.[7] Consequently, it is important to be cautious when drawing conclusions from the differences between participants' denominational backgrounds and their current affiliations.

These statistics do not accurately reflect the importance of the Pentecostal and related charismatic or neo-Pentecostal movements.[8] While very few IVCF students are members of explicitly Pentecostal congregations, the general liturgical, spiritual, and rhetorical tendencies introduced or embodied by this tradition have had a significant influence on (especially young) evangelicals in North America. The pop-

Table 1. Inter-Varsity Christian Fellowship study group demographics (60 participants)

	Denominational Background*	Present Church Affiliation
Anglican	3	0
Associated Gospel	0	3
Brethren	6	0
Canadian Reformed	2	0
Christian Reformed	6	3
Convention Baptist	10	8
Fellowship Baptist	4	24
Mission Baptist	0	4
Nazarene	2	0
Pentecostal	3	3
United Church	9	2
Vineyard Christian Fellowship	0	2
Other Evangelical	11	9
None	4	0

N = 60: male, 26; female, 34.
Age at time of study: 19 years old, 15; 20 years old, 9; 21 years old, 16; 22 years old, 9; 23 years old, 5; 24+ years old, 6.
Age at time of conversion: 4–7 years old, 17; 8–11 years old, 8; 12–15 years old, 9; 16–20 years old, 16; no specific date, 10.
Academic disciplines: engineering, 8; humanities, 8; kinesiology, 5; natural sciences, 10; nursing, 5; social sciences, 19; social work/occupational therapy, 5.
*Refers to the churches in which students received the majority of their religious education.

ularity of highly enthusiastic and demonstrative public worship, the prevalent use of full-scale folk-rock bands in churches, and the renewed interest in speaking (and praying) in tongues are just three examples of practices that have been cultivated (though not invented) by these movements. The impact of these traditions is quite evident in the IVCF and is just beginning to be discussed by members of the group. Although an exhaustive consideration of this influence is beyond the scope of the present book, in several places in subsequent chapters, I engage in focused discussions of the role of this element in IVCF discourse.

Ethnography, the social-scientific tradition that undergirds this work, is barely a century old. Nevertheless, even in its short history, ethnography has undergone major upheavals. Since the mid-1970s, ethnographers have largely abandoned the positivistic ideal of scientific objectivity in favor of a more modest and reflexive dialogue with the people they study.[9] Marcus and Fischer (1986) argue that current shifts in cultural anthropology are derived from a "crisis of representation," which has affected most human sciences. Marcus and Fischer are referring to the thorough undermining of academic confidence that it is possible to represent a group of people adequately without objectifying or diminishing them. In response to this predicament, previously well-respected divisions between academic disciplines and modes of writing have been deteriorating. Two decades after Geertz's groundbreaking work (1973), ethnographer Robert Pool wrote: "The blurring of boundaries within ethnography and between ethnography and other disciplines and genres has, especially since Geertz and the literary turn, become commonplace. The boundaries between fact and fiction and personal and subjective and interpersonal anthropological experience have become less sharply defined" (1991:325).

While early ethnographers assumed they could visually engulf their subjects, coolly observing them with an unwavering scientific eye, in *Writing Culture*, James Clifford observes that current ethnographic approaches are based on "a discursive rather than a visual paradigm" (1986:12; Marcus 1994:48). A discursive paradigm allows both the writer's and the participants' "voices" to be "heard." Whether one calls this new approach "experimental" (Marcus 1994), "post-modern" (Tyler 1986), "reflexive" (Myerhoff and Ruby 1982), or "discursive," this form of ethnography has elucidated the larger "social discourses" (Geertz 1973:20) in which our participants' discrete utterances make sense.[10] Instead of the putatively clear separation between scientist and subjects that exists in other social sciences, recent ethnographic work has opted for a relational mode of study which allows these boundaries to be both criticized and compromised.

Although most contemporary ethnographers are aware of the dangers of what Edward Said (1978) has called "orientalism," the projection of a brittle and sometimes romantic otherness onto one's participants, ethnographic research typically entails the study of an exotic or at least distant community of people who, on the surface at least, are very different from most residents of modern, Western, capitalist societies.[11] There is an implicit assumption among some ethnographers that serious fieldwork requires traveling, learning new languages, and some measure of physical danger or discomfort. The distance and danger entailed in most field studies not only create an aura of authority around both the project and the ethnogapher but also may result in turning an ethnographer's subjects into ossified, remote others.

Moreover, ethnographers may also depersonalize their subjects though the medium of time, as well as through geographical space. Ethnographers often implicitly or explicitly treat their others as existing not simply "over there," in a fundamentally mysterious place, but "back then," in a simpler, more traditional time. Ethnographer Johannes Fabian argues that conventional ethnographies often promoted western hegemony by accommodating "the schemes of a one-way history: progress, development, modernity (and their negative mirror images: stagnation, underdevelopment, tradition). In short, *geopolitics* has its ideological foundations in *chronopolitics*" (1983:144).

Largely because of the work of researchers such as Marcus and Fischer (1986), Fabian (1983), and Clifford and Marcus (1986), ethnographers are more aware of the spatial and temporal modes of objectification, both of which have been part of anthropology since its inception. But even in the midst of our growing awareness of our complicity in objectification, we might more optimistically propose that contemporary ethnographies may now allow the "voices" of others to be heard in a more nuanced manner than once was the case. Moreover, understanding these others in a less arrogant, more dialogical way may enable us to grasp more critically the assumptions on which our own cultures are based.

It is not necessary for groups of people to head-hunt, practice ritual scarification, or fire-walk to merit ethnographic attention. Careful consideration of the North American groups and institutions that are our less remarkable cultural neighbors often reveals profoundly unfamiliar cultural practices (DaMatta 1994; Jackson 1987). In fact, the cultural heritage and symbols North American ethnographers share with these apparently familiar others may present a more difficult and interesting obstacle than unfamiliar languages, unusual foods, and illnesses do in the ethnography of exotic peoples. A great deal can be overlooked when the "natives" being studied dress, eat, speak, and, for the most part, behave in the same way as the ethnographer. However, when geographically and culturally proximate ethnographies are at their best,[12] they can elucidate the creative ways in which people rearrange superficially familiar symbolic and cultural patterns to suit their unique situations and needs. In so doing, such studies offer us an opportunity to hear a previously unheard "voice."

Ethnographer Renato Rosaldo writes: "If classic ethnography's vice was the slippage from the ideal of detachment to actual indifference, that of present-day reflexivity is the tendency for the self-absorbed Self to lose sight of the culturally different other" (1989:7). Such an effacement of the other is always a possibility in explicitly postmodern ethnographies, especially those which emphasize "discourse," "poetics," and the coconstruction of ethnographic texts (Clifford and Marcus 1986; Tedlock 1983; Tyler 1986:126). While the deprivileging of the hermeneutical conventions that once guided ethnography clearly allows us, as it were, to hear a fuller and more dynamic range of voices, I would suggest that it is also important not to abandon too hastily the empirical (and admittedly sometimes positivistic) tools on which anthropology was dependent until the 1970s.[13]

Since ethnography requires the collaboration of a writer and a group of others, it is crucial that the writer includes in the text some sort of reflection on his or her impressions; otherwise, a central and definitive element of the encounter is missing from the ethnography. In short, ethnography is always part autobiography. However, while this personal, or interpersonal, component is arguably a vital element of any ethnographic study, Rosaldo fairly warns scholars not to use this method to pursue their own self-justification or self-exploration. Following this caution, I include my psychological and emotional impressions and reactions in this study, but I attempt to do so judiciously.

As a Unitarian Universalist, I was raised in family and religious milieux extremely suspicious of religious conservativism.[14] While tolerance is a core religious value of Unitarianism, early in my prefieldwork period I realized that I was predisposed to be tolerant of almost everyone except evangelicals and fundamentalists, whose rational faculties, I once supposed, must be repressed or overly enchanted. However, my sense of their intellectual immaturity (if I am to be honest about my previous view) was radically challenged as I learned during my fieldwork that many of my assumptions about evangelicals were not simply incorrect but unfair.[15] Throughout my research, my resistance to several aspects of evangelicalism was mollified as I came very close to viewing our world through evangelical eyes.

Many of the IVCF students I encountered were at least nominally aware of my religious background. Consequently, several of them were eager to discuss and debate Unitarian theology. I was drawn again and again (and sometimes slightly against my will) into conversations about heaven and hell, my more inclusive understanding of salvation, my egalitarian views about women, and other topics on which we often fundamentally disagreed. Although such conversations could have driven a wedge between myself and IVCF members, in most cases, our theological, ideological, and moral differences served as points of entry into many issues we might otherwise have never discussed.

The IVCF students usually adopted a thoroughly respectful approach to my own religious tradition, even when they politely informed me of its errors and of the grave eternal ramifications. They sought to understand and refute my faith; however, this endeavor stemmed not only from their radically different convictions but also from the friendship and respect that had emerged between us. Although I was initially irritated by their concern for my endangered soul, eventually I came to appreciate that my friends, almost all of whom have very well-defined ideas about the afterlife, simply wanted to prevent me from burning in hell for eternity. The sincerity of my new friends' fairly regular (and sometimes, it seemed, almost scheduled) attempts to "draw me closer to Christ" affected me considerably. I could discern the anguish on their faces when I remained respectfully steadfast. "You know so much," an earnest second-year student said during an interview, "and we know you're close. We just don't understand why you won't become a Christian."[16]

One day in Lithuania, a member of the IVCF mission team revealed just how "close" he thought I was to conversion. The IVCF participants sometimes speak of the "God scale," a scale on which zero represents being born, fifty represents the decision to become a Christian, and one hundred represents the end of a life fully devoted to God. "Sometimes our job is just to help someone move from twenty-nine to thirty on the God scale," Buff Cox explained one day. "Eventually they have to make the decision. And of course there is no telling what the Holy Spirit can do in that process," she continued. During the mission to Lithuania, I asked a team member where he would situate me on the God scale. He paused for a moment and then responded flatly: "Forty-nine. No question." "Forty-nine and holding," I teased.

The repeated and loving questioning of my IVCF friends, in so many voices and from so many angles, has compelled me to come to terms with several of the inherent problems of my own tradition. As a result, I understand my own form of Unitarianism much better, now that I have lived with evangelicals who in most significant theological and ethical senses are categorically different from Unitarians.

From the point of view of some IVCF members, their interactions with me led to spiritual growth and development as well. To my knowledge, no one has been "led away from Christ" by my participation in the group. Much to my surprise, many IVCF members told me weeks after an interview that our conversation had actually strengthened their faith. In fact, several members claimed that God had "used me" to show them something. To say the least, this is an unusual statement for a Unitarian to hear from an evangelical.

Surprisingly, the IVCF has a historical link with Unitarianism, although few members are aware of this fact. The Canadian IVCF was founded in 1929 as a result of the missionary efforts of the British Inter-Varsity Fellowship (IVF). However, the IVF itself emerged as the conservative side of a 1910 schism in the Student Christian Movement (SCM), which was a fairly loose agglomeration of evangelical students from Oxford and Cambridge universities. The SCM broke into two (liberal and conservative) wings over a variety of issues.[17] One of the most divisive of these involved the question of whether the SCM "Basis of Membership" could be broadened to include Unitarians, who were liberal Christians at that time (Stackhouse 1993:91). "This was the inclusivist principle gone mad!" claimed Oliver Barclay, one of the leaders of the conservative faction (Donald 1991:12). Although I was unaware of this historical episode when I started my research, it stands as a constant and somewhat ironic reminder that the estrangement I sometimes felt from the group has, in fact, a well-entrenched historical precedent.

Terminology

The terms "evangelical" and "fundamentalist" appear regularly in the major media and are often used interchangeably. Although there continues to be debate on their precise meanings (cf. Marty and Appelby 1991), it is important to develop an operational definition of these terms. Throughout this text, I use a modified version of George Marsden's 1991 definition,[18] which lists the defining characteristics of evangelicalism as its emphases on (1) the Reformation doctrine of the final authority of the Bible, (2) the belief that the real historical character of God's saving work is recorded in scripture, (3) the belief that salvation to eternal life is based on the redemptive life of Jesus Christ, (4) evangelism and missionary work, and (5) the necessity of a spiritually transformed life (1991:5).

Unfortunately absent from Marsden's definition is a factor that I have found to be a central and perhaps the definitive element of contemporary evangelicalism as it is expressed by IVCF members—namely, the emphasis on having a "personal relationship" with Jesus Christ.[19] The five elements Marsden describes are definitely important to the evangelicals I met during this project. However, all but the fifth criterion describe theological commitments, which for IVCF members are not as crucial to their faith as their personal relationship with Christ. Marsden's fifth criterion alludes to what IVCF students mean when they speak about the consequences of their personal relationship with God; but since a "spiritually transformed life" absolutely requires this relationship, I think the latter element belongs explicitly in the operational definition I use throughout this study.

What, then, distinguishes evangelicals from fundamentalists? The term "fundamentalism" is normally attributed to Curtis Lee Laws, a Baptist preacher who between 1910 and 1915 published a series of texts titled *The Fundamentals* (Marsden 1988). The term "fundamentalist" originally referred to a person who believed in the conservative, evangelical orthodox teachings explained in *The Fundamentals* (Marsden 1980:107; 1991:57). However, as recent scholarship makes abundantly clear,[20] the contemporary meanings of the term now have little to do with Laws's texts. Furthermore, the term is now used in scholarly and nonscholarly discourse to refer to a wide variety of non-Christian and even nonreligious phenomena throughout the world. Although no single definition of the term can apply to all so-called global fundamentalist phenomena, let me propose a definition of the term in a North American Protestant context. Protestant fundamentalists in the last decades of the twentieth century adhere to all of Marsden's criteria for an evangelical but add to these characteristics a typically militant opposition to (1) liberal theology or (2) what they perceive as the relaxation of cultural values in North America during the past century (Marsden 1980, 1991) or (3) what Bruce Lawrence describes broadly as the ideology of modernism (Lawrence 1989), which undergirds the two previous options and which promotes individualism, feminism, secularism, higher (biblical) criticism, scientism, pluralism, and, ultimately, some form of relativism.[21]

Fundamentalists, in other words, are evangelicals who are, on some level, angry about what they perceive as the disenchanting (Weber 1948) and liberalizing effects of contemporary culture. Radical fundamentalists are inclined toward separation from what IVCF participants call "non-Christian" institutions, but this perspective is indicative of only a minority of North American (mainly U.S.) fundamentalisms.[22]

Although Canadian evangelicalism shares many roots with the analogous American movement, John Stackhouse, perhaps the leading scholar of twentieth-century Canadian evangelicalism, argues that this tradition is neither a "branch plant operation of American groups" nor a "colonial residue" (1993:196).[23] The fundamentalist-modernist split of the 1920s, which continues to shape the relations between evangelicals and fundamentalists in the United States (Wuthnow 1988:12),[24] was not a significant influence in shaping the Canadian tradition (Stackhouse 1993: 200; Gauvreau 1991:11), which is less militant than the analogous American phenomenon (Stackhouse 1993:198). Moreover, while evangelicals in the United States tend to be vocally conservative in their politics (Simpson 1994), it is important to note that this trend has had a limited appeal in Canada (J. Grant 1988:237). McMaster IVCF students reflect this distinction: on the whole, they espouse conservative moral and political sensibilities, but most of them do not identify passionately with a particular political party or ideological movement.[25]

Provided that an emphasis on a personal relationship with Christ was added to his criteria, IVCF members would almost very likely see themselves reflected in Marsden's 1991 definition of evangelicalism. While the IVCF caters to both sides of the theological and moral spectrum within Canadian evangelicalism, the majority of the group's McMaster members may be described as conservative evangelicals or fundamentalists,[26] although they are obviously not of the separatist variety (otherwise they would not attend a "non-Christian" university). But there are also participants who describe themselves, or could be described, as liberal evangelicals in that they accept a less literal interpretation of the Bible, the ordination of women, and a comparably progressive ideology. These two constituencies within the McMaster IVCF are discussed throughout the following chapters.

Although students do not have to agree formally to the following principles to become members, the five official goals of the IVCF are:

1. To witness to the Lord Jesus Christ as God incarnate and to seek to lead others to a personal faith in Him as Saviour and Lord; EVANGELISM IS A PRIME OBJECTIVE;
2. To deepen and strengthen the spiritual life of students and others by the study of the Bible, by fellowship, and by prayer; THE SPIRITUAL DEVELOPMENT OF CHRISTIANS IS AN EQUALLY IMPORTANT OBJECTIVE;
3. To encourage Christians under the enablement of the Holy Spirit to demonstrate responsible Christian love; THE LOVE OF ONE'S NEIGHBOR IS A COMMANDMENT OF THE LORD;
4. To assist Christian students and faculty to explore and assert to the educational community the relevance of the Christian faith to every issue of private life and public concern; ALL TRUTH IS IN CHRIST;
5. To affirm our vocations as full-time service to God; to pray, give and serve in the global mission of the church. EVERY CHRISTIAN IS CALLED TO BE SENT INTO THE WORLD.[27]

I have only met one IVCF student who has referred to this statement explicitly. However, it seems clear that even though most students are probably unaware of these official goals, such principles are already inherent in their own faiths.

Theoretical Issues

Although the present study is neither a defense nor a refutation nor an elaborate discussion of the theory of secularization, this contentious theory forms part of the backdrop of virtually all contemporary discussions about the nature and role of religion in the modern world. Consequently, some kind of consideration of secularization seems in order at this point. Moreover, we need to address the specific relevance of the secularization debate to understanding the Inter-Varsity Christian Fellowship at McMaster. The IVCF is, de jure, nondenominational and open to students of all backgrounds. At many IVCF events, worship leaders encourage participants to "worship in whatever manner you feel comfortable" and advise the audience that the IVCF is neither exclusively Protestant nor a denominationally affiliated group. However, as we shall see, the worship, preaching, and biblical hermeneutical styles commonly practiced at IVCF events are, de facto, broadly evangelical and Protestant.[28]

Because the IVCF is thoroughly evangelical and Protestant in its self-presentation and membership, it is helpful to understand the major interpretations of the evident conservative Protestant vitality in the midst of some degree of mainline religious inertia and, according to many evangelicals, a secularized, permissive society run amok. Because these interpretations are elaborated primarily in discussions about the so-called increasingly secular nature of North American life, it is important to outline the theory of secularization, as well as two of its hermeneutical competitors, and to reflect on the ways they are relevant to an ethnography of the McMaster IVCF. Following these theoretical considerations, I outline the general contours of the argument I present in the next seven chapters.

British sociologist Bryan Wilson, one of the major proponents of the theory of secularization,[29] offers an operational definition of secularization as "a process of transfer of property, power, activities, and both manifest and latent functions, from institutions with a supernaturalist frame of reference to (often new) institutions operating according to empirical, rational, pragmatic criteria" (1985:12). Wilson points out that while "religion once provided legitimacy for secular authority; endorsed and at times sanctioned public policy; . . . was seen as the font of 'true learning'; socialized the young" (1992:200), it no longer officially nor in most cases even unofficially functions in this way. Although Wilson's definition describes the formal role of religion in institutional contexts, secularization may also diminish the intimate role of religion in the cognition and moral sensibilities of believers (Luckmann 1967; Stout 1988).

The inherited model of secularization, Wilson explains, does not necessarily predict the complete disappearance of religion as such. Religion may occasionally reconfigure itself and emerge elsewhere in the culture (Wilson 1985; cf. Stark and Bainbridge 1985). However, when it does reemerge, it does not wield as much social power as it once did. Once it is driven out of government and public education, unless these two institutions opt in the future to reclaim this part of their history, religion cannot play the role it once played and is likely to survive mainly in "a privatized form, at society's margins or interstices" (Bruce 1992:20).

On the surface, "secularization" does not seem to describe the situation of religion in the United States, where (with the exception of the 1960s) personal and public commitment to religion in general has been fairly stable in the twentieth century.[30] As well, of course, the resurgence of conservative Protestantism in the United States in particular seems to constitute a striking refutation of the secularization thesis (Berger 1992). If, on the whole, Americans are, on both public and personal levels, as religious now as they were before World War II (although the nature and dimensions of this spirituality have changed) and are, according to most measurements, more religious than citizens of other Westernized countries, we might argue that the secularization theory must be fundamentally flawed or at least inapplicable to the American scene. According to George Rawlyk (1996), Canadian data also support this critique of the secularization thesis. Rawlyk suggests that liberal scholars have incorrectly assumed that since they and their well-educated peers are less committed to traditional faith, therefore, the majority of the populace must share this experience. On the contrary, Rawlyk argues that ordinary (or, to use his terminology, nonélite) Canadian Christians have retained and, in some cases, increased their personal loyalty to traditional religiosity (1996:54). Canadian surveys continue to evidence a high (86%) and generally stable level of belief in God (Rawlyk 1996:56). The majority of Canadian respondents also maintain some form of affiliation with the denomination in which they were raised (Bibby 1993:128). So, while Hammond and Hunter (1984:221) observe that "it is, beyond debate by almost any definition, that modern society is more secular" than ever before, and while fewer people are explicitly involved in religious groups, survey data seem to support Rawlyk's claim that, on the whole, Canadian Christians are no less personally devout in the 1990s than they were in the nineteenth century (1996:225).

Although this evidence illustrates some of the flaws inherent in what might be called a "vulgar" or positivistic form of secularization theory—which predicts that religion in all forms will simply disappear—it does not nullify a more modest theory of secularization. James D. Hunter, an advocate of such an approach, suggests that the apparent empirical stability of American religiosity may disguise a central shift in its essence. Hunter (1985) contends that the contemporary interest in evangelicalism in North America obscures the fact that to attract members, evangelical churches and parachurch organizations such as the IVCF have succumbed to or compromised with certain aspects of the dominant secularity of the surrounding culture. Hunter writes: "Conservative Protestantism's survival in the modern world can . . . be brought into question. Modernization, in other words, exacts costs from orthodoxy—costs expressed in terms of accommodation" (1985:159).[31]

Thriving evangelical groups in a secular society challenge the secularization thesis and force us to rethink the questions we might ask when studying contemporary religion. Should we understand burgeoning evangelical groups as institutional embodiments of the compromises these groups have been compelled to make with the secular ethos in order to survive (Hunter 1985)? In other words, are these groups growing or even persisting because they have, as it were, sold out to the non-Christian world? Or should we understand these organizations as resolute uprisings against the overwhelming disenchantment (Weber 1948:155) supposedly concomitant with contemporary culture? This second explanation suggests that evangelical groups are temporarily among the most vigorous Christian organizations in the country because they are perceived by adherents as being the least complicitous in the disenchantment cultivated by secularization. Neither one of these interpretations is sufficient. The first approach is valuable because it reminds us to pay attention to the compromises a given group has made with its surrounding cultural milieu (Wagner 1990). However, while many evangelical groups and individuals make compromises with nonevangelical institutions, as we shall see, believers living within secular institutions also find ways to protect and, more to the point, strengthen central elements of their conservative worldviews. The second approach helps us to reflect on the role of conservative groups as embodiments of critiques of a liberal society. However, as this book demonstrates, the vitality of conservative religiosity cannot be fully understood as a protest against secularism. To be sure, these believers have a tremendous amount of disdain for several key elements of the ideology of secularism.[32] As well, these students have made compromises with the secular world. But analyses based primarily on either one of these two processes fail to convey adequately the social or existential conditions of these students' lives. To my mind, a better approach to groups such as the IVCF (and the approach I hope to adopt) would combine a sensitivity to the ways the group facilitates both compromises and confrontations (or, to use the main metaphors of this book, bridges and fortresses). I return to this issue later in this chapter.

Now, if some (even merely institutional) form of secularization seems to be evident in North American culture in general, it is especially evident in the social and academic contexts of secular universities. Although most universities in North America began as outgrowths of Christian denominations, during the past century the majority of these institutions have become explicitly secular (Marsden and Longfield 1992).

For an excellent example of this process, we need look no further than McMaster University itself. McMaster was founded as a Baptist university in 1887 by an affluent Canadian senator, William McMaster. Although there was no "theological litmus test" for its students, George Rawlyk observes that McMaster students were to be educated by evangelical teachers "and thoroughly equipped with all the resources of the best and most liberal culture to enable them to meet the polished shafts of a refined and subtle infidelity" (1992:285). The university sought to offer its students the best of the liberal and scientific disciplines, partly so graduates could fight for the place of Christian faith in a world increasingly characterized by liberal and materialist sensibilities (Johnston and Weaver 1986). Until 1957, the governors of McMaster University were elected by the Baptist Convention of Ontario and Quebec. After the passage of the McMaster University Act, 1957, McMaster became a nondenominational private institution, which was funded then, as it is now, from a combination of endowment income, gifts, tuition, and annual grants from the city, regional, provincial, and federal governments (Johnston and Weaver 1986).

There are a variety of explanations for the changes that have occurred in Canada between the nineteenth century, when a broad (and broadly evangelical) consensus on the seminal role of Christianity in a university education was well entrenched (Rawlyk 1992), and the end of the twentieth century, when such a consensus is completely alien to most universities.[33] However, one common denominator among these explanations is the observation that by the late 1920s universities that had once been guided mainly by evangelical principles had become "enthusiastic proponents of secular learning" (Rawlyk 1992:280).

The secularization of the Canadian academy seems to have occurred for a variety of reasons. Historian A. B. McKillop writes that the "English Canadian university of the first quarter of the twentieth century, like the society itself, was in a precarious balance between the weight of tradition and the currents of change" (1979:229). Eventually, this balance tipped definitively in favor of the currents of change, powerfully embodied in the advent of higher criticism[34] and the liberalization of Protestantism (1994:206, 230). These forces, writes McKillop, problematized evangelical religious assumptions "by pointing in the direction of historical relativism and a liberal ethical religion" (1994:204).

In 1909, the McMaster University Senate wrote: "While complete freedom should be accorded in the investigation and discussion of facts, no theory should be taught which fails to give its proper place to supernatural revelation or which would impair in any way the supreme authority of the Lord Jesus Christ" (from the minutes of the McMaster University Senate meeting of 2 December 1909; in Rawlyk 1992:287). Near the end of the same century, teaching or assuming supernatural revelation and the "supreme authority of the Lord Jesus Christ" would be fundamentally opposed to McMaster University's largely publicly funded secular mandate.

The senate's 1909 prohibition indicates both the prevailing evangelical conviction that traditional Christian faith and modern science were essentially compatible (Rawlyk 1992:288) and the portentous evangelical anxiety about the power of the increasingly liberal nonevangelical culture. McMaster was the stage for a clash between the evangelical tradition in which it had originally been rooted and the currents of change rushing in from an increasingly liberal culture (McKillop 1994: 209). If the senate's bold 1909 statement can be likened to sandbags added to reinforce the dike built to protect evangelicals from the corruptions of modernism, by the mid-1920s, the dike was almost completely ruptured. By the early 1920s, the sciences and liberal arts (rather than the Bible or Christ) were emphasized as the best vehicles for, as Chancellor Whidden put it in his 1923 inaugural address, "the modern emancipation of the mind" (Rawlyk 1992:297).

In the late 1920s, plans were drafted for the relocation of McMaster University from Toronto seventy-five kilometers southwest to Hamilton. The original plans for the new university featured a beautiful chapel as the focal point of the campus. The chapel was to be, in Chancellor Whidden's words, "a silent symbol of the place of true Religion in relation to the study and pursuit of truth as contained in the Arts and Sciences" (McKillop 1994:316). However, when Cyrus Eaton, a patron of the new university, reneged on his promise of a large donation, Chancellor Whidden chose to cancel construction of the chapel, leaving the rest of the construction plans intact. McKillop writes: "In such ways did the place of religion slowly recede in the hierarchy of priorities of this university and others" (1994:316). In fact, by the end of the 1920s, virtually every Canadian Protestant university and college had evolved in the McMaster manner: "the conservative evangelical consensus was replaced by an accommodating liberalism" (Rawlyk 1992:298).[35]

The process of institutional secularization that led to the marginalization of evangelical faith and sensibilities within most Canadian academies continues to this day. Contemporary evangelicals still interested in expressing, exploring, and cultivating their faiths on contemporary Canadian university campuses find the social and academic contexts within these secular institutions less and less open to their goals. Dozens of IVCF students told me that their professors offer them no opportunities to relate the Christian faith to the subject matter of their courses and that in many cases faculty seem to be determined to destabilize and mock the evangelical beliefs on which the university was originally and quite explicitly founded. On this topic, James Dobson, a popular American evangelical leader, writes, "I doubt if many students or their parents realize just how antagonistic many of our state schools have become to anything that smacks of Christianity. The Christian perspective is not only excluded from the classroom, it is often ridiculed and undermined" (1995:233).

Many evangelicals would argue that Dobson's comment could easily apply to contemporary Canadian secondary and postsecondary educational institutions. With this in mind, it is probably not entirely coincidental that the first IVCF groups in Canada were established in 1929 (Stackhouse 1993). At the end of a decade that had witnessed the quiet banishment of evangelical Christianity from the mandates of most Canadian universities, evangelical students, perhaps sensitive to this rapid de-Christianization, began to organize IVCF chapters.

Now let us return to the theoretical level to consider alternatives to the theory of secularization. Interpreted according to the less widely used framework of differentiation, the role of religion in our society appears to be more enduring and complex than the secularization framework seems to suggest. The roots of this alternative to the theory of secularization may be found in Durkheim, who asserted in his pioneering work on the division of labor that modern societies are characterized by "organic solidarity," in which activities within institutions are differentiated, that is, assigned to specific subgroups (1973). Niklas Luhmann, a contemporary differentiation theorist, asserts that differentiation "is not simply a decomposition into smaller chunks, but rather a process of growth by internal disjunction" (1982: 231). Moreover, according to Luhmann, the form of ("functional") differentiation most typical of modern societies "is not simply a process of delegation or decentralization of responsibilities, and not simply a factoring out of means for the ends of society. The displacement [in our case, of religion] integrates each specific function into a new set of system/environment references and produces types of problems and solutions which would not, and could not, arise at the level of the encompassing system" (1982:241). According to the differentiation thesis, religion is not expelled from the larger social system in which it might previously have been relatively undifferentiated. Rather, religion simply becomes more concentrated in a different part of an increasingly complex social system (Luhmann 1984).

Interpreted in this light, the IVCF might be understood as a well-defined group, existing within a system of other religious and nonreligious groups, all of which must determine their difference from each other (Luhmann 1982:245) and from the larger system of which such groups are constituent members. Within differentiated groups such as the IVCF, religion continues to exert a powerful influence on believers and perhaps even on the larger social system (Luhmann 1984:32). Nevertheless, since religion is no longer diffused throughout the entire social system (as it arguably once was), this process of differentiation must be correlated with some sort of secularization. But this secularization need not be construed as a reduction in the absolute "quantity" of religion within a larger system such as the university[36] or as a confirmation of Weberian disenchantment. Rather, one might understand this form of secularization as Luhmann does, as a result of functional differentiation (Luhmann 1984; 1982).

For example, McMaster is secular in the sense that it is not the responsibility of the didactic or administrative elements of the larger university system (of differentiated functions) to promote any religious tradition. But obviously religion still exists on campus, in differentiated groups and in individual lives. Although IVCF students may occasionally perceive themselves, as one member put it, as "aliens" in Mc-Master's non-Christian ethos, the differentiated academic, administrative, and student governance components of the university continue to exist alongside and even in some ways to support these allegedly endangered groups. In the case of religious "clubs" such as the IVCF, this support comes in three forms: the McMaster Student Union's annual financial grant (derived from student fees) to each club, the university's provision of free meeting space for all clubs, and McMaster's official anti-discrimination policy that prohibits discrimination against any student on the basis of "creed," among other factors. This new, institutionally protected, and perhaps more concentrated form of religion is evident at McMaster, which was transformed from a "Christian school of learning"[37] to a pluralistic institution in which the tradition on which the university was founded is now best represented by the IVCF, one club among others, some religious, some not. However, it is important to note that while the IVCF may be supported by (and thus actually dependent on) the university's ethos of differentiation and pluralism, like many other evangelical groups, it "asserts a de-differentiated world in which all spheres of life are knit together by a single divine will" (Ammerman 1994:150). Surely it is at least ironic that a pluralistic institution such as McMaster cultivates an ethos in which an essentially antipluralist group such as the IVCF can thrive. These issues are explored in greater depth in the following chapters. For now, I would like simply to suggest that the changing status and locus of evangelicalism at McMaster may be fairly interpreted as evidence of some form of secularization.[38] However, by attributing this kind of institutional secularization to differentiation (Dobbelaere 1981) and by underlining the persistence of faith within the subunits of the larger system, the differentiation thesis may more clearly portray the complex position of religion in contemporary society.

In *Fragmented Gods* (1987), sociologist Reginald Bibby advances another interpretation of the place of religion in contemporary society. Bibby argues that in lieu of the all-encompassing worldviews previously embraced by Canadians, believers now select "fragments" of established faiths. According to this interpretation, Canadians have adopted the same "selective consumption" approach to religion as they have to the purchase of clothing and other consumer goods. While people continue to have the same psychospiritual needs—for a supportive community, mystery, unconditional divine love, and answers to spiritual questions—mainline Protestant churches in Canada have not found a way to meet these needs in a manner that inspires their members or "affiliates" to return to the pews (1993:177). Bibby maintains that people might be members of a particular church or believe in God but that they pick and choose among the social, moral, and theological offerings of their church. For Bibby, many Canadian believers are eager to engage in what sociologist Peter Berger calls "cognitive bargaining," a process in which one negotiates with another (often diametrically opposed) worldview to determine which ideas one should embrace and which one should reject.[39] Such bargaining, Bibby and Berger both suggest, often leads to a highly precarious faith. As Berger puts it, "One needs a very long spoon indeed if one is to dine with the devil of doubt; without it, one is liable to end up as dessert. Or, to vary the metaphor, the very first step in this bargaining process lands one on a slippery slope whose foot lies on the debris of shattered faith" (1992:42).

Although Bibby is not a proponent of the secularization thesis, his fragmentation thesis does depict religion as reduced to "a privatized [fragmented] form" (Bruce 1992:20), so to some extent his perspective trades on—if not presupposes—elements of the secularization thesis. In any case, it is important to note that, according to Bibby, evangelical Christians are less willing than other Canadians to adopt fragments of traditional religious worldviews. Bibby and Rawlyk suggest that although evangelicals constitute only between 8% (Bibby 1993; Bibby and Brinkerhoff 1994) and 16% (Rawlyk 1996) of the Canadian population,[40] their members are far more committed to and involved in their churches than are nonevangelical believers.[41] Bibby argues that compared to Canadian mainline Protestant churches, which are failing to attract and keep Canadian believers involved, evangelical churches are succeeding not only at attracting new members but also at keeping these members very active.[42] While Bibby laments the increased hegemony of consumeristic spiritual sensibilities (1987; 1993), which has led to the fragmentation of traditional worldviews,[43] he maintains that the victors in a secular, fragmented Canada are evangelicals and avowed secularists. The latter group might celebrate the movement toward fragmentation as a harbinger of the disintegration of religion, and the former group succeeds partly because it offers adherents all-encompassing worldviews which are explicitly critical of the permissivism, liberalism, and pluralism that have become central themes in North American culture. According to this interpretation of religion in contemporary society, the success of the IVCF may suggest that its members have rejected the fragmented religious sensibilities of their non-Christian peers. Or, since some degree of fragmentation is likely to occur even within the worldviews of evangelicals, Bibby's thesis may help us to understand the contradictions evident in the discourse of some IVCF members.

When considering religion in contemporary society, we may use at least three interpretations. First, it is possible to interpret the contemporary role of religion in Canadian life (or on a university campus) as manifesting an overall reduction or marginalization of religion in society or in individual lives. Second, we might interpret the same role as implying that religion has simply become concentrated in its own differentiated sphere(s). Third, we might argue that the place of religion in Canada suggests the increasingly selective consumption of traditional religiosity in general, on the one hand, and the successes of evangelical churches in particular at responding to this situation on the other hand. Throughout this book, I blend elements from these three approaches.

There can be no doubt about which approaches seem most plausible from a believer's perspective. For IVCF students, institutional and cognitive secularization and the fragmentation of orthodox Christianity are clearly evidenced on the McMaster campus and in North American culture in general. Thus, many IVCF students described the group as "a light in the darkness" of indifferent or inhospitable North American and campus cultures. Most IVCF students would likely perceive that the differentiation thesis does not adequately capture what Clark Pinnock, an evangelical professor at McMaster's Divinity College, described convincingly as McMaster's "bias against God" during a lecture to the IVCF.

From a social-scientific outsider's perspective, however, the most credible theory is not so clearly apparent. While institutional secularization seems to be quite evident at McMaster, the presence of cognitive secularization is more difficult to establish. Since my study did not involve a comparison between IVCF students and non-IVCF members, I cannot theorize with much confidence about whether secularization, differentiation, or fragmentation best characterizes the general processes at work in the religious lives of non-Christians at McMaster. Moreover, it is also difficult to determine whether cognitive secularization is occurring in the broader Canadian society among non-Christians in this age group because there is a paucity of Canadian ethnographic data focusing on this specific generation and educational category.[44]

We could argue that religion at McMaster has become localized in what the McMaster Students Union calls "clubs," such as the IVCF and the Muslim Students Association, and thus that religion remains a potent element of McMaster life. However, I would argue that by being relegated to one of many clubs, alongside the chess and ski clubs, the IVCF is, de facto and de jure, diminished in broad systemic influence and significance, compared with the historical position of this form of Christianity at McMaster. Students may proclaim the universal significance of their gospel, but they must do so as members of one group among others with competing truth claims.[45] Moreover, as I discuss in subsequent chapters, IVCF students tell me that as a result of the unofficial hegemony of liberalism on campus, they are neither encouraged nor comfortable in introducing their convictions into the context which drew most students to McMaster: the classroom. Students seem to be either intuitively or intellectually aware that introducing their beliefs about the "Lordship of Christ" into the academic discourse of the classroom or the social discourse of the cafeteria would be considered, in Ingram's terms, an unwelcome "frame intrusion" (1989; cf. Goffman 1974). Throughout the following chapters, evangelical students describe many incidents that seem to confirm their impressions.

The McMaster IVCF chapter may be thriving, but it is doing so on what is arguably the periphery of the university system. Moreover, it is surviving in a milieu if not dominated, then at least distinguished, by pluralism, moral secularization (Stout 1988), and the selective acceptance of traditional worldviews (Bibby 1987). Whether such groups will survive further marginalization is impossible to predict.[46] But the contrast—and perhaps even the antagonism between the IVCF's interests (as embodied in its statement of purposes) and McMaster's pluralistic ethos—reminds us that differentiation may entail more than simply a new locus for religion but rather a devaluation of its position within the broader social system. It is my task in this work to explore the individual and corporate responses to the marginalization or differentiation (both negatively evaluated by evangelicals) of evangelical beliefs and values from McMaster's central academic and social contexts.

Conclusion

I want to problematize the secularization thesis by underlining Rawlyk's (1996) illustration of the endurance of religion in Canada. The endurance and vitality of religion in the United States even more thoroughly undermine a simple version of this thesis. As I mentioned, my own approach combines the insights entailed in the theories of secularization, fragmentation, and differentiation. However, I find myself more compelled by the argument that instead of being simply repositioned in the ongoing discourse of Canadian or McMaster society, conventional expressions of religion are now less welcomed by institutions and less wholly or unquestioningly accepted by individuals.

In the following chapters, I argue that McMaster's IVCF students have each made what might be understood as an implicit metaphorical "contract" with the dominant secular ethos in which they live. The development of these contracts (cf. Bruce 1992:18) is an ongoing process which occurs so that evangelical students can reduce the cognitive dissonance (Festinger 1962) or cognitive contamination (Berger 1992:39) generated by their participation in an institution in which the evangelical claims of biblicentrism, apocalypticism, and conservative morality must compete (perhaps on an uneven field) with the secularists' (and some liberal Christians') claims of liberalism, relativism, secularism, and moral permissivism. These contracts are not always negotiated consciously or in a neat, finite period. Furthermore, the level of awareness about such contracts depends primarily on the extent to which each student perceives either (or both) the academic and social experiences he or she has at university as threats to his or her worldview. All IVCF students, however, negotiate contracts, even though the exact nature of these vary, depending on the personalities of the students involved. In some cases, these contracts were negotiated with the help of parents, pastors, youth groups, and evangelical camp counselors years before students began university. For these students, the transition to university life was not especially traumatic. In other cases, however, students explained that when they began studies at McMaster, they found themselves completely unprepared for the secular and often Dionysian environment they encountered. For this group of participants, the IVCF is large and well organized enough to act as a supportive alternative community and a socialization context in which students can learn to negotiate their own personal contracts with the dominant secular environment.[47]

My analysis suggests that as an alternative institution within an institution, the IVCF enables students to cope with their essential social and spiritual estrangement from the lifestyles, values, and relative irreligiosity of their secular peers. For every secular student social function, the IVCF offers a unique evangelical counterpart. The group also organizes regular meetings in which participants refute elements of classroom teachings, such as evolution and relativism, and critique aspects of their peers' behavior, such as promiscuity and drinking.[48] These meetings, small group workshops, and social events provide students with an alternative social network which not only equips them with a sense of social solidarity but also provides them with opportunities to address the cognitive dissonance often generated by being an evangelical on "the world's turf," as Buff Cox once put it. However, as we shall see, the IVCF is not a "total institution" (Goffman 1961; cf. Peshkin 1986; Wagner 1990) because the wall between itself and the surrounding culture is often highly permeable; moreover, the group seeks to complement and not supplant the main functions of the university.

During my fieldwork with the IVCF, I noticed that these students relate to the nonevangelical world in two distinct ways. Throughout this book, the "fortress strategy" denotes the defensive posture believers assume to protect themselves from the evils of the non-Christian world. Hammond and Hunter employ 1983 quantitative data to explore issues closely related to those I discuss in this book. They examine the apparent paradox that evangelicals on non-Christian university campuses tend to retain and even cultivate their religious commitments, while their coreligionists at explicitly evangelical colleges demonstrate a tendency to abandon their faiths (1984:230). Hammond and Hunter assert that believers on non-Christian campuses employ a variety of defensive (and faith-strengthening, believers said) strategies to maintain the plausibility of their worldview. The pattern Hammond and Hunter illustrate exemplifies what I describe as the "fortress" strategy. In support of their thesis, they argue that "groups such as the Inter-Varsity Christian Fellowship . . . encourage the development of 'Christian ghettos' on public university campuses. . . . In this situation the believer's identity *qua* believer is accentuated and reinforced; one's worldview is annealed" (1984:232).

Moreover, Hammond and Hunter assert that the practice of witnessing to non-Christians "elicits a seige mentality . . . and provides an opportunity to hone and renew one's own faith" (1984:232). This observation is true in the case of some and perhaps many IVCF students. However, I find no evidence to support the severity of their generalization about the IVCF. Far from being ghettoized, McMaster's IVCF members are actively involved (albeit selectively) in campus life. Furthermore, Hammond and Hunter ignore the friendships between evangelicals and nonevangelicals that sometimes precede, sometimes result from, and often have nothing whatsoever to do with such witnessing. In other words, while Hammond and Hunter's survey data clearly evidence the "fortress strategy" and the insiders' experiences of otherness to which this approach responds, their findings do not reflect the existence of a second distinct strategy. I call this second approach the "bridge strategy" to suggest the way the IVCF facilitates a constructive, friendly, and not directly evangelistic rapport between its members and non-Christians. McMaster IVCF participants use these two strategies so they can belong (though not unproblematically) to both the evangelical and nonevangelical worlds.[49] Compromises have definitely been written into many of the contracts forged by IVCF members, but it would be a mistake to ignore the faith-sustaining function of these contractual negotiations with the nonevangelical world.

When I began my fieldwork among the IVCF, I expected to find examples of what Peter Berger describes as "cognitive retrenchment" (1992:43), the erection of a fortress of resistance to secularism and pluralism, and indeed I was not disappointed. However, what I did not expect to find (and what made this study so interesting to me) were so many bridges, so many examples of what Berger calls "cognitive bargaining" (1992:41), the relatively conciliatory negotiation with the "other's" (in this case, non-Christian) worldview. It struck me fairly early that I was observing and participating in a group that is, for a variety of reasons I discuss throughout this book, able to combine tendencies of compromise and resistance.[50]

The "fortress" and "bridge" ideal types describe two sometimes simultaneously deployed strategies oriented toward establishing both clear boundaries and possible commonalities between Christians and non-Christians. I doubt that these two strategies and the contracts to which they contribute are unique to the IVCF. On the contrary, I would suggest that all three of these elements are evidenced in other situations in which evangelicals (and other religious minority groups) must interact with a secular ethos. I would expect to find analogous strategies and resolutions manifested in the interactions between Muslim students and McMaster's academic and social contexts. Moreover, I would also contend that these two basic ways of approaching the other would be evident in the relationships between dominant and minority groups outside the sphere of religion. For example, the relationships between female surgeons and their mainly male peers might also involve contracts and the two styles of interaction I have outlined as the means of negotiating the control of contested "turf."

In addition to elucidating the fortress and bridge strategies, this text demonstrates that evangelical students employ what I call a "selectively permeable membrane" that operates according to fortress and bridge approaches, which themselves are designed to generate contracts. This metaphorical filter is sufficiently permeable to ameliorate the tension between evangelicals and their non-Christian peers but sufficiently impermeable to enable evangelicals to achieve a strong sense of separateness and solidarity or, as one IVCF participant described it, "a good sort of alienation." In other words, evangelicals both suffer as a result of their difference from the culture of their secular peers *and* employ a "good sort of alienation" as a central strategy in their efforts to survive and thrive in a secular context.

The sense of otherness experienced by IVCF students has at least two sources. First, in their extra-IVCF social lives, IVCF members (especially those participants who live in the campus residences) are exposed to relative moral permissiveness with respect to homosexuality, nonmarital sexual activity, and alcohol and drug consumption; in the context of their classrooms, many of these students are exposed to challenging ideas such as biological evolution, relativism, and pluralism. In other words, Hammond and Hunter are correct to argue that "the threat to the sustained plausibility of this worldview is not just fancied in the minds of adherents but is, in fact, *external* and *communicated*" (1984:232). The differences believers perceive between themselves and their non-Christian peers and professors are indeed based on real differences of worldviews, ethics, and theologies. Nevertheless, the second source of their perceived otherness is IVCF members' practice of utilizing elements from their experiences of difference as symbolic instruments with which to *define themselves* as different, as Wuthnow writes, "in a positive sense" (1989:182).

To date, there have been no ethnographies published on any North American IVCF chapter. Indeed, I have found no ethnographies published on any evangelical campus group in North America. Thus the present ethnography is both exciting and challenging. It is exciting to break new ground. However, it is challenging not to be able to stand in a tradition of insights and methods from recent work and not to be able to test or disprove previously articulated theories advanced by other ethnographers working on this particular subject. Nevertheless, the present study is not written in a vacuum. In addition to utilizing the wealth of scholarly literature related to the history and theology of evangelicalism in North America, throughout this book I discuss numerous social-scientific studies of evangelical denominations, movements, and churches.

By using the ethnographic method to study this group, I intend to add a new dimension to the study of Canadian and, more broadly, North American evangelicalism. Although the apparent paradox of a large and vigorous evangelical group on a non-Christian university campus forms the central focus of the present study, my interests extend well beyond the IVCF chapter at McMaster University. Throughout the following ethnography, my focus alternates between the specific features and individuals of this group and the broader issues surrounding the relationship of conservative faith to contemporary North American social institutions.

In the present chapter, I have described the group and tradition I am considering. I have also laid the foundations for the larger arguments I make throughout this study.

To provide readers with as "thick" (Geertz 1973) an account of this group as possible, in chapter 2 I outline and interpret the life histories of four group members. Although these members are not intended to represent "typical" IVCF participants, their spiritual and personal biographies feature themes and issues that would be familiar to most members.

Chapter 3 includes a consideration of the rhetorical practices of the IVCF. At all IVCF meetings and events, specific forms of speaking and singing are employed to establish an atmosphere of solidarity among participants and a sense of distinction from the surrounding secular milieu. While social-scientific research on the nature and function of evangelical rhetoric confirms that evangelicals employ forms of speaking and singing that set believers apart from nonbelievers, previous studies mostly concern groups such as the Primitive Baptists, who are already relatively isolated (either geographically or culturally) from the non-Christian world. In contrast, I discuss the extent to which IVCF rhetoric evidences the attempt to employ both the fortress and bridge strategies in the context of living within an urban, educated, non-Christian social context.

Virtually every student I interviewed reported feeling worried about his or her role in what is perceived as an unpredictable if not hostile postuniversity economy. Moreover, in addition to experiencing a sense of separation from the postuniversity world of careers and families, evangelical students often experience estrangement from the mores and intellectual commitments of their secular student peers. In chapter 4 I explore what might be termed the "double alienation" I have encountered among IVCF participants. I focus on the process whereby this compounded sense of otherness motivates IVCF members to band together for protection and support. Significantly, while most students confirm this experience of estrangement, all of the members I interviewed believe God will protect and guide them through their lives. As a result of this conviction, these evangelical students do not experience a perpetual sense of anxiety about their futures. Nevertheless, members frequently described having to guard constantly against what one participant called her "human" tendency—and what another called "Satan's temptation"—to fall into periods of doubt and anxiety about their economic or personal prospects.

In chapter 5 I explore the role of women in evangelicalism to determine possible explanations for the high female-to-male ratio of IVCF participation (approximately

70% females to 30% males). Randall Balmer (1994) argues that the feelings of cultural and political alienation experienced by evangelicals are to a significant degree the result of the changing roles of women. Although this assertion is fairly representative of other social-scientific work on the role of women in evangelicalism, it is only partially helpful for understanding the place of women in the McMaster IVCF. If, broadly speaking, evangelicalism is supposed to be inhospitable toward women, why are women found throughout the IVCF, and not simply as administrators but as executive members, worship leaders, staff workers, and preachers? I argue that while all evangelical students experience two forms of otherness (cf. chapter 4), female students may experience an additional complex form related to being evangelical women in an androcentric institution that paradoxically celebrates egalitarian gender roles. The most likely explanation for the high proportion of women in the McMaster IVCF chapter is that the group is able to respond to women's triple sense of otherness at McMaster.

In chapter 6 I analyze the role of the figure of Satan in the lives of IVCF participants. Satan is often described by these students as both the mediate and immediate source of evil in the universe, evil that ranges from murder to lustful thoughts. A consideration of Satan's crucial significance in members' personal lives and the group's forms of worship illustrates a central element of their shared theological sensibilities and raison d'être. From an IVCF or emic point of view, Satan is a formidable, persistent, and personal foe; from a social-scientific or etic perspective, the figure of Satan for the IVCF may be a symbolic or metonymic reflection of the secular culture's antagonism toward conservative Christianity.

In the seventh chapter, I consider the practice of "witnessing," both during the mission to Lithuania and at McMaster. Throughout the 1995–96 academic year, I attended a small group that focused on the practices of witnessing to non-Christians. These practices are also known as "friendship evangelism." This form of evangelism is nonconfrontational and, from what I have observed (and experienced myself as one of the "friends"), quite sensitive to non-Christian convictions. This relatively tactful form of witnessing allows IVCF members to maintain and express their sense of the absolute and exclusive veracity of their faith as they ensure their positive rapport with their non-Christian peers. During all IVCF events, the value of missionary work is stressed, whether the missionary "field" is conceived of as the campus, the workplace, or a foreign country. In chapter 7, I also discuss my participation in and observation of the IVCF's annual mission to Lithuania to foster that country's evangelical college groups. This trip serves as a case study of the role international missionary work plays among group members.

My general argument that the IVCF serves as an alternative social and religious institution in which believers can negotiate contracts with their surroundings is woven throughout the seven major chapters. In the final chapter, I discuss the larger implications of the theoretical framework I develop for understanding the relationship between conservative Christianity and secular institutions in the broader context of North American society.

Four Life Histories

What then are we to say? Should we continue in sin in order that grace may abound? By no means! How can we who died to sin go on living in it? Do you not know that all of us who have been baptized into Christ Jesus were baptized into his death? Therefore we have been buried with him by baptism into death, so that, just as Christ was raised from the dead by the glory of the Father, so we too might walk in the newness of life.

Romans 6:1–4

Apart from adapting theory and other constructs to under-stand the subjectivity of particular life histories in different cultures, we might want to reverse the process and start with the life history as a basis for constructing theories about the role of individual behaviour in culture change and culture transmission. If we look carefully at the life history as a subjective document, we can see the individ-ual's self-perceived impact on his social environment.

Watson and Watson-Franke

When talking about their lives, people lie sometimes, forget a lot, exaggerate, become confused, and get things wrong. Yet they *are* revealing truths.

Personal Narratives Group

One of the challenges of ethnography is that it requires one to enter into a community and become enmeshed in the web of affinities, opinions, gossip, rhetoric, and beliefs that characterize this group. Then, at the end of fieldwork, one must step outside the others' world and interpret it for (other) others and oneself. This analytical stage, however, compels one to condense one's experiences and, indeed, one's newly acquired friends, to make them more manageable, less inde-terminate elements of an academic study. This challenge constitutes both ethnog-raphy's strength and its weakness. Moreover, such a challenge is what makes eth-nography a social *science*: that the vast array of fieldwork experiences must be distilled and communicated in a nonidiosyncratic manner. Unfortunately, the very analytical processes by which the ethnographer's personal experiences are rendered communicable often flatten out the most interesting parts of the "other." Ethnog-rapher David Mandelbaum describes this dilemma with poignant clarity:

> When an anthropologist goes to live among the people he studies, he is likely to make some good friends among them. As he writes his account of their way of life, he may feel uncomfortably aware that his description and analysis omitted something of great importance. His dear friends have been dissolved into faceless norms; their vivid adventures have somehow been turned into pattern profiles or statistical types. (1973:178)

Such diminishing of the unique features of specific individuals is rarely the inten-tion of the ethnographer; rather, this effacement is a natural by-product of analyses in which one attempts to make, as I do, for example, broader claims about the place and coping strategies of traditionally religious individuals in a secular culture. Even when the means of making such assertions is a "thick" description (Geertz 1973) of a religious group, it is inevitable that individual differences are sometimes effaced by broader conceptual reflections.

Throughout the following chapters, I refer to and often quote many IVCF mem-bers at length. The ideal way to render these students' comments comprehensible would be for me to provide a life history of each speaker before quoting him or her. Because I refer to most of the sixty students I have interviewed (and several I have not formally interviewed) throughout this study, however, thorough contex-tualization would impose an onerous burden on the reader. Nonetheless, since I have been drawn into these evangelicals' religious and personal lives, I am reluctant to begin this work without providing readers with a "thicker" sense of the multidi-mensional and irreducible people I met in the course of my fieldwork with the IVCF.

As a partial solution to this problem, I offer in the present chapter brief life histories of four IVCF students.[1] In preparation for this chapter, I reread my field-notes from the sixty interviews I had conducted and then requested a second inter-view with four students who were chosen for a variety of reasons. First, I had spent a month in Lithuania with three of these participants and had established a positive rapport with the fourth. Second, all of these students had demonstrated during our interviews and their testimonies that they were both capable of and comfortable with discussing their religious and personal lives. Third, two of these participants are women and two are men. Fourth, two of them "became Christians" when they were children, and two had converted more recently. Fifth, these members seem to me to be fairly representative of the ideological and theological diversity within the McMaster IVCF.[2]

David Mandelbaum, whose pioneering study of Gandhi has become a classic in the life history approach in anthropology, observes that no single person "can be

labelled 'typical' in all respects" (1973:183). While these four IVCF students were
not selected to represent all "types" of IVCF students, meeting them should allow
the reader to appreciate the diverse life situations in which IVCF students are
embedded and the personal histories from which they have emerged as evangelicals.
Most IVCF participants would find in these stories significant similarities between
themselves and at least one, if not several, of the four people I introduce in this
chapter.[3]

Since the 1970s, scholars have become increasingly aware of the powerful influence exerted on ethnographic interpretations by the assumptions, biases, and pred-
ilections the researcher takes into his or her fieldwork. This general insight has
begun to permeate most social-scientific methodologies, including the life history
approach. In fact, so sensitive are many life history interpreters about their roles that
they now describe the life history as "a joint production" (Watson and Watson-
Franke 1985:12) and "a collaborative venture" (Langness and Frank 1985:61). The
ethnographer and the "other" "co-produce" (Kapchan 1995:484) the life history. The
person telling his or her story alters it in some ways to be understood (and often
appreciated) by his or her listener, while the researcher "simply" recording the story
imposes his or her own set of expectations on the narrative in the process of con-
veying, paraphrasing or interpreting its details and major themes.[4] Thus readers must
bear in mind that I mediate all of the narratives in this chapter; I also situate these
narratives and their speakers within what I consider to be the relevant academic
discourse(s). For these reasons, it seems responsible to try to make my interpretive
presence as apparent as possible.[5]

As part of a larger project, the life histories contained in the present chapter are
comparatively limited in their length and depth of interpretation. Moreover, my
exposition and minimal interpretation of these four people does not culminate in
an argument as such. Rather, the following four life histories are meant to evoke a
richer sense of the complex identities of IVCF members than would be possible if
these individuals were simply referred to sporadically throughout this book. Now,
let me introduce these four students.

Gabrielle

Gabrielle[6] is a twenty-one-year-old English student who was raised in Waterloo,
Ontario, approximately fifty kilometers west of Toronto. Her parents were nominal
Christians, raised in the United Church. When she was five years old, a friend
invited Gabrielle to attend her Sunday school at the Gospel Hall, the local Closed
Brethren church. "They had this great little bus and they'd come right to your
house on Sunday morning and pick you up and then drop you off after," Gabrielle
recalled. Eventually, her father decided he should investigate the church his daughter was attending because he "was curious about what kind of Bible teaching we
were getting, not that this was super important to him at the time, but he was
interested. So he came and checked it out and then started coming on a regular
basis. One day he went out to the church picnic, and I can just see him sitting
there between two of the church's elders, talking."

Gabrielle's father increased his involvement in the church and eventually decided to become a Christian. Considering that these events occurred when she was seven years old, Gabrielle remembers her conversion and that of her father with unusual clarity.

Dad became a Christian on July twenty-fourth, 1983, a couple of years after he started going to church. I guess I remember these details so vividly because I've heard him tell his story so many times. My mom was a bit stand-offish about the whole thing. She wasn't hostile or anything. That's just the way she is, sort of reserved and cautious. She wasn't saved until 1986. She had to make sure it was right for her.

One of the most striking features of Gabrielle's life history is the prominent role played by her father. Her own conversion is intractably bound up with her father's, and as she tells his story, she weaves parts of her own into his. At several points during our interview, it was difficult to distinguish between these two narratives. When describing her conversion, Gabrielle commented:

I can't exactly pinpoint what brought me to the point that I knew I needed to be saved. It was partly because of all the stories from the Bible I'd heard for so many years. But really, I guess what brought it home for me was the issue of baptism, which became a big thing for me when my dad was about to get baptized. I remember my dad was going through the interviews before baptism and one day when he was talking about it I heard him and started asking him questions.

Then, on the day itself, it was September eleventh, I got really curious. In our church at that time we had a baptismal pool that we could put together or take down whenever we wanted. I can remember the pool being put up and watching the water being poured in. It was a Sunday afternoon, after church, but before the evening service when my dad was going to be baptized. I went into the room where my dad was getting dressed for his baptism, with shorts and a T-shirt under his robe, and I started asking lots of questions, but especially why he needed to be baptized. He said to me that it was a public expression of faith, a spiritual dying to your sinful nature and being resurrected like Christ. Of course, he said this in simpler words, so I could understand. I asked him what being baptized had to do with being saved and he said it had to do with obedience to scripture, since Christians in the Bible were all baptized. We talked about that and ended up back on the topic of salvation. He said that the only way for Christ to save us from our sins was for him to die on the cross. Up to that point the whole thing was just a story—it didn't really mean a lot to me. But gradually the fact that Jesus Christ did all these things so we could be saved from our sins became real for me.

So, I guess you could say that my father led me to the Lord, for sure. I told him that I wanted to be saved and that I had done some bad things. Like I remember cutting off my sister's hair when I got some new scissors, and sometimes telling lies or disobeying my folks. I told him I wanted to have these sins forgiven. Dad said that the only way to do this is to ask Christ for forgiveness. Then he read some biblical verses which emphasized the act of asking and then we prayed. Actually, he did something for me I'll never forget: he let me pray myself. It was around 3:00 P.M. on September eleventh, 1983, just a few hours before he was baptized. I can still see the shadows on the wall. I was baptized four years later

on March twenty-second, 1987, when I was eleven. Nothing major happened
between when I became a Christian and when I was baptized, except for going
to church a lot.

After ten years as members of their Closed Brethren congregation, Gabrielle's
family moved to London, Ontario, and joined another less conservative Brethren
church. When I asked her to describe the differences, she replied, "Like in this
one, women were allowed to cut their hair and wear earrings as long as they weren't
really obvious about it. That was a real change from the Waterloo church we were
at." However, because this new church placed very little emphasis on religious
education and was far from their home, they only remained there for a year and a
half. For the rest of their five and a half years in London, they were members of
the Highbury (Fellowship) Baptist church:

> My own spiritual walk [after her conversion] until I went to Highbury, and even
> a little while after, was pretty stagnant. I mean, at the Gospel Hall there wasn't a
> lot of creativity—mainly there was an emphasis on repetition, and there were no
> instruments allowed in worship. But at Highbury, there were drums and guitars
> and pianos—it was great. And at Highbury, women took a more active role,
> compared to the Gospel Hall, at least.

In Gabrielle's Roman Catholic junior high school:

> There were only two Christians there, and I wanted to fit in with the non-
> Christians, so I went to dances and even started swearing sometimes. Actually,
> and you'll get a kick out of this, one day my friend and I, the other Christian,
> were kicked out of religion class, if you can believe it. The teacher was talking
> about the importance of priests, and I asked why they were so important since
> people could talk to God themselves without priests as mediators. So she said we
> should leave the class. Bizarre, eh?

After grade nine, Gabrielle transferred to a public French immersion school, which
many of her friends from Highbury attended. As well, the Inter-School Christian
Fellowship, the IVCF's high school equivalent, had an active chapter at her new
school, which provided her with an explicitly Christian alternative to the secular
academic and social contexts: "This was such a huge relief. It meant I didn't need
to lead a double life. That's what it felt like—one with my school friends and
another with my church friends. I was starting to feel badly about this, the difference
between the ways I'd act at school versus the ways I'd act at church. This way I
could hang around with my church friends at school and I could continue to be a
Christian there, too."

At the age of sixteen, Gabrielle's "Christian walk" became infinitely more complex and arduous after she was sexually assaulted by a family acquaintance. This
traumatic experience challenged and destabilized her faith and personality. Gabrielle adapted to this experience by "retreating into a kind of Christian bubble,"
as she described it during a conversation we had in Lithuania. She attributes her
psychological survival to her Christian community:

> If I hadn't been at public school with all my church friends and Highbury, I
> don't think I would have made it. Things got pretty rough. Before this I had been

growing spiritually, reading my Bible regularly, focusing on discipleship. . . . The crisis with that creep when I was sixteen led to a bunch of little crises with my family and teachers. The burden just grew and grew. I didn't tell my parents about the creep for months and they didn't know what to do. Then I started therapy with a Christian therapist from my church. If it wasn't for her, I'm not sure what would have happened to me. God placed her in my life as a support and to reassure me that what happened wasn't my fault. She was a Godsend, literally.

This whole experience made me more cautious, and I was angry at God for a long time. I mean, how could he have let this happen to me, I kept wondering. You always hear Romans 8:28[7] whenever someone needs to comfort someone. Or else you hear people saying something about Job. I've used both of these with people I've been trying to help. But when you're experiencing the suffering your-self, this isn't always a big help. Time helped me get over the anger and just helped the healing process—not just as a Christian, but as a human being. Just like it says in that "Footprints" poem, you know. God was carrying me when I was too weak to walk.

Shortly before she began her studies at McMaster, Gabrielle's family moved again, this time to a town outside Ottawa. Her move to McMaster further tested the staunch fundamentalism of her childhood and adolescence. "I mean, Highbury is more liberal than the Gospel Hall, but not as liberal as Buff [the IVCF staff worker]," Gabrielle related.

Gabrielle's stories of her first experiences with McMaster's secular ethos echoed the accounts shared by many IVCF members. Moreover, her recollections illustrate the liberating role the IVCF can play for evangelical students at McMaster. For example, to explain the social estrangement she felt at the university before she discovered the IVCF, Gabrielle shared the following story. Since she was living off-campus and had few friends in Hamilton, Gabrielle joined the Society for Off-Campus Students (SOCS), an alternative social group for people who do not live in the residences. At her first SOCS event, "They put a beer down in front of me and said 'Drink!' That event was modeled on the Olympics—you had to drink a beer after each event. But, as you know, I had never had a drink in my life. I was just '*no thanks,*' and got out of there." Soon after this incident, Gabrielle went to an IVCF event and met Janice, the 1996 Lithuania team leader. Janice invited Gabrielle to the Church at the John, "and I was just so stunned. I loved it." After this initial excitement, Gabrielle became a regular participant in the McMaster chapter, an environment in which she encountered:

A lot of new ideas, especially on the role of women—it was a real eye-opener. I mean, I guess I knew people thought this way, but not that they felt it so ada-mantly. I came away with new things to think about, but I still think the same way as I used to, like about women's role in the church. I think it's okay and biblical for women to be deaconesses, as long as that doesn't mean that they have spiritual authority over men. If they're going to be in administrative roles, that's fine.

Gabrielle's faith has been, to use evangelical rhetoric, "stretched" by her asso-ciation with the IVCF. However, while her growing awareness of the diversity (and especially the liberal component) within the evangelical world has led her to make some adaptations, as she explained, she continues to embrace most of the fundamentalist values and beliefs she brought with her to McMaster. She continues to believe in the "young earth hypothesis,"[8] the literal truth of the Bible, and the subordinate role of women in her church. In subsequent chapters, I discuss the way the IVCF paradoxically facilitates both this stretching and the entrenchment of previous (and usually fundamentalist) convictions.

At the end of our conversation, I asked Gabrielle why her mother is almost completely absent from her story of her spiritual development. Gabrielle responded: "My mom doesn't play a very active role in my faith, you're right, but that's probably because women don't play active roles in our church in general. Like they can't speak, for example, as you know. She just hasn't been that involved in this part of my life. It's not that she's not a Christian or isn't supportive of me; but she's not the driving force behind my faith." Gabrielle's general acceptance of women's ancillary roles in her community may be interpreted as a reflection of her will to assume the feminine roles[9] played by her mother and sanctioned by her father. She describes these roles as biblically mandated, but the centrality of her father in her narrative suggests that biblical authority may be less important for Gabrielle than her father's authority and approval.

However, in response to a question about how she would describe her father's present role in her faith, Gabrielle smiled and commented: "I'd like to say that my dad plays a small role, but he still has a huge influence because I really respect him. He's just taught me so much. But his word is not final; otherwise I wouldn't have gone to Lithuania or applied to Moody [see later]. He wasn't crazy about either of these ideas, to say the least. But I went anyway."

The mission to Lithuania was an important turning point in Gabrielle's IVCF "career."[10] Although she had been active and comfortable in the IVCF prior to the Lithuanian trip, by the end of the mission there were some misunderstandings and disagreements between Gabrielle, the staff worker (Cox), and the mission team leader. As Gabrielle explained, these disagreements alienated her from the chapter's core responsibilities and from Cox herself. In theory, since the chapter is entirely student-led, Cox's impression of Gabrielle should not impede Gabrielle's career within the group. However, Cox is, in fact, what ethnographers call a "gatekeeper," a person (typically, a group leader) who implicitly and explicitly determines one's access to a given group. Cox played this role with respect to my own research and, more subtly and less decisively, for the group's members, whose level of participation she can influence. In the final analysis, Cox cannot ostracize anyone from the chapter. The group and its student executive are open to and welcoming toward anyone; nevertheless, because Cox is the group's oldest participant, an ordained minister, and a highly respected Christian, the executive members and other core members hold her and her opinions in very high esteem.

Gabrielle had hoped to increase her involvement in the chapter, perhaps even leading a small group or becoming a member of the executive. However, Gabrielle said that during phone conversations Cox discouraged her from assuming such responsibilities. According to Gabrielle's interpretation of these interactions, Cox had decided that Gabrielle's behavior before, during, and after Lithuania reflected her need for "discipling." "Buff basically said I should step back and think about not taking such a prominent role in the group for a while," Gabrielle said during an interview. She also commented:

> The flak between me and Buff after Lithuania has never been resolved. I've tried several times to set up a time to meet with her and talk it through, but she never gets in touch with me. I know she's busy. I don't think her not calling me is on purpose; just a matter of timing. But still, I want things between us to be better, but that may not work. She and I have never seen eye to eye. There's just no connection there between us. I don't have bad things to say about her. I just don't have anything to say about her. But I guess I would have appreciated more support from her.[11]

One morning during the long return train trip to Vilnius from the mission team's four-day holiday in Saint Petersburg, Gabrielle announced to the team that the previous night she had had a "vision" that: "God wanted me to do mission work in Eastern Europe. Remember that day we sort of had to ourselves? Well, I think I was sitting in the Winter Gardens and thinking about how I was going to fit what had happened to me in Lithuania into the rest of my life. And then, you know when something just feels right? Well, that's how it was. I just got a real sense that this was where God wants me to be."

Gabrielle suffered the worst culture shock of anyone on the 1996 Lithuania team. She spoke of this culture shock during several of the team's evening debriefing sessions. She also had trouble sleeping, was often ill, and was occasionally frightened when walking with the mission team through the narrow, bustling streets of Vilnius during the day. When she told the rest of the team about her vision, one of the members of the team (apparently confused by Gabrielle's seemingly dramatic transformation) asked, "Are you sure it wasn't just a dream?" Gabrielle insisted, somewhat defensively, that it was an authentic spiritual vision. A few days later, Gabrielle told me that this vision's imperative was augmented by:

> All of the conversations we all had at night [in Lithuania]. Do you remember the one you and I and Kelly and Janice had in Vilnius that night? We talked about the role of women. We totally disagreed with you in some ways, but because of these sorts of conversations, and others I had had before, I was already questioning the things I was taught. I mean, I still would never be a pastor, because I don't think women should have spiritual authority over men, but I think God wants me to do mission work.

After returning from Lithuania, Gabrielle applied to and was accepted by the fundamentalist Moody Bible Institute in Chicago, where in September 1998 was to begin working toward her Masters of Arts and Biblical Studies. She continued to pursue her B.A. in English, which she was to finish at McMaster before she enrolled at Moody.

Simon

Simon is a twenty-two-year-old second-year geography student who was raised in Burlington in what he describes as "an ideal Christian environment." His father and mother were both raised in fundamentalist communities, and most of his uncles and aunts continue to be affiliated with evangelical churches. Although Simon's family attends a relatively moderate fundamentalist Baptist congregation, his family still has ties to strict fundamentalism. Simon explained, "My grandmother, my dad's mom, who lives with us, is still a strict Brethren. She thinks rock music is the devil's tool, that sort of thing, and she prays for me when I go to movies. But I admire her—she has a great Christian faith, but she's from another time. There's no point in trying to change her."

During our interview, I asked Simon to discuss his conversion and its role in his life. His account is typical of a small minority of IVCF participants whose faith has been part of their lives since childhood and who did not experience a profound moment of conversion. When I asked Simon when he became a Christian and what that experience means to him, he replied:

> My conversion? I can't really remember, you know. My mom told me it happened when I was five and I prayed and asked Jesus into my heart. So I guess that's when it happened. But the exact date is not really important to me. I've just always been a Christian as long as I can remember. I guess the actual moment is significant, but I can't really remember it. [pause] When I have kids, though, I think I will ask them to receive Jesus at an early age. Even though what happened when I was five was important to God, I think he was always working within my life. . . . It was a starting point for me.

Within the evangelical community, one is often expected to be able to remember the moment, or at least the period, of one's conversion.[12] One might become a Christian over a period of days, weeks, and sometimes even months (Rambo 1993: 165), but ideally, one is expected to be able to specify this moment or period with some certainty. One of the reasons for this ideal is that in sharing one's testimony with non-Christians, it is more effective to focus on a particular moment or period in one's life. According to Susan Harding (1987), this strategy helps non believers imaginatively situate crucial elements of the convert's salvation narrative in the context of their own lives (cf. chapter 3). In cases such as Simon's, in which no memorable or profound experience marks the inauguration of evangelical faith, believers often emphasize what many have described as a "second conversion" experience, which usually occurs during their teen years. Such experiences are major turning points for these individuals. As Simon described it, "Well, you know how it is. As you're growing up, you look to the older Christians for guidance on how your faith should develop. Now it's definitely more my own faith. Around when I was sixteen or seventeen was when I sort of took control over my own faith. I guess you could call this a second conversion."

I asked Simon what led to this second conversion:

> It was probably a number of things, like a few retreats and a bunch of conversations I had heard or been a part of. But there wasn't a single big moment, even in this second conversion. Maybe it was a little more random. But I think the main thing that happened personally is that there was an acknowledgment of God, that he cares deeply for me personally. If I was the only one on earth, Christ would still have come down to die for me. For *me*. That's just so awesome.

Also, there was an acknowledgment of the forgiveness of sins around that point. When I was a kid, I asked God to forgive my sins, you know, but it was like blah, blah, blah, forgive me, like what all little kids ask for. But really, what sort of sins had I committed? Not many when I was five. Now [when I ask for forgiveness] it's a total humbling before God because I understand more clearly that I need my sins forgiven. Now when I sin, I feel a real separation between me and God. Not that he's left me, but that I've left him. Sometimes I think I've done something so bad I need to let God have some time to cool off to forgive me, but that's so not true. I might need time, but he's always there. This need for the forgiveness of sins was pretty new for me back then.

Throughout Simon's childhood and adolescence, he was involved with church youth groups, an involvement which provided him with an alternative milieu in which he felt more confident than he did at school: "In school I was short and skinny, and I didn't really share my faith much. Like I said, I stuttered a lot and actually failed the second grade. So, it was great to have church. But still, it's not like I had a terrible time in school. I had a good time. I wasn't a leader or a follower, but maybe more of a follower if anything."

Another major factor in Simon's life has been the example of his older brother, who was also an active IVCF participant when he was at university. Simon actually began attending the McMaster IVCF meetings with his brother before he became a McMaster student:

I had a bit of an in, I guess. People always teased me about being Kevin's little brother, but that's okay, because I liked being that. I guess there has been a lot of copying between him and me in my time at IV. I mean, Kevin was asked to go to NSLC [the IVCF's national student leaders conference] one year and then to be on the NSLC committee the next year, and he also went to Lithuania. Then I did all of that stuff. But that doesn't bug me.

By the time Simon arrived at McMaster, his brother had already introduced him to many of the group's most popular and active members. This familiarity meant that he avoided what younger members often describe as the bewildering experience of trying to feel comfortable at some of the group's large events. Simon is acutely aware of the special treatment he enjoyed because of his brother and previous exposure to the group. As a result, he makes a concerted effort to welcome younger students to IVCF events and make sure they never feel abandoned.[13]

In his first year at McMaster, Simon was asked to attend the NSLC with several other prominent members of the chapter. That same year, he decided to join the final Lithuania mission in May 1996. When I asked him what led to his decision, he replied, "Well, I know it might sound bad, but my brother went to Lithuania three years ago, and I wanted to go, too. Also, I wanted to travel and see Christianity in another country. I had never been anywhere really, and since Kevin had been there I sort of knew what to expect, but sort of not, you know?"

In an attempt to confirm his own inclinations to go to Lithuania, Simon asked the 1995 mission team's trip leader how it was possible to be sure that God wanted one to go on missions. "He just told me that that shouldn't really be an issue because it already says in the Bible that all Christians should go. I just said hmmmm, okay."

In his second year at McMaster, Simon was asked to be a member of the NSLC committee to plan and facilitate the December 1996 conference:

> [The conference] was great. The people who came were just so spiritually thirsty it was unreal. [A leader of a mission for street youths in Toronto] spoke and the whole group of us went on a "street walk" down Yonge Street. He told us to pretend we were fifteen-year-old girls who have to survive. He also told us to go into strip clubs and porno theatres and sex shops. I didn't do this, but some of us also went to the Church and Wellesley area of town, which is where a lot of the homosexuals hang out. [At the conference,] I attended a workshop on homosex-uality where a former homosexual told us about how God helped him stop being a homosexual. It just really gave me hope. You know, before, if I had walked around the Church and Wellesley areas and had passed all these gay people, I might have somewhere deep down in me said, "Oh no, these people are doomed. There's no hope for them." But listening to him just really made me see that this was not true and that there is always hope for them.

Simon's participation in the IVCF and especially his involvement in the Lith-uania mission cultivated his already strong faith and growing confidence as an adult. His comfort, popularity, and prestige within the IVCF have been mirrored on the extracurricular level as well, since he has recently assumed new responsibilities at his Baptist church as a member of the missions committee and a coleader of the junior high school group.

By his own accounts, Simon has had to face only minor faith crises during his spiritual "walk." However, in ways that will become clear in subsequent chapters, the IVCF has exposed Simon and many others from similarly "ideal Christian environments" to the diversity within the evangelical tradition and to the major issues with which this tradition is struggling. One of these issues concerns the ar-guably inferior status of women within many churches in the evangelical tradition (cf. chapter 5). I had not intended to discuss this issue during our conversation. However, although (or perhaps because) he is aware of my strong opinions on this topic, Simon raised the subject independently:

> You know, I went to Sunday school all my life as a kid. And I was thinking the other day that all of the teachers who had such a huge influence on me when I was a kid, all these people who taught me so much about the Bible and God, were women. I remember all those conversations we all had in Lithuania about that issue. Remember? I don't know, I guess I have some confused feelings about it. I think I'm leaning toward equality. At least that's what I want to think, that's the direction I want to be heading. But then, maybe not, you know? I mean, I want there to be evidence behind what I think. I don't just want to say, "Hey, I want to believe this, so it's true," you know? I'm just not sure about this any more.

Simon's experiences with Lithuanians and Canadians whose family histories have been less "ideal" than his own have had a significant impact on him. Because of his growing awareness of the privilege he has enjoyed, he feels compelled to support the faith development of "new Christians," new members of the IVCF, and potential Christians in other countries. Near the end of our conversation, Simon commented:

I know I've been raised in the totally ideal Christian environment. Great parents, great church, great friends. It's hard to imagine how it could be better. I mean, I come home from school and my mom comes up and kisses me and asks me about my day and then on Sunday the whole family gets up and goes to church together. I know this is an ideal situation, and because of this I think God probably has more expectations of me than other people, since I've had it so easy all my life. I look at what Steve's experienced, for example, and how much more difficult his life and faith have been than mine and I'm just blown away. I mean, I've seen God's grace throughout my life, but watching God work in other peoples' lives really brings that home to me.

Steve

Steve is a twenty-two-year-old student at McMaster's Baptist Divinity College. His parents were born and raised in the West Indies. Each of his parents had eleven siblings. Steve is an amiable, extroverted, soft-spoken, and extremely handsome West Indian of East Indian descent. Steve's narrative began with his father's life in the West Indies and his eventual immigration to Canada twenty-two years ago. Steve's father quit university at nineteen to support his brothers and sisters after his own father's death. Steve's grandfather "was super strict, which might explain my dad's way of relating to us. My dad is basically the head of the house and he dictates what's going to happen and we are all supposed to accept it. . . . I come from a basically noncommunicative family."

Soon after Steve was born in 1974, his parents moved to Canada and earned enough money to sponsor other members of their family to become Canadian citizens. The family lived in Toronto until Steve was four years old and then moved to Oakville, a suburb of Toronto, where they have lived ever since.

When he was sixteen, "spiritual questions" began to trouble Steve. These questions were:

> Mainly about the meaning of life, and life after death, and stuff like whether there was a God, and are humans the only life in the universe. These were mainly philosophical questions, especially the question of life after death. For me, I couldn't separate the question about the meaning of life from the question of life after death. I thought that, I mean, if everything about me just ended after my eighty years on the planet, then my life now would be totally meaningless. I still think that.

Steve's search for answers to these questions led him back to the faith of his forebears:

> I really didn't have any answers to these questions, so I started looking into Hinduism, which was the religion of my family. I thought maybe I'd find answers there. . . . Well, it's not really just the religion of my family; it's more a question of Indian culture or their way of life. Religion is just a part of that. Where my family is from, Hinduism and just their culture totally determine everything you do or who you should be.

Anyway, I looked into Hinduism a little and just couldn't find any answers there. Buddhists believe in reincarnation, right? I thought a lot about reincarnation, too. Yeah, I looked into reincarnation, into Buddhism and Hinduism, and I still didn't find answers. But I just had a strong sense that the answers were somehow outside of me. I just wasn't convinced by the whole "the truth is within you," or the "God is inside me" idea. These things just didn't satisfy me.

Although "at that point in my life [grade eleven] I . . . didn't have a lot of friends," Steve decided to try out for his high school's volleyball team, a decision which was to have profound consequences for his life. He made the team and also met Jeff, a committed evangelical teammate (and later an active McMaster IVCF member), with whom Steve spent a lot of time during volleyball training:

One night Jeff invited me out to an outreach at his church, so I went. I was totally interested in this sort of thing, like I said, so I figured I should check it out. Of course, I was really intimidated and totally ignorant. I had no idea about Christianity, about denominations, or the Bible. I thought that whatever happened at Jeff's church must just be Christianity. For me, it had always seemed like the cultural religion of white people like Hinduism seemed like the cultural religion for Indians. But I knew three of the people there that night, so it was okay. Actually, it was great.

This experience aroused Steve's curiosity:

After this I got my hands on a Bible. The only one I could find around the house was a children's picture Bible my mom had given me when I was a kid. I have no idea why. In any case, I was really drawn to it as I started reading. Just the possibility of finding spiritual answers was exciting to me. Also, I felt really welcomed by the community at Oakville First [a Fellowship Baptist congregation]. That was a first for me—a strong community worship experience. I had been to the Hindu temple a few times, but it was totally different, and in another language.

One of the pivotal experiences in Steve's spiritual journey occurred on a church hayride with Jeff a week after Steve began reading the children's Bible. Steve recalled that during the hayride, "Jeff had his evangelist hat on, for sure." As they drove through the night on the hayride, Jeff turned to Steve and said, " 'I know where I'm going when I die.' Man, that really set off bells for me," Steve remembered. Jeff's fateful questions, his cultivation of Steve's budding spirituality, the power of the children's Bible, and the warmth of the Oakville First community all played roles in Steve's eventual commitment to Christianity. However:

What clinched it for me was that two thousand years ago, the crucifixion and resurrection actually happened. I don't know if I believed him right on the spot, but I was a vacuum about this stuff. I was amazed. I remember just looking at him with wonder. On the bus ride home, I was just processing what he had said. When I got home, I felt a real heart feeling, an excitement, like something was about to explode in me. Like I said, the actual events of the crucifixion clinched it for me. This is where the Holy Spirit comes in. I'm not going to simplify it and say that the Holy Spirit put these thoughts in my mind or anything like that.

But when I look back, I believe the Holy Spirit worked in me. I don't know exactly how it worked, but I know those first questions were of God. It's not really far-fetched for me to believe that God or the Holy Spirit personally interacted in my life. I mean, look at how Jesus interacted with people. I'm not totally sure if what was happening to me is an innate part of the human being to seek God, or the Holy Spirit working in me. I just don't know yet.

According to Steve, Christianity became compelling or, in his words, "inescapable," not because of the social acceptance he found at Oakville First or the support he received from his new friend, Jeff. The two "clinchers" are, respectively, more scientific and more mysterious than these influences. In Steve's narrative, the historical truth of—and not simply blind faith in—the events of Christ's life, death, and resurrection and the gracious activity of the Holy Spirit played the two most significant roles. In other words, his faith is supported by both historical reality and the work of the third person of the Trinity.

During our formal conversations, I became convinced that perhaps the single most crucial element of Steve's Christian self-understanding is that his own establishment of the veracity of the Bible (or at least the death and resurrection of Christ) provided him with an eminently valid and inescapable basis for conversion. I asked Steve how he determined when he was sixteen that the major events described in the Bible had actually occurred. He replied:

> I didn't research it in a history book, if that's what you mean. I can't really remember. . . . Umm. . . . The way I looked into it was by, hang on, it was so long ago. I think I did it by talking with other Christians and reading the Bible and thinking about the longevity of the Bible, you know, how long it's been around, and how long people have been believing what it says. I don't know, but I think I looked into the archaeological evidence, like the Dead Sea Scrolls. Part of me needed to see some scientific evidence, some hard evidence. But the majority of it came from reading the Bible itself and looking at it as a historical document and seeing the prophecy of the Old Testament coming true in the New Testament. All of these things contributed to my seeing it as true, but the historical truth of the Bible was crucial to me. Without this, I'm not sure I would have become a Christian.

I decided to ask Steve to describe how he verified these facts because he had mentioned the importance of this evidentiary fait accompli three times during our conversation. However, the tone of uncertainty I detected in his normally calm voice when he tried to recall how he had determined that Christ's resurrection actually happened might suggest that *maintaining the belief* of having firmly validated these facts is a crucial (and perhaps at that time not fully stable) pillar of his self-understanding. His apparent uneasiness might be a function of the cognitive dissonance generated by the need to protect his self-understanding as a person who knows rationally that Christ died and rose again when his own memory and explanation seemed to suggest (perhaps on different levels, to both of us) that his adolescent investigations were preliminary.[14] As Charlotte Linde argues, the factuality of elements in personal narrative has little bearing on the more interesting question of how and why these stories provide individuals with a sense of "coherence" de-

manded both by society and the individual psyche (1993:222). Recognizing this need
for coherence, I did not pursue my question for very long once I intuited Steve's
discomfort about the topic of proof for the resurrection.

Steve's conversion was not instantaneous, but nevertheless had a profound impact on his life:

> I don't think there was an exact moment when I became a Christian, like as
> though I came home that night after the hayride and just, boom, all of a sudden
> I was a Christian. It was an experiential thing. I found out about a month later
> about the sinner's prayer, so I prayed it, but that itself was not the turning point.
> I think if I had to pinpoint my moment of becoming a Christian, I would say it
> was in the week between reading the book and after the hayride, or maybe in the
> few weeks between the hayride and the sinner's prayer.

This conversion was the beginning of a lengthy, painful, and radically transformative process for Steve. After he became a Christian, he started frequently attending Oakville First and gradually reorienting his values, ambitions, and self-
understanding.

> [His conversion] totally changed my priorities. For three months after I became
> a Christian, there was this uncontrollable energy in me, kind of an unfocused
> curiosity. I was so excited I just went *aaaahhh*, you know? I just wanted to know
> more and more and be fed.
>
>   But then my parents reacted. I mean, in a sense they were right, because my
> grades were slipping since my focus was totally on learning about Christianity.
> My parents said I was a Hindu, not a Christian, and had to stop being a Christian,
> and that was that. The church I was at had a mission to Central America, and I
> wanted to go on it, but my parents really put their foot down at that point. So,
> after that, Christianity became quite nominal for me. So, I hid my Bible and kept
> lots of secrets from them. But it was also embarrassing to me that I didn't have
> Christian parents like all the other kids in my church. I was so frustrated. I just
> wanted to know why I couldn't know God better.

After his parents virtually forbade him to be a Christian, Steve felt "spiritually
two-faced." On the one hand, he knew he was a Christian, but on the other hand,
he was not allowed to develop fully the new consciousness or lifestyle associated
with this new state of being. Nevertheless, as a result of his parents' restrictions, his
marks improved, gaining him acceptance to every university to which he applied.

Although many students from staunchly fundamentalist communities tell very
different stories of their early years at university, Steve's first year in residence at
McMaster was exciting and nurturing because of the relationships that developed
between people on his floor, relationships that were "intimate, but not sexual, like
in a lot of residences. I was having a great time here. But I was also empty." After
the winter break in his first year at McMaster, he decided he "didn't want to live
like this any more":

> It wasn't anything against the residences or anything. I know a lot of IV people
> hate the residences, but I loved it. No, I mean I didn't want to live without God
> any more. This was like a second conversion for me. I remember it so clearly. It

was the first Sunday back in January after Christmas, and I took a long walk down Cootes Drive talking and crying and yelling and whispering things to God.

At that point—again I have to use the word "inescapable"—I wanted the intimacy I knew when I became a Christian in high school. Then I went to the [Church at the] John and sang and it was amazing. I believe this is the work of God. I felt like a prodigal son coming home from another country. It was a hugely significant moment in my life. I could just feel God telling me that something special was going to happen to me. The Holy Spirit was saying that this was the beginning of something new. Within a week of this, I was asked to be outreach coordinator on the next year's exec. Buff said I was the risk on the executive, because I hadn't been out very much, really just a few large groups and some small group meetings in my first year.

Being asked to be a member of the executive committee represents an enormous honor and responsibility for IVCF students. As I explained in chapter 1, the executive is organized according to portfolios. Each member's job requires not only attendance at weekly two- or three-hour executive meetings and most other major IVCF events, but (primarily) completion of the usually quite time-consuming tasks included in his or her portfolio. Although Steve accepted the nominating committee's proposition in the early part of the winter term, by the summer of the same year (1994) he decided that he could not assume this position: "I felt I would be lying to my parents and to IV people because a lot of them didn't know my parents were non-Christians—not to mention Hindus—and that they were so against my being a Christian." However, the woman who was to assume the job of president for the 1994–95 academic year convinced Steve to accept the responsibility of outreach coordinator. Nevertheless, this was not the end of Steve's dilemmas. In November 1994, he was asked to attend the NSLC in Vancouver as one of the McMaster chapter's delegates. He worried both about whether he should go and whether he should tell his parents:

> But at the Church at the John, I heard a presentation where the speaker asked: "Is Your God Able?" He was talking about Shadrach, Meshach, and Abednego [Daniel 3], you know, the three Jews who refuse to bow down to Nebuchadnezzar. At some point they say something like "If our God is able to deliver us from the furnace, . . . then let him. But if not, we will not serve you or the Gods you worship." That really hit home for me. I told my parents about going to the NSLC, and they weren't happy, but they had a wait-and-see attitude. I guess they just hoped it was a phase.
>
> Then, just before I left [for the NSLC], [the nominating committee] asked me to be next year's president (1995–96). I remember asking myself if I was going to keep letting my parents rule my life. And then a while later, Buff asked me the exact same question, and wow, it just really had an impact. Buff was great. Even when I was thinking about whether or not to become president, she took the pressure off me, and was really supportive throughout the whole process. I accepted the job as president, and I'm not really happy about this part, but I decided not to tell my parents.

Obviously, not all coping strategies (or, to use Mandelbaum's [1973] term, "adaptations") are beneficial for a person for a long period of time. Just as Gabrielle retreated into a "Christian bubble" as a means of adapting to her crisis, Steve adapted to the conflict he experienced between his parents and his faith by keeping them radically separated. However, this strategy required lying to his parents, a decision supported by neither his Hindu past nor his Christian present. However, this choice allowed him to forestall a potentially self-destructive conflict between himself and his parents for long enough to entrench his new Christian identity, and therefore Steve considered it a necessary moral sacrifice. While his deception postponed a conflict with his parents, the consequent "incoherence" (Linde 1993) between the family and faith elements in his life's narrative generated significant anxiety for Steve.

In addition to concealing his steadily increasing executive responsibilities (as outreach coordinator in 1994 and then president in 1995) from his parents, Steve also had not revealed his dwindling interest in medical or graduate school. By the winter break in his third year at McMaster (when he was the president), Steve had decided to graduate in April 1996 with a three-year degree in science, rather than a four-year honors degree (which his parents assumed he would complete en route to medical or graduate school). More important, he had decided that he would apply to enter McMaster's Baptist Divinity College the following September (1996).

Steve agonized about lying to his parents and remembers a Boxing Day conversation he had with his cousin, in whom he confided his situation. His cousin urged him to tell his parents what he wanted to do with his life. "Again, it was inescapable," Steve said.

> I racked my brain trying to think of a good way and a good time to tell [my parents] about what I was going to do. I'm not very proud of this, but I didn't actually tell them about div college and graduating in April until March of that year. I was just so fearful. I knew that the worst-case scenario would be total rejection. I guess in my family, even among my dad's siblings and cousins, I'm kind of looked upon as sort of the son of the godfather; you know, nothing could go wrong with me, that sort of thing. So, I knew it would be a huge embarrassment to my dad that I was not going to be a doctor or whatever, and that I was going to go to div college.
>
> I remember around January receiving the verse in Matthew 6:24–25, you know, about denying yourself and taking up the cross. Jesus said, "For those who want to save their life will lose it and those who lose their life for my sake will find it."

I asked Steve what he meant when he said he "received" the verse. He replied:

> I guess I was already reading this chapter, but somehow I was really drawn to this part, but this was definitely spoken to me by God. Don't ask me how, like if he actually spoke or what, but I knew I received it from him. This verse alone carried me through that period. Paul, it was awful, just horrible. I never thought about killing myself or anything, but there were some times that I thought it would be better to be dead than going through this. It was my own personal Gethsemane. That's how I think of it now. I told my parents on March twenty-eighth. The week before I did this I prayed like I've never prayed before, and received messages of comfort and support and more than any other time I knew that God was speaking to me through the Bible. I told them on the phone. I look back on it

and feel horrible about how I did it, but then I just couldn't face them in person. I was just so fearful that I'd get the same kind of response I got when I told them [about becoming a Christian] when I was sixteen.

His parents were "shocked and angry," but they were also highly suspicious that someone had coerced Steve to make these major decisions, a misgiving he has still not completely allayed. The conflict between Steve and his parents had been developing since he was sixteen but reached a new and acute level when he became deeply involved in the IVCF. The period surrounding the phone call, Steve said, "was the hardest time in my life. I felt shattered. I didn't talk to them for a month after."

Not surprisingly, the tensions between Steve and his parents were exacerbated by the fact that at roughly the same time he told them he was going to the seminary, he also decided and told them that he was going to join the IVCF's 1996 mission team to Lithuania. His parents reacted very coolly to this latter idea, but such a chasm had already opened up between them and Steve that the news did not categorically alter their relationship.

At his emotional nadir in April 1996 (after he had told his parents everything), Steve had a dream that confirmed not only his decision to go to Lithuania but also Christ's power to save him from his tribulations. As Steve relates it, in his dream he is falling down a narrow, dark shaft, with his hands immobile at his sides. Although he is unable to see what is beneath him, he can hear the screams and hisses of monsters and demons. Just as the noises become almost deafening and his death seems imminent, he succeeds at placing his hands in front of him in the traditional Christian prayer position. The moment he is able to pray, his descent ceases, and he immediately and rapidly ascends toward the light above him.

Steve's experience in Lithuania served as a further affirmation of his convictions. During our conversation, Steve said:

> Lithuania was the best thing for me. Especially in the way the Lithuanian Christians received God and worshiped so passionately. It just really lifted me, and it felt like God had wiped off all my tears. The whole trip just really showed me God again. And then, listen to this: after this great, awesome experience, I came home, my mom picked me up at the airport, and as soon as we got in the door, she asked me if I could clean out the garage. My sister said, "Hey, take it easy on him, he just got home." My mom said, "Yeah, but he's been on holiday for a month." It was just *boom.* I was so totally up from Lithuania and then all of a sudden [making a fist and punching the air dramatically] *poooowwww,* back to reality.

Currently, relations between Steve and his family "are as good as they can be now, all things considered. But I know there still needs to be a lot of healing, emotionally and spiritually."

Every year, several of the McMaster chapter's members attend a conference in Urbana, Illinois, to learn about international missions, to develop their faith, and to network with Christians from other North American evangelical organizations. The international planning committee for Urbana 1996 asked Steve to speak briefly to an audience of approximately twenty thousand students about the McMaster team's mission to Lithuania. "This was a huge thing for me, too. I'm not sure why, but speaking at Urbana was a kind of a turning point. It was redemptive, too. It's hard to explain why, though." I speculated that with the invitation to speak not about his conversion but about his experiences in international evangelism (a prestigious calling), the conference may have symbolically marked his full immersion in and acceptance by the evangelical community. "Yeah, I guess that makes sense," he agreed tentatively.

Steve's life since he began classes at the Divinity College during the 1996–97 academic year has been challenging but satisfying because he now knows, to use evangelical rhetoric, what God wants him to do. Steve now considers the anguish he experienced, especially during the two years he was on the executive, as a lesson from which other Christians can learn. In fact, in his eyes, his suffering has assumed biblical proportions and significance (cf. Harding 1992:74). Steve reflected:

> I definitely see that there is some kind of redemption in my suffering. I'm not totally sure how that is. I think my testimony has been something for other Christians to see as an example, as something to edify other people. I now see that I was not just lying to my parents and to IV people, but to God, as well, and I had to stop that, too. You know, more than anything, I think that if I can relate at all to what Christ experienced, it's what he went through at the Garden of Gethsemane. The bottom line for me now is that I want to live my life with Christ. That's the basic guiding principle which guides my specific decisions about my faith and my life.[15]

Rosenwald (1992:286) describes the subject's "longing to become identical with its story" as the impetus for dramatic changes between and within major self-understandings. Steve's joy at finally being able to live the kind of public Christian life he has wanted to live for six years may indicate that while he may not yet be identical, at least he bears a stronger resemblance to the character he wants to play in his preferred "story."

Carole

Carole is a twenty-three-year-old woman who grew up in London, Ontario, in a United Church context. Her parents continue to be affiliated with the denomination. The United Church of Canada does not emphasize the necessity of an intimate relationship with God or the centrality of the moment of commitment, as most evangelical churches do. Consequently, as Carole puts it, "I guess I was just always aware of Christianity; I mean, I had the biblical cartoon books and that sort of thing. But the United Church doesn't stress the personal relationship with God thing. Looking back now, I can see some truths in my religious background, but they're buried in the United Church's political correctness and social justice orientation." Carole's involvement with the United Church continued during her adolescent years, when she was involved with her high school youth group:

> We went on retreats and that sort of thing, but the adults in charge didn't really monitor us closely or set very good examples. Actually, I can remember kids going

off together into the bushes. I'm not sure I was really aware of what was happening back then, but now I've figured out that they were probably fooling around. . . . I would have been considered one of the more religious kids in my youth group and in high school in general. When I look back, I suppose I was searching even then. In grade thirteen, I wrote my independent study essay on the Song of Solomon—as if you can say anything about that at that age.

Carole was not a rebellious teenager, "but after I turned eighteen I started doing things I should have gotten in trouble for but was careful enough to avoid getting caught." In the summer after grade twelve, she joined the army reserves, a summer occupation that introduced her to a subculture in which alcohol and sexual activity played major roles. The summer after she graduated from grade thirteen, she went to Manitoba with the army, at which point (and perhaps as an adaptation to the morally permissive ethic of her military surroundings) she began to drink and became increasingly sexually active. Carole continues: "During the summer in Manitoba, I went to church occasionally. [laughing] Actually, once I remember I got all excited because I met a Christian guy on the base, and I thought I could go to church with him. That was great, but on Saturday nights we'd go out and drink so much we were often too hung over to make it to church the next day."

Carole recalls, "The key thing during all of this period, when I think of it, was that I desperately wanted to be accepted. I'm still dealing with this need now, but it's less important to me." During my interviews with IVCF students, participants often spoke of their need to be accepted by their peers. Sometimes they spoke of this need in the past tense, as a requirement that was fully supplanted by their awareness of God's acceptance and love. And sometimes they spoke, as Carole did, of this need as a gradually (and still) diminishing part of a process of psychospiritual maturation. Nevertheless, in Carole's self-understanding, she has made great progress. "In my memory, there are two different sides of me: the social side that craved acceptance and the Christian side which was still there, and learning, but not as central to me for most of my life."

After she finished her work with the army, she entered an engineering program at a university in southern Ontario. As Carole put it:

I don't know if you know this, but the engineering culture is all drink drink drink, so I maintained the same habits I had developed in the army. One night at a campus bar, I saw a guy with an IVCF T-shirt on with scriptural verses on the back, and I went up and started talking to him, and thought great, now I can get a ride with someone to church. I went with him to the Mennonite Brethren Church in London for a while.

It was through this connection that Carole became involved in the IVCF. Since Carole was enrolled in a "co-op" engineering program, she alternated between spending one semester on campus and the next at an engineering work placement. This situation led to living what she described as "a double life." She explained:

I was heavily involved with [her university's IVCF chapter], but also with the engineering culture of drinking and picking up guys and all that. There were a couple of people from the IVCF who were also in engineering, and I remember feeling so ashamed whenever they would see me with the other engineering people being drunk and stupid. I guess that's called conviction, right? Being caught was not the worst part—it was realizing that I was leading two lives.

During the fall semester of her second year, Carole and a small group of her engineering peers had planned to spend their co-op work placements in Toronto, "having a great time and getting crazy. When we all planned to be together [in Toronto], this looked great, because by the summer before this term, I was drinking a lot and was with a new guy almost every weekend, even though I don't think I was really happy about it." However, as part of her casual involvement with the IVCF during this pre-Toronto period, she decided to attend Campus in the Woods, an IVCF retreat at the end of August. Her memory of the impact of this weeklong experience is quite vivid:

I thought it would be mainly a social thing, but it was a lot more. I was in the Explore Your Faith Track, which was about teaching us about prayer and concepts of God. During one of these workshops, I remember drawing a picture of God. There was this bright light in the center of the paper and then a maze all around the outside, with little traps and dead ends, like drinking and sex. I wanted to be in the middle but kept getting caught in the traps around the maze.

Suddenly in that week I realized that I. [pause] Before, I thought I had to earn the approval of everyone, like my parents, and God, too, and because of the accumulated crap, but especially because by this time I had slept with more than one guy, I was ashamed of myself and thought I was beyond redemption. The fact that I had slept with these guys still haunts me. Not just because it happened, but because I should have known better and I couldn't blame it on my ignorance or youth or drunkenness. I remember several times before, setting all these goals for myself. I even made a list one day and put it up in my room, saying I would stop doing this and that, especially having sex and drinking. I wanted to get out of this pattern, but every attempt I made failed totally. Then I realized that I couldn't do it by myself. If I had to pick a moment, I would say it was at the Campus in the Woods one day when I heard this song. I had heard it before, but suddenly the words just really made sense to me. The words were "I will bring you home, whatever's the matter, whatever's been done, I will bring you home." Home—that's what I wanted more than anything. That's when I realized God's love was unconditional. I wouldn't be comfortable saying the song made me think this. I mean, I knew this philosophically before, but that's when it finally sunk in.

I asked Carole why God's unconditional love and acceptance finally became a reality for her at the Campus in the Woods. She responded:

I could realize this then because until then I hadn't realized how much I needed it to be true. It could be that I was harboring enough pride until then that I thought I could do it all myself or that I could earn the acceptance I craved so much. I remember crying at the time and feeling relief and gratitude. What I knew at that moment that I didn't know before was that I would not be continuing that lifestyle. I knew the acceptance I wanted was not going to be found among the people I drank with.

Because Carole had been so active in her church youth group (unlike Steve, for example), I asked her whether she was a Christian before her conversion at Campus in the Woods:

I would have said I was a Christian, but. [pause] I'm not happy about making that distinction [between Christians and non-Christians], although I know a lot of IV people are totally happy to do this; but in terms of the sheep and the goats and the wheat and the chaff, I was probably part of the chaff before. I guess the difference was that I didn't have a personal relationship with God before. At the Campus in the Woods, my beliefs finally started to have an impact on my life.

When she moved to Toronto the week after Campus in the Woods, she disappointed her peers from the engineering department who invited her to go out with them to drink and meet men. At Campus in the Woods, she had met and started to date a Christian man from Brampton, a suburb of Toronto. She quickly became very attached to his family, whose invitations to participate in their family life provided her with "good excuses to escape what all my other engineering friends were doing in Toronto."

After this work term in Toronto, her university lifestyle changed dramatically. She became heavily involved with the IVCF and ceased her participation in the drinking and courting associated with the engineering ethos. The following summer, during a work term in Ottawa, she decided to transfer to McMaster, where she was accepted into the computer science program. "I had really started to dislike the stupid elitism of most of the engineers, and their whole subculture. And also, academically, I lost all interest in it."

Because of the support she had previously received from the IVCF, when she arrived at McMaster in 1995, she joined its IVCF immediately. Her sexual history sets her apart from the vast majority of female IVCF members, most of whom are not sexually experienced. However, as an adaptation to her new role as a fully committed Christian woman, and in an attempt to grapple with the role of men in her life, Carole recounts:

In the summer of ninety-five, I committed myself to not dating for a year, because I realized that I had still been seeking approval from the Christian guys I had been dating since Campus in the Woods. I felt I needed to learn to be content in the sufficiency of God. Now it's been more than a year and a half since that commitment. In the last year, I've been growing into myself more. My long-term goal is to become a Godly woman. And part of that is figuring out the whole role of women thing and what sort of woman God wants me to become.

Although Carole is acutely aware (more than most IVCF women I interviewed) of the issues associated with the subordinate role of women in her tradition, "for now that's on the back burner for me,"[16] she said. Nevertheless, she characterized her current opinion in the following manner:

I was studying the passages on the role of women in the church in Ephesians a while ago. It says that wives should submit to their husbands, and husbands should love their wives like Christ loved the church. Well, Christ loved the church so much he was willing to die for it and always put its needs above his own, so I guess if a man was willing to treat me like that I would be willing to submit to him. But I still haven't really worked out the women preaching thing yet. In London, I go to an Associated Gospel Church, where women can't preach. But in Hamilton I go to an Anglican church, because I love the form and structure of the liturgy. But it's hard to get good teaching at the Anglican church, you know, because it's more and more like the United Church, so interested in political correctness.

Since Carole is enjoying self-directed faith development and involvement with her small group of Christian friends (many of whom are IVCF members), her participation in the chapter has dwindled to occasional attendance at social events. Nevertheless, she remains aware of the group's activities and still considers herself an IVCF member, albeit a loosely affiliated one.

Although at twenty-three, Carole is (chronologically) one of the oldest members of the group, other group members would consider her one of the chapter's "youngest Christians." Measures such as abstaining from serious involvements with men help to diminish her need for the approval of others and, simultaneously, to dull the shame she still feels when she thinks about her previous sexual experience. Even though her experiences in the United Church had familiarized her with significant elements of Christianity, what she perceived as the distant and politicized God of her childhood and adolescence could neither inspire nor empower her to change her life. Only an intimate, awe-inspiring, and categorically different sort of God could accomplish this. Her personal introduction and moral submission to this God have had such a profound affect on her life that "I have a hard time believing that my pre-Christian life was really me. I just sort of look back and think of that person as a totally other person. Since the conversion experience, what I've gone through is very much growing into the kind of woman God wanted me to be all along. Now I finally know this, that's all."

Conclusions

The four lives explored in this chapter are in many ways distinctive. I have not encountered an instance of familial resistance to evangelicalism as profound as Steve's, nor are the vast majority of IVCF students members of a visible minority. I have encountered very few women in the chapter who share Gabrielle's austere fundamentalist convictions yet are also committed to traveling to foreign lands to evangelize and who are as friendly toward and appreciative of a committed non-Christian such as myself. I have met no other IVCF woman with as much or as thoroughly analyzed sexual experience as Carole, nor have I met many students in this chapter who can articulate their faith in as thoughtful and self-conscious a manner. Finally, I have met few lifelong Christians in the IVCF who are as gentle and considerate as Simon is toward others, especially non-Christian others, and who are as self-effacing as he is about his faith and life experience.

Although Steve, Carole, Gabrielle, and Simon are unique individuals, their life histories include situations and themes found in the stories other members of the chapter tell. In the next six chapters, I explore most of the major narrative motifs evident in these histories and the larger patterns and tensions they reveal. However, some of the major strands woven through these four histories bear mentioning at this point, both to summarize some central issues in these four lives and to fore-shadow the following chapters.

The status of women in the evangelical and, more generally, Christian tradition, surfaced in all life histories except Steve's. This is ironic, in that Steve is the only one of these four participants who supports the full equality of women in the church. His advocacy of this position is not, however, unambiguous; he continues to affiliate himself with a church and denomination that do not allow women to preach. The other three participants' views on the role of women in their tradition are still, to varying degrees, in a state of flux. This uncertainty reflects the growing problematization of the issue of female pastors and the role of women in general within the evangelical community. The IVCF participants' dynamic and ambiguous views of women reveal the significant influence of feminism on evangelicalism generally (Stacey and Gerard 1990). In addition, these students' views may also reflect their exposure to McMaster's egalitarian academic and relatively egalitarian social ethos. In chapter 5, I discuss the ways in which the IVCF offers evangelical students a forum in which to entertain often equivocal feelings about women in their faith.[17]

The role of evangelism at McMaster and abroad is a significant issue for these students. In the narratives recounted in this chapter, the mission to Lithuania is highlighted, largely because I shared this experience with three of the four students. The trip to Lithuania forced Gabrielle, Steve, and Simon to formalize their beliefs in order to communicate them and to come to terms with the tremendous privilege they enjoy as North American Christians. The mission also altered (in Gabrielle's case) and consolidated (in Steve's case) the vocational course of their lives. In the following chapters and especially in chapter 7, I explore what I term the "apostolic self-understanding," which undergirds so many IVCF participants' relations with non-Christians in North America and elsewhere.

Throughout this book but especially in the next chapter, I explore the system of body language and spoken language that has come to characterize the group and, conversely, those outside the group. In this chapter's life histories, the meanings of words such as "spiritual walk," "Christian" as opposed to "non-Christian," a "personal relationship with God," "salvation," and "sin" may strike readers as elements of an unfamiliar jargon. This perception is accurate: Steve, Gabrielle, Simon, Carole, and all of the other IVCF members whom I have come to know employ well-defined spoken and acted rhetorical signs, some of which are derived from the broader evangelical community, some of which seem to be unique to the IVCF, and all of which are used as tools to effect personal self-transformation (Staples and Mauss 1987). The role that key words such as "Christian" play in this process are explored in detail in the next chapter, in which I discuss the IVCF's distinctive rhetorical signs and the larger semiotic system underlying them.[18]

One of the most conspicuous features of IVCF students' life history narratives is the prevalence of what might be termed the discourse of psychospiritual bifurcation. This discourse is also evident in the four narratives I have explored in this chapter. With the exception of Simon, these students spoke of God, Christ, the Holy Spirit, or the evangelical community as helping them to cease leading "double lives" (for

Gabrielle and Carole) and being "spiritually two-faced" (for Steve). Psychiatrist Charles Strozier writes:

> The most general psychological observation about fundamentalists[19] one can make is that they demonstrate inner divisions that find expression in their beliefs. *All* fundamentalists I met described their personal narratives as broken in some basic way. Before rebirth in Christ they described their lives as unfulfilled, unhappy, and usually evil. Their stories were discontinuous and full of trauma; faith healed them. That moment of finding a "personal relationship with the Lord," as they put it, was the great divide in their lives. (1994:42)

Strozier notes that for those who became Christians after their childhood, the divergence between their former lives and, as IVCF students sometimes say, their "new life in Christ" is often construed as categorical (1994:43). Hence, Steve and Carole interpret their transformations (or "turnings," to use Mandelbaum's [1973] term) to have altered and elevated their spiritual essences in a dramatic manner.[20]

Whether one is born into the faith as Simon was, chooses at a young age to enter the faith as Gabrielle did, or has a life-altering conversion experience as Steve and Carole did, one is a Christian by virtue of one's will to initiate a relationship with Christ. For IVCF students, conversion involves a process of personal reorientation in pursuit of what ethnographer Salvatore Cucchiari describes as "more integrative systems of meaning, personal autonomy and moral responsibility" (1988: 418). In some cases, a second conversion is required for assurance that faith is more than a function of family tradition or adolescent needs, but in practically all cases, IVCF members describe having made conscious decisions to forsake one life in favor of another.

Once one begins to analyze both the conversion experiences described by these students and the larger biographical reorganizations which flow from these rebirths, one quickly becomes mired in a basic social-scientific dilemma. Some examples should illustrate this problem. Gabrielle's description of the intimate relationship between her own conversion and that of her father seems to suggest that she was partially motivated to become a Christian because she wanted to participate in the new endeavor in which her beloved father was so passionately engaged. It would be possible and interesting (but beyond the scope of the present work) to offer a Freudian or more generally psychoanalytical interpretation of Gabrielle's relationship with her father and his role in her conversion. For Steve, the fact that his family was emotionally distant, authoritarian, and uninterested in addressing his existential questions seems to have played a significant role in his desire to become a Christian: through this new community, he could find emotional support, achieve self-actualization, absorb an encompassing and ethnically nonspecific theological and cosmological framework, and have an opportunity to participate in leadership. Carole seems to have required the imposition of binding rules and mores from an authoritative transcendent source, a source that could forgive her sins and control both her sensual appetites and her need to be accepted. And finally, Simon's wish to participate fully in his family's and his community's religious life may have prompted him both to become a Christian when he was five years old and then (more memorably) to reappropriate his faith between his sixteenth and seventeenth years. The former transformation secured the love of his parents, and the latter commitment secured his self-definition as a mature Christian and a *bona fide* member of the wider evangelical community.

When I ask IVCF students what led to their conversion(s), I usually hear two distinct explanations (not always in this order): first, these students speak of their shallow, unsatisfying if not simply desperate pre-Christian lives. Second, students also speak of the role of the Holy Spirit (or Christ) in drawing them to God. When asked to explain the relationship between their pre-Christian psychosocial conditions and the Holy Spirit, students normally explain that the Holy Spirit used their existing predicament to draw them to God. If I suggested to Gabrielle that her "real" motivation for becoming a Christian was to secure the love of her father or to Steve that his "real" motivation was to find a supportive alternative family in which his personal gifts would be welcomed and his concerns about mortality would be resolved, both students would be puzzled. On the one hand, Steve and Gabrielle would agree that becoming a Christian greatly improved their personal lives. On the other hand, they would suggest that I had missed the ultimate point—that they chose to take advantage of the opportunity provided by the Holy Spirit. For IVCF students like Steve and Gabrielle, any interpretation of conversion which restricts itself to psychological or social explanations is patently reductionistic and neglects the more pivotal and irreducible divine element.[21]

One might argue plausibly that these students' searches for "new lives in Christ" are expressions of the basic existential quest for meaning and purpose, which might have been satisfied in other ways, such as converting to Buddhism or Islam or devoting their lives to a political movement. However, almost none of the students I met would accept the religious relativism implicit in the previous sentence. For all but one of the sixty IVCF participants I interviewed, the choice to become a Christian is absolutely and universally required for a truly fulfilled life and a desirable afterlife. However, as a social scientist, I cannot even begin to determine either whether the God to whom IVCF students are so devoted exists or whether the Holy Spirit actually participated in these students' conversions. I do not mean reductively to dismiss these students' shared belief that their "new lives in Christ" were influenced by or led them into intimate contact with God. However, I am not content to enclose these students' conversions in a mysterious "black box" (Cucchiari 1988: 417) and focus only on the consequences of such enigmatic processes. I can interpret or translate for non-Christians what I think these believers mean when they speak of salvation, conversion, faith, and so on. I can also relate that from a believer's viewpoint, becoming a Christian decreases these students' alienation from God. As well, from an outsider's perspective, I can posit that conversion also satisfies these students' psychosocial needs, such as belonging to a group, possessing an exclusive truth, and being directed by an established moral model.[22] Nevertheless, I will not subsume IVCF participants' postulations of the ontological independence of God and the veracity of the Bible under the common social-scientific postulation of God and the Bible as symbolic fulfillments of essentially psychosocial needs. Clearly, this study must ultimately propose a social scientific (rather than a theological) interpretation. However, I am inclined to allow the evangelical and social-scientific truth claims to coexist, albeit distinctly and uneasily, throughout this study.

As I outlined in the introduction to this chapter, the life history method is an inherently "collaborative venture" (Langness and Frank 1985:61). In choosing which portions of the transcripts of our conversations to include and when to interrupt the voices of my interlocutor to paraphrase or make theoretical observations, I have molded these narratives into concise packages that serve as introductions to four individuals.[23] In so doing, I have of necessity omitted many details from these accounts. As Crapanzano (1980) argues, this "collaborative venture" probably reveals as much about the writer as it does about his or her subjects.[24] Nevertheless, ethnography is, or at least aims to be, more than an anthropologist's autobiography in disguise. Rather, my obvious presence in these life histories is intended at least to problematize if not shatter what Kirshenblatt-Gimblett describes as "the illusion that nothing [stands] between the reader and the subject, that one [is] in the presence of a culture authoring its own text" (1989:130). I am present in these life histories, but (I hope) respectfully and reflexively.

Most important, the four histories in this chapter are intended to remind the reader that the broader arguments I advance in subsequent chapters emerge out of my experiences with real people who wrestle with and wonder about the issues I explore. I hope I have been able to depict Simon, Gabrielle, Carole, and Steve in such a way as to convey some of the complexities of their personalities and to make these four individuals seem, as much as possible, familiar.

THREE

IVCF Rhetoric

> In the beginning was the Word, and the Word was with God, and the Word was God.
>
> John 1:1

> Among orthodox Protestants, and especially among fundamentalists, it is the Word, the gospel of Jesus Christ, written, spoken, heard, and read, that converts the unbeliever. . . . It is the Word of God, the gospel, and believers would add, the Holy Spirit, God himself, that converts, that "changes the heart." We cannot understand Fundamental Baptist conversion by looking only at what causes a person to listen to the gospel; the causes are innumerable. We must listen too, and we must explore the consequences of listening.
>
> Harding

> You know, everyone in this country says they're Christians, but very few actually are. We talked about this whole thing in my small group. We tried to come up with a different word, like "believers," or "born agains," and I think these are maybe better. At least they're a way to separate ourselves from all the people who just say they're Christians but don't have a personal relationship with Christ.
>
> Denise, from fieldnotes

Anthropologist James Clifford asserts that "the return of rhetoric to an important place in many fields of study . . . has made possible a detailed anatomy of conventional expressive modes." This new focus on rhetoric, Clifford continues, "is less about how to speak well than about how to speak at all, and to act meaningfully, in a world of public cultural symbols" (1986:10). Even when groups use the same official language as the mainstream culture in which they exist, a distinctive pattern of communication usually emerges within each group. In various ways, this new pattern separates the group's members from nonmembers. This pattern of speech is often unique in terms of its characteristic intonation (cf. Tedlock 1983), or a group may distinguish itself through the rhetorical medium of song by virtue of the use of archaic language, as in the case of Roman Catholic monastic chanting, or through the employment of slang, as in the case of rap music.[1]

As anthropologist James Fernandez has observed, a sensitivity to local figures of speech is necessary for any good ethnography (1974:119). The most obvious distinguishing feature of a group's mode of communication is the array of insider's words—for example, words such as "outing" among gays and lesbians, "fly" among young inner-city African American men, and "away" among residents of Prince Edward Island.[2] These words are not always incomprehensible to people outside of the group; I am neither homosexual, African American, nor an Islander, but I know what many of these group-specific terms mean. However, these terms originate in local communities and have a special significance within them that casual observers cannot always fully appreciate. In this chapter, I introduce and interpret the IVCF's insider words, phrases, and gestures and the broader rhetorical and social contexts that give these phenomena their meanings. My experiences with non-IVCF evangelicals lead me to believe that the majority of IVCF rhetoric is shared by believers in the wider evangelical community. Therefore, the strategies manifested in IVCF students' uses of distinctive rhetoric may shed some light on the role of the same or similar terms and gestures in North American evangelicalism in general.

Instead of understanding expressions of distinctive rhetoric as disconnected episodes, it is more plausible to interpret them as elements of complex "performances," which folklorist Deborah Kapchan defines as "patterns of behaviour, ways of speaking and manners of bodily comportment whose repetition situates actors in time and space, structuring individual and group identities" (1995:479). By using the word "performances," I do not mean to suggest that IVCF participants are "merely" acting or pretending to believe or feel what they say they do. The paradigm which undergirds the present analysis follows anthropologist Victor Turner (1969, 1974) and conceives of social life as a drama with all individuals as actors. This model does not, however, dismiss the performers or their convictions as insincere. Rather, it suggests that we should pay close attention to the ways a person's surroundings and self-understanding combine so that he or she feels compelled or inspired to assume a role in an unfolding play and thus is, to some extent, bound by a script. The IVCF rhetorical performances clearly manifest the students' religious sensibilities and the social networks in which these individuals find themselves. Construing these students as performers simply reminds us of the drama's constructed and dynamic nature.[3]

Although much of intra-IVCF communication strikes me as being what Kapchan calls "habitual practices," the more public rhetorical expressions (such as those rhetorical conventions evident at large and small group meetings) fall into the category she describes as "heightened performances" or "stylistically marked expressions of otherness, lifting the level of habitual behaviour and entering alternate, often ritualized or ludic, interpretive frames wherein different rules apply" (1995:

479). Usually, performers are aware (albeit to varying degrees) of the nonhabitual and dramatic nature of their actions and words.

While it is tempting to emphasize the theological references and subtexts inherent in religious language, in most religious contexts believers rarely speak about or strictly because of theological ideas per se. The theological substructure of religious language is an important component of any consideration of religious rhetoric. But religious language consists not simply of speech acts which communicate prior and more important ideas.[4] Rather, religious utterances (including speaking, praying, and singing) are themselves unique acts or commitments (Bloch 1989:37), which may bear only a slight family resemblance to the beliefs or ideas on which such acts are supposedly ultimately based. In other words, more important (at least in the present study) than the cognitive processes at work behind or prior to these rhetorical expressions is the cultural context within which such utterances are made and are expected (by the speakers) to make sense.

The rhetorical practices associated with conservative Protestant groups such as the IVCF represent conspicuous manifestations of specialized rhetoric. For example, when one IVCF member said, in the context of a small group meeting I attended, "We should let God lead and not try to go off on our own, because if we let God lead, then he'll go ahead of us and prepare the way for us," this student was accomplishing more than the simple communication of a religious belief. His assertion expressed a conviction that he could be certain was shared by the rest of the group. This performance—note how the final part of his sentence assumes a biblical tone (Harding 1992)—distinguishes the student (to himself and his listeners, including myself) as an insider, an obedient "Christian."[5] This use of rhetoric to define oneself and one's nonself was quite common among the IVCF. During my association with the IVCF, I kept a list of spoken and sung terms, phrases, idioms, and patterns of speech that struck me as either atypical for university students or central to the way IVCF participants talk about their religious beliefs, moral standards, and relationships with their non-Christian peers.[6] By the end of my research, I noticed that numerous elements on this list embody the group's central religious values and organizing principles. Consequently, a consideration of IVCF students' rhetorical practices should be an effective means of understanding these believers.

Just as there are ways of determining good and bad performances in the theater, so, too, are IVCF rhetorical presentations subject to evaluation, usually by the performers themselves.

One of ethnographer Dennis Tedlock's interlocutors describes a Zuni criterion for a good or true performance. Speaking about a "good" or "true" story, Andrew says, "You're right with that story, like you were in it. Some guys, the way they tell it, it seems like they were really in it" (1983:166).[7] Likewise, the main IVCF criterion for a good story or a good witnessing narrative is, similarly, that the teller is credibly "in" the story and that auditors may be able to place themselves "in" it as well. Wayne Booth, a scholar of English literature, commented that testimonies are "not just showing listeners how to be saved, with the consequences of the listening postponed until afterward; it is giving them the experience of salvation here and now, in the act of dwelling in story. Citizen listeners experience a transcending of this world, 'for the time being'—from the first time they 'buy into' the world of the story. . . . The listener is lifted into that world in the act of listening or reading" (1995:386).[8] The IVCF witnesses are obviously not always successful at transporting listeners to another imaginative world in which their convictions will appear compelling to the nonbeliever (or perhaps "not-yet-believer"). However, this ideal gives rise to a widely, though implicitly maintained criterion which might be described as "semiotic sincerity" or perhaps "semiotic plenitude." One must, at the very least, be sincerely "in" one's words. In other words, the words must come across as sufficiently authentic to enter the listener's mind, to encourage him or her to dwell "in story," as Booth puts it. Students use the term "Christianese" to describe a semiotically insincere use of their rhetoric in which the terms are banal or opaque to both outsiders and participants. For example, during a conversation about God's plan for her life, Candace reiterated a motto I had heard several times during interviews. She said, "I'll do my best. God will do the rest," and then stopped abruptly. She continued, "*Oooh*, sorry. That was Christianese. I try not to talk like that, but it's just the way I think sometimes." As soon as Candace recognized that her thoughts were expressed in the form of a rhyming slogan, and thus I might perceive them as artificial, as semiotically empty, she became immediately self-critical. She followed her apology with a lengthy elaboration of the intellectual content of the saying.

Fernandez (1974) argues that the language used in explicitly religious contexts is not usually designed merely to express ideas and communicate personal experiences. Whether the words in question are used within the group to discuss important issues or more selectively in the context of a member's conversation with an individual from outside the group, this rhetoric is laden with metaphors and symbols which both convey meaning and condition the possible interpretations a participant in the conversation might make. In other words, rhetoric opens up and closes off potential interpretations. For example, when one IVCF participant says to another, "Last year I was saved and it changed my life," this statement transmits specific information within the limitations inherent in this common evangelical statement. The possible meanings of this sentence are limited by the conviction (which the evangelical speaker can assume is shared by virtually all evangelical listeners) that being "saved" cannot refer to an experience one can have without Christ. People are theoretically free to reject the limitations imposed by their group's language. However, most of us rarely choose to exercise this freedom (Fernandez 1974:132). Most of us enter (at birth or later voluntarily) a set of established rhetorical practices; by and large, we gradually accept these practices, even though we might also subtly adapt them to our personal needs. For example, in response to this hypothetical statement, an auditor might reply, "That's great. A friend of mine experienced the same sort of thing when he joined Alcoholics Anonymous." But IVCF rhetoric has evolved to facilitate and condition a particular sort of discussion about faith. As loyal advocates of the beliefs and values reflected and sustained by IVCF rhetoric, in this example, other IVCF members would quickly deploy their rhetorical tools to demonstrate to this nonconformist that the Bible clearly limits salvation to Christ.

Although there is some diversity when it comes to the theological and moral beliefs held *abstractly* by IVCF students on religious issues,[9] I observed only minor differences between the ways members *actually* expressed themselves (in the contexts of interviews, prayers, and small and large group events). In his study of a Primitive Baptist church, Brett Sutton observed that worshipers are encouraged to do whatever the Holy Spirit leads them to do but that their subsequent conduct and speech invariably fall squarely within the traditions established within the church for "normal" behavior (1980:172). Similarly, near the beginning of most large IVCF events, participants are encouraged to express themselves in the manner to which they are accustomed (and to which the Holy Spirit leads them). However, subsequent behavior at IVCF events also conforms to narrow standards of decorum.[10] As in the Primitive Baptist setting, neither the Holy Spirit nor IVCF participants seem inclined to transgress the implicit expressive conventions of the group.

The following two examples demonstrate the constraining function of IVCF rhetoric. During one of our conversations, Martina, a fourth-year science student with IVCF executive committee experience, warned me that she had a very different understanding of Satan from that of other IVCF members. However, when she began to share this view with me, she used the same expressions, sentences, and illustrations as most other participants. The second example is set in Lithuania, where Jocelyn, a second-year social work student, was reluctant to share her "testimony" (her account of her conversion) with the other team members or the Lithuanians because she believed that her experience of "coming to Christ" was not only different from but also not respected by the majority of IVCF members.[11] Since I had interviewed her at length months before the 1996 mission, I was aware of these differences and understood her hesitation. When she finally shared her testimony with the Lithuanian students and the mission team, however, the structure, style, and content of her narrative were identical to the testimonies of the other team members and bore little resemblance to what she had told me months earlier.[12]

The IVCF's official openness to a variety of forms of evangelical rhetoric is a function of the diverse denominational backgrounds of its members. In the words of Buff Cox, the IVCF staff worker, "We want to make sure students are learning about Christianity, not 'churchianity.' " However rhetorically open the group may be in principle, in practice it may be that the virtual homogeneity of IVCF rhetoric is what mitigates against interdenominational and intradenominational tensions and idiosyncratic religiosity. In any case, the fact that I observed very few manifestations of idiosyncratic religious behavior during my fieldwork seems to confirm John Stackhouse's assertion that the IVCF participates in the "transdenominational evangelicalism" (1993:12) rooted in the common ground of Canadian conservative Protestantism.[13]

Ethnographers must avoid at least two intellectual traps when interpreting the unique argot of the group they are studying. The first is a tendency toward strictly textual criticism. Titon argues that "The meaning of language performed orally . . . is often so context-bound that attempts to work primarily from the transcribed texts are misguided" (1988:12). For the IVCF, it is primarily during singing that Durkheim's collective "effervescence" (1973:181), the communal enthusiasm which binds a group together and enshrines (and often creates) many of its values, is the most striking.[14] Titon contends that when dealing with language in the context of music, the narrow application of literary theory to songs is particularly inappropriate because the meaning of a song may have little to do with its lyrics. "You cannot argue

with a song," Bloch writes (1989:37), underscoring the primarily nonlogical essence
of songs and singing. For example, "Sin Jacket," one of the street dramas performed
by the IVCF in Lithuania, is set to the popular 1980s rap song "Can't Touch This,"
performed by M. C. Hammer. The literal message of this song is diametrically
opposed to the meaning ascribed to it in the IVCF context. During this drama, the
mission team uses a jacket to represent sin. At the beginning of the performance,
a IVCF actor, playing Jesus, forbids a female member, playing a mortal, from touch-
ing the jacket. Eventually, the woman succumbs to temptation, puts on the jacket,
dances around the stage jubilantly, but then is unable to take the jacket off. The
jacket becomes so heavy it causes her to collapse. Then the student playing Jesus
steps in, removes the jacket from the prone woman, painfully puts it on himself,
and then dies, an act of sacrifice which restores the woman to life. In the song
playing in the background of this drama, Hammer sings: "You can't touch [compare
yourself to] this [Hammer]," and brags about his greatness. The dramatic use of
this song, by contrast, seeks to communicate the (transformed) messages that we
"can't [should not] touch this [sin]," as well as Christ's sacrifice for our failure to
heed God's demands. In fact, only the title of the song is related to the skit's
message. None of the members of the mission team seemed to be aware of the
contradiction between the egocentric lyrics of the song and the theocentric message
they were trying to convey in the drama.[15]

One may not be able to argue with a song, but this does not mean that one
must ignore the messages implicitly and explicitly encoded in the song's lyrics.
During this and other chapters, to support the arguments I am making, I discuss
the lyrics of songs sung during IVCF events. I hope, however, to avoid an excessive
preoccupation with or reliance on the literal meaning of the lyrics.

The second difficulty in interpreting performances is the more traditional temptation to treat the rhetorical practices of a group of people as simple and secondary
functions of the group's values, structure, or ideological commitments, functions
worthy of study only once all the truly important research has been completed.
Titon argues that even the serious considerations of religious language often ignore
its crucial performative elements and focus instead on the way language reflects
philosophy, poetry, or theology (1988:192). In this chapter, I attempt to avoid this
problem as I depict the two major forms of rhetoric apparent in the forms of speaking, praying, and singing that are characteristic of the McMaster IVCF.

In her 1987 text, based on fieldwork among fundamentalist Baptists in the United
States, anthropologist Susan Harding proposes an explanation of evangelical rhetoric
which is helpful for a study of the McMaster IVCF. Harding's main thesis is that
fundamentalist rhetoric insinuates itself into the listener's "subliminal mind" in the
form of "a biblical rhythm of alternatives, a vibrating template" (1987:179), which
strongly encourages believers to understand their world in sharply dualistic terms:
one is either saved or damned, bound for heaven or hell (cf. Strozier 1994; Wagner
1990:104). The more one uses and hears this rhetoric, the more thoroughly it becomes integrated into one's imagination, and the more completely it disengages one
from one's pre-Christian self-understanding. This highly specialized rhetoric helps
evangelicals construe their experience of the world in a manner which emphasizes

the essential antagonism between their values and practices and those of a fallen world.[16]

A study of rhetoric rarely involves the consideration of a single word in isolation. For the most part, what follows is a necessarily selective reflection on conversations or public performances in which I emphasize particular words or manners of speaking. My present task is to provide the reader with a brief account and demonstration of the spectrum of IVCF rhetoric. This account should prepare the reader to interpret other examples of rhetoric as they appear throughout this ethnography.

Fortress Rhetoric

The Harding model describes rhetoric which corresponds with what I described in chapter 1 as the fortress approach to the non-Christian world. This strategy allows participants to repel what one older IVCF student described as "the onslaught of secularization." In this strategy, the perforations in the "selectively permeable membrane" between the secular ethos and the evangelical world are fully or almost fully constricted. Rhetoric in this scheme is designed to distinguish IVCF participants from the secular milieu, normally by framing the differences between these two subcultures in sharply dualistic terms, with the evangelical ethos portrayed as under seige by the hegemonic if not demonic ideology of secularism.[17]

An examination of particular instances of fortress rhetoric can elucidate these oral practices and the antagonistic dualism that underlies them. The examples of rhetoric I have selected are arrayed on a continuum, with some terms nearer what I call the "active divisive" end and others closer to the "passive divisive" end.

On the "passive divisive" side of the continuum are terms and concepts such as discipling, angels, prayer, visions, Trinity, free will, and repentance. Because terms in this category are also sometimes employed by people outside the evangelical fold, these words are not the most potent examples of fortress rhetoric.[18] Nevertheless, according to IVCF students, non-Christians (a technical evangelical term meaning, usually, nonevangelical Christians) do not use these terms within the crucial legitimating framework of a personal relationship with Christ and a belief in the authority of the Bible. As well, IVCF students commonly exhibited a variety of degrees of awareness and discomfort that the rhetoric they use to describe their most cherished beliefs is considered obsolete or quaint by most of their peers (most of whom would be considered by IVCF members to be merely nominal Christians). Consequently, when members use these terms on the McMaster campus, it is usually in the safe context of an IVCF event. Moreover, students are well aware that the same room that houses occasional IVCF discussions about creation science and obedience to God could be at other times the setting for McMaster-sanctioned classes on evolution or humanistic psychology. This reminds IVCF members that they are not in entirely friendly territory.

In the middle of the continuum I have described are more active terms employed to separate IVCF students and other evangelicals I have met from non-Christians. A great deal can be learned about the McMaster chapter's theology and social structure by the way its members use the common evangelical active-divisive terms "saved" and "salvation." During the sixty interviews I conducted, participants spoke freely about salvation. As I mentioned in chapter 2, approximately 85% of participants were able to describe (and some to name) either the day or the month of their salvations. Even though more than two-thirds of these conversions occurred before the participants were thirteen years old (and more than half of these between the ages of four and eight), the events are invariably described as crucial turning points in the participants' lives.

In some cases, the language IVCF members use to describe salvation evokes the children they were when they were saved. In other cases, the experience is communicated in more mature terms. As Kirk, a first-year kinesiology student, described it, "I was saved one night when I was twelve. After I finished playing Nintendo with my friend Doug, he just got out [the Book of] Revelation and read it to me. That scared me like crazy. That night I went home and prayed to God. I said, 'Lord, I don't know you now, but my friend Doug does, and I want to be with him in heaven.' And from then on, it slowly affected my whole life."

Brenda, a first year humanities student, said of her salvation, "Oh yeah, I remember being saved. A pastor one day in church—I was six—told us that our parents' faith would not take us to heaven, that there were no guests allowed, if you know what I mean, and that really hit home. At that moment, I felt a real weight lifted from me and I felt a peace I had never felt before. That was it."

Frank, a second-year kinesiology student, told me, "When I was six, I knelt beside my mom and became a Christian because I really knew that Christ died for me and that I didn't want to go to hell." I asked him what that experience meant to him, and he replied, "Well, as much as it can mean to a six-year-old. I mean, I was just a kid then—what do you know when you're six? But I believe you can start with something small and build on it."

As Lewis, a third-year student, recalls:

Yeah, I guess I was saved around twenty. This is getting pretty personal, but [pause] okay, I guess I can tell you. I was having an on-again off-again, relationship with this woman. It all escalated until one night we just had this really bad sexual experience. I mean really bad. This sort of made me bottom out spiritually and in other ways. I had no idea what to do at first. Eventually I began to accept Christ and start to rebuild myself.[19]

Once redemption is secured—for most members, years before they entered university—students understandably speak of this experience among themselves less frequently. Nonetheless, one of the main contexts in which they speak of being saved is when they offer their testimonies to an IVCF group or to a non-Christian.[20] As well, IVCF students may speak of their salvation in the context of a general admission of their own wickedness and a celebration of God's goodness, as when Frank included the following confession in a brief testimony he shared with a large group meeting: "I mean, I can't believe it, you know, that God wanted to save a sinner like me. Isn't that awesome?"

The "saving work of Christ" also constitutes one of the central elements of the songs many participants have sung for years at Bible camps, church services, and

IVCF events. Psychiatrist Anthony Stow notes that "at an emotional level, there is something deeper about hearing than seeing; and something about hearing other people which fosters human relationships even more than seeing them" (Stow in Warner 1997a:228). An effective means of generating solidarity-galvanizing collective effervescence and celebrating their salvations is provided by IVCF songs such as "Salvation," which includes the following lyrics:

> Salvation belongs to our God
> Who sits upon the throne
> And we the redeemed shall be strong
> In purpose and unity

More than simple descriptions of the spiritual status of IVCF students, the terms "saved" and "salvation" function as wedges driven between IVCF participants and the vast majority of non-Christians. The distinction between IVCF participants as "saved" and non-Christians as "unsaved" casts the latter in the dim light of spiritual waywardness, if not damnation. One day at the end of an engaging small group discussion, the conversation turned toward the possibility—gently suggested by me—that salvation of some sort might be available through non-Christian religions. As tensions increased between myself and the other group members over the course of the discussion, Oscar, a third-year psychology student, tried, somewhat unsuccessfully, to put me at ease. "Well, I don't think we have to believe that non-Christians are all bad and we are good," he said, smiling sweetly and shrugging his shoulders. "I mean, the only difference between me and you, Paul, is that I'm saved and you aren't. That's it."

Closest to the "active divisive" end of the IVCF's rhetorical continuum is a term that is central to the way IVCF members understand themselves and their relationships with their secular peers. Throughout this and the previous chapters, I have used "non-Christian" in the same ways members of the IVCF (and many other evangelicals) use it—to denote the vast majority of individuals in our culture who do not have what evangelicals call a "personal relationship with Christ." According to recent survey data, approximately 80% of Canadians describe themselves as Christians of one variety or another (Bibby 1993:128; Rawlyk 1996).[21] From the perspective of IVCF members, however, the number of people who can be said to have a personal relationship with Christ—that is, the number of "real" Christians—is much lower. Although IVCF members are reluctant to make estimates about the number of real Christians in the general population, when they do, these approximations are usually expressed in terms such as "very few," "way less than what you'd think," or "I doubt it would be more than about ten percent." Interestingly, although none of the members I interviewed indicated familiarity with social-scientific studies of religion in Canada, the figure IVCF students normally quote is roughly equal to the proportion of Canadians Bibby (1993:34) and Rawlyk (1996:8) estimate can be considered to be evangelicals.

During my fieldwork, only three IVCF members indicated any discomfort with the exclusive implications of the term "non-Christian."[22] Martina, a science student, echoed the other two women's comments when she said, "I think ['non-Christians'] is a really good example of Christianese. I try to avoid using that word. I like what

Clark [Pinnock: a professor at McMaster's Divinity College] says—that non-Christians are really not-yet-Christians." The use of the inherently oppositional label "non-Christian" obviously reveals a great deal about the use of that even more central term, "Christian." Defining who is and is not a Christian is a sensitive issue for and among these students. For example, when I noticed that members of my small group commonly used the terms "non-Christian" and "Christian" in what seemed to me to be a fairly precise manner, I asked them to elaborate on whom they would consider to be Christians. Jane, a third-year social work student, said that she prefers to leave this judgment to God—a reservation several students expressed when asked to determine if a particular person is a Christian. However, after this comment, Jane offered a definition which used behavior as a major criterion. Describing her roommate, she said, "You know, this girl is totally into the United Church. She knows all about its history and theology and all of that. She goes to church sometimes, too. But still, she drinks and swears like a sailor and has sex and all of that sort of thing. I mean, is that Christian? But still, I try not to call her a non-Christian to her face."

Representing a slightly more rigid position, Sean, a third-year kinesiology student, said, "Yeah, well, I think my parents, for example, aren't Christians. I mean they go to church and that. But I'm not sure how much it means to them, or if they have a relationship with Christ. We don't talk about it, but I kind of doubt it." During the same small group discussion, Cindy, a kinesiology student from a Brethren background, said:

> Well, I tend to take a hard line on this issue. I'll actually call them [non-Christians]. I mean, I don't necessarily call them this to their faces, but, like with my father, for example, even though he'd say he was Christian on a census form, I really don't think he is. I mean, it's not that he's a bad person or anything, but it all comes down to the issue of the relationship with Christ, and I know he doesn't have that, so it seems fine to think of him as a non-Christian. And he knows I think this, which makes things a little tense sometimes. I really worry about him and pray for him a lot.

One day in Lithuania, I asked Denise, a first-year student team member, whether her definition of Christian would include the elderly woman who had sat behind us the previous day on the bus. The woman was evidently a devout Roman Catholic; she spent the two-hour trip engrossed in a well-worn manually typed devotional book while she held her rosary beads, prayed, smiled, and kissed the pictures of Mary.

"Well, she was a Catholic, right?" Denise asked.

"Yes," I replied.

"Then no, I don't think she would be a Christian."

One of the Canadian mission team leaders overheard our conversation and politely (but with a tone of irritation in his voice) disagreed with Denise's assessment of the elderly woman's faith. "But how do you know she doesn't have a relationship with Christ just because of the way she worships? How can you make this judgment without even talking to her?" he asked. Denise replied that she would consider the team member's opinion, but that she thought that some ways of worshiping, including the practices of the elderly woman, were overwhelming obstacles to a person's relationship with Christ.

Since its inception in Canada, the IVCF has wrestled with the spiritual status of Roman Catholicism.[23] Denise's comment reflects the anti-Catholic tradition (and a common definitional boundary to what the term "Christian" signifies) inherent in the IVCF and Canadian evangelicalism in general. In the "debriefing" session the day after my conversation with Denise in Lithuania, we addressed the anti-Catholicism implied in the common assumption that Catholics are, by definition, non-Christians. The group leaders took pains to remind the team that Lithuanian Catholics are not necessarily non-Christians. The group appeared to accept this exhortation without contestation, but throughout the month I continued to hear team members describe a Lithuanian by saying, for example, "Well, no, he's not a Christian. He's a Catholic."

At McMaster, the small group I joined was organized as a study group to read Paul Little's popular guide to evangelism, *How to Give Away Your Faith* (1966; expanded 1988). Little quotes an old evangelical adage: "Going to church no more makes you a Christian than going into a garage makes you an automobile" (1988: 88). At one small group meeting, Cindy augmented Little's aphorism by adding another version: "Going to church no more makes you a Christian than going into McDonald's makes you a hamburger," she said.

These sayings were quoted as if they were self-evident truths; the discussion continued without pausing to reflect on them. However, there was something puzzling to me about the second parts of these two adages. After the meeting, I asked two of the members to explain why the words "automobile" and "hamburger" concluded these metaphors, rather than, for example, "mechanic" and "cook." Taking a deliberately provocative stance, I argued that it was just as improbable that one would instantly become a mechanic or a cook upon entering either of these businesses than that one would become an automobile or a hamburger. Cindy replied that the words "automobile" and "hamburger" were probably used because cars and food are the things most commonly associated with garages and McDonald's restaurants. While this explanation is certainly plausible, I think these amusing metaphors also bespeak common evangelical beliefs about what it means to be and become a Christian. For these students, being a Christian is not something one simply "does," nor is it a matter of adopting a role, as a person does who becomes a mechanic or a cook. Fernandez suggests that metaphors such as those implied in these two sayings are especially well suited as vehicles for the "transformation or transcendence of [a given] state" (1974:131). The metaphorically mediated transformation entailed in becoming a Christian represents a total existential change, just as profound as the metamorphoses that would be required for a person to become an automobile in the first aphorism and a hamburger in the second one. Little's analogy captures the literally essential difference between Christians and non-Christians. However, the chasm between Christians and non-Christians, although wide and deep from an evangelical perspective, is not untraversable. The unsaved "not-yet-Christians" have equal access to their own salvations, if they but seek it.

In the epigraph to this chapter, Denise expresses her frustrations about the conventional words used to describe her faith. "Christian," she knows, is a word many people apply to themselves, in her view mistakenly. Her alternatives—"born agains," "believers"—are occasionally employed by IVCF members, but "Christian" and "non-Christian" remain the self- and other-descriptors of choice among IVCF participants. These terms reflect and, more important, help create the deep spiritual fissure between IVCF students and their non-Christian peers.

Bridging Rhetoric

Fortress rhetoric, the form of discourse outlined to this point in my discussion, subtly or sometimes blatantly estranges IVCF students from their non-Christian peers. In so doing, it fulfills Harding's (1987) thesis that evangelical rhetoric divides believers from nonbelievers. However, her model does not explain the second "bridging" form of rhetoric, which I would suggest is central to the survival of evangelicals in officially secular institutions.

Unless evangelicals opt to become fundamentalist separatists (and almost none do), they must interact with educational, governmental, and commercial institutions, which are usually designed and staffed by non-Christians. How do evangelicals maintain their religious integrity in their associations with institutions and individuals espousing values and beliefs that many evangelicals consider bankrupt? One solution to this dilemma would be simply to maintain an exclusively evangelical frame of reference in all secular contexts, deploying in all interactions the specialized rhetoric used in evangelical churches. However, while most evangelicals believe that after their conversions they are the same redeemed person in all settings, most also consider it to be inappropriate to employ explicitly fideistic language in every social interaction.[24] Evangelicals intuit (probably correctly, as far as I am concerned) that most non-Christians would view such a believer as a zealot.[25]

I would argue that bridging rhetoric complements the fortress language described in the previous section. Both rhetorical strategies enable IVCF participants to guard their religious integrity in a fallen world. There are two major types of bridging rhetoric.

First, as I have mentioned and as most IVCF participants accept, in their interactions with secular institutions, evangelicals conform to the rhetorical practices of the larger group. For the most part, this does not present a problem, since IVCF members are not so naive as to believe that the solemn and often biblical fortress language characteristic of the evangelical ethos would be appropriate or practical in the majority of secular contexts. However, the need to have a store of evangelically acceptable language for IVCF members to employ in conversations with non-Christians has led students to adopt what I describe as a strategy of substitution. The best illustration of this strategy involves profanity.

University student life is profane, not simply in the Durkheimian (1973) sense of nonsacred but in the common use of this term: people swear a great deal. This profusion of profanity represents a considerable challenge to IVCF students, many of whom consider it immoral to swear for any reason. One small group conversation dealt with the awkward social situations in which Christians find themselves in non-Christian settings. When the conversation turned to the problem of profanity—or, as Little calls it, "filth" (1988:72) — there was an immediate expression of frustration from all members of the group. I asked them to explain why they perceived swearing to be so problematic. In response, Sean said that one's language "should be pure and oriented toward God." Before he could elaborate on this, Jane added, "I think it's more the attitude behind swearing that bugs me. And also, it says in Matthew, I think, that what comes out of the mouth flows from the heart. So, if you are swearing, it should make you wonder what condition your heart is in. But really, what I hate the most is when people use Jesus' name as a swear word. That drives me crazy. I could just never do that." As soon as their non-Christian friends know that IVCF members do not swear, Cindy said, they "put us up on a pedestal. I mean, my nickname with my department friends is 'the angel,' just because I don't swear or go to their parties."

"Yeah," said Charles, a first-year science student, "my non-Christian friends are always apologizing to me when they swear. But I don't want them to think I'm condemning them for their lifestyle, because I'm not. That's not my job, and anyway, it's not a very good way to witness to them."

Faced with their peers' often profane rhetoric, many IVCF members feel that abstaining altogether from swearing of any kind would deepen their separation from non-Christians. Consequently, in the form of an array of often homonymic and putatively neutral words, IVCF participants have developed an alternative to swearing (cf. Wagner 1990:131–135). The sound and context of these alternative words are so comparable to the words they are replacing that a "translation" is unnecessary. A simple list should suffice to depict this form of rhetoric. When students are frustrated, they often say, "Ah, frig" or "Chuck this." When they are irritated at someone, they sometimes hiss, "Frig you" or "Chuck you." When participants are amazed at something—positively or negatively—they might exclaim "Holy barf," "Holy hernia," or "Holy frig." As a substitute for saying "God," students say the common "Oh, my goodness" or, in amazement, "Oh my hernia."[26]

It might be argued that the presence of these terms among the chapter's rhetorical conventions is a function of the personalities of the group's present leaders and not reflective of a "rhetorical strategy," as I have described it. This is a plausible argument, and it surely accounts for the particular words that have made their ways into the group's vernacular (i.e., "hernia" instead of "tumor," "frig" instead of "frick"). However, the necessity for these terms was not invented by individuals or elites within the group. Ultimately, these usages arise out of a combination of what Fernandez calls the "metaphorical innovation" (1974:132) of certain individuals, the tacit social acceptance of such rhetorical alternatives, and the underlying evangelical aversion to profanity of all varieties.[27]

These unique terms and phrases function in three ways for the chapter: first, members can avoid profanity; second, they have something to say to each other when a situation arises that would commonly elicit a swear word (a disappointing grade); and third, participants have some alternative words and phrases at their disposal when they are involved in circumstances in which their non-Christian peers are using profanity. The last two functions in particular decrease the alienation of IVCF students from their non-Christian peers. This aspect of the bridge strategy, in other words, helps to soften the boundaries between IVCF members and non-

Christians maintained by the fortress strategy. These in-group terms are sufficiently analogous to the words they are replacing that their public use does not call attention to IVCF students, but these alternatives are sufficiently different, as far as IVCF students are concerned, to validate their membership in a rhetorically righteous group.

The second major category of IVCF bridging rhetoric represents an attempt to prevent students from being either proud of their salvations or patronizing toward non-Christians. Earlier in this chapter, I discussed the way terms such as "saved" and the opposition between "Christian" and "non-Christian" serve as the pillars of a fortress designed to protect IVCF students from an environment sometimes perceived as inimical to Christian faith and morality. However, in addition to fulfilling its defensive role, the fortress also lends to students a strong sense of their chosen status. Almost all of the IVCF participants I met are fairly certain that non-Christians are going to suffer in hell for eternity and that Christians will receive the ultimate heavenly reward for what many members refer to as their "obedience" to God. At the January 1995 Church at the John, two IVCF members performed a skit in which one student drew parallels between "the divine shepherd" Psalm (Psalm 23) and professional baseball to explain to the other student the ways in which God is like the ultimate baseball manager. Near the conclusion of the skit, one of the performers said, "The reward for following the rules of the coach is the Hall of Fame: heaven." Moreover, IVCF members are reminded by pastors, youth leaders, scholars (Balmer 1989; Cox 1995; Rawlyk 1996), and the media that evangelical congregations and parachurch movements are arguably the most robust forms of Christianity in North America. The students' awareness of their movement's power is underlined in boisterous songs such as "Rejoice," which includes lyrics such as

> Now is the time for us to march upon the land
> Into our hands He will give the ground we claim
> He rides in majesty to lead us into victory

Occasional feelings of superiority would be predictable for a group of people who consider their own and their group's spiritual vitality to be categorically superior to those of the vast majority of their neighbors. And such a sense of supremacy would surely deepen IVCF participants' sense of separation from their peers. However, regular "leveling" or "humbling" rhetoric tempers any pride that might be generated by members' certainty of their salvation and the occasional triumphalism of contemporary conservative Protestantism.

Expressions such as "Fathergod," "children of God," and "kingdom of God" are examples of this form of rhetoric. The father-child model of the God-believers relationship is prevalent throughout evangelical rhetoric in general. The song "Children of Light" includes the following lyrics:

> We are the children of God
> Made in the image of Christ

and the popular "Father of Lights" includes:

> Father of Lights
> You delight in your children.

In most IVCF songs and prayers, God is described and experienced as a protective, compassionate, stern, and just father, a transcendent paragon of virtue who resembles an idealized form of the traditional patriarchal father. In fact, terrestrial and celestial paternal roles have practically merged in the word "Fathergod," which begins many students' prayers. Since this familial model of the relationship between humanity and the divine seems to privilege or at least include primarily Christians, it may appear to function as an example of fortress language. Indeed, this paradigm does appear sometimes to affirm the students' uniqueness. However, IVCF participants tell me (as a matter of fact and of witnessing to me) that non-Christians are also members of God's family. Non-Christians have simply either forgotten or rejected this spiritual fact. But non-Christians are always, in a sense, prodigal children who would be welcomed home at any moment by their "Fathergod." Consequently, "Fathergod" helps to remind these evangelicals that regardless of the righteousness of their behavior, all people are united by being children of the same God.

A closely related bridging strategy is apparent in the phrase "kingdom of God." In the song "We Declare," participants sing:

> We declare that the kingdom of God is here
> Among you, among you

In "King of the Nations," students sing:

> Come let us worship Jesus
> King of Nations, Lord of All
> . . . Voice, race, and language blending
> All the world amazed
> . . . Bring tributes from the nations
> Come in joyful cavalcades
> One thunderous acclamation
> One banner raised

In IVCF rhetoric, the kingdom of God, like the family of God, includes everyone (in principle at least), although participants are encouraged regularly to work toward bringing everyone into the "joyful cavalcade" in a fully conscious sense. Construing all people as inhabiting the same kingdom or being members of the same family may diminish participants' sense of separation from and superiority to their secular peers.[28]

Two other illustrations of this form of rhetoric are the use of the term "just" and the clicking sound worship leaders make with their mouths during public prayers and scripture interpretations.

When Martina complained about the prevalence of "Christianese" in IVCF rhetoric, I asked her if she could provide me with an example. She said, "Oh yeah: the way they use the word 'just.' It's really starting to drive me nuts. You know, I think it started out being a humility thing. But now I think it's just become filler. It's as though every good prayer now has to include the word 'just.' " In what sense is the use of "just" a "humility thing"? Its most common syntactical location is near the beginning of approximately half of the prayers offered at IVCF events. For example, a customary beginning to IVCF prayers is "Fathergod, we just come before you tonight to," a variation of which might be "God, we just want to sing your praises tonight because we've just seen all the wonderful things you do in our lives." This term seems to muffle the students' demands somewhat, underlining their indirect and humble approach to God. Without "just," their prayers would be comparatively bold. For example, they would be reduced to the overly direct alternatives: "We come here tonight to" and "God, we want to."

An analogous role is played by the "click" sound worship leaders often make with their mouths.[29] Its location in their rhetoric is similar to and often follows the word "just": "God, we just [pause . . . click] want to thank you for your son and to ask you" or "Fathergod, we come here tonight to ask if you will [pause . . . click] help us see how we can share your love." By implying that the speaker is unable to finish a prayer because he or she is overwhelmed by the opportunity to communicate with God, this sound softens the believer's petition and, again, emphasizes his or her respectful love for and approach to God. The word "just" and the common click sound have no obvious relationship to the secular ethos. However, insofar as they humble those who use them, these rhetorical expressions reduce the sense of superiority that might otherwise develop as a result of IVCF participants' perceived exceptional spiritual status and the successes of the evangelical movement of which they are a part. Thus, these practices ensure that IVCF students do not isolate themselves unnecessarily by their arrogance.

Conclusion

Susan Harding's model of the conversion rhetoric or "gospel talk" used by fundamentalist Baptists emphasizes the "biblical rhythm of alternatives" (1987:179) implicitly conveyed in this language. The IVCF's rhetoric regularly introduces into believers' minds exactly what Harding predicts: a schism between non-Christian and evangelical worldview(s) and a sense of the categorical difference between Christians and their secular surroundings and peers. I have described this form of language as "fortress" rhetoric to evoke the believers' self-understanding as an embattled minority protecting itself from secularism.

If this fortress rhetoric was the only form of discourse operative in IVCF circles, Harding's thesis would suffice to explain IVCF rhetoric. However, the deployment of a quite different form of speaking and singing is apparent among these students. I have called this form "bridging" rhetoric to suggest its power to maintain and even improve the relations between IVCF and non-Christian students. The terms in this category provide alternatives to profanity and mitigate against the potential arrogance associated with the members' self-understanding as chosen and saved.

I would suggest that the IVCF can accommodate these two forms of seemingly opposed rhetoric for two reasons. First, the group seeks to meet the needs of both liberal and conservative (fundamentalist) evangelicals. Consequently, the language used in its worship settings and heard in interviews combines the compromising rhetorical tendencies of the former group of students and the unyielding expressive conventions of the latter.

However, IVCF discourse also includes both bridging and fortress-making language because its members are committed to what appear on the surface to be somewhat contradictory goals. On the one hand, many students (from across the evangelical spectrum) feel occasionally that they are in hostile territory. Many of them describe feeling unprepared for the intellectual and moral challenges to their faith that they have to face in the university environment. Consequently, students sometimes seek the shelter provided by fortress rhetoric. On the other hand, they cannot afford, so to speak, simply to strengthen their defenses and burn their bridges. They want—many of them desperately—to be accepted by their non-Christian friends. The complementary rhetorical strategies outlined in this chapter help these students both (and sometimes simultaneously) befriend their secular peers and reinforce their difference from these others.

FOUR

Otherness

Beloved, I urge you as aliens and exiles to abstain from the
desires of the flesh that wage war against the soul. Conduct
yourselves honourably among the Gentiles, so that, although they malign you as evildoers, they may see your
honourable deeds and glorify God when he comes to judge.

1 Peter 2:11

[As suburban children] life was charmed but without politics or religion. It was the life of children of the children
of the pioneers—life after God—a life of earthly salvation
on the edge of heaven. Perhaps this is the finest thing to
which we may aspire, the life of peace, the blurring between dream life and real life—and yet I find myself speaking these words with a sense of doubt. . . . I think there
was a trade-off somewhere along the line. I think the price
we paid for our golden life was an inability to fully believe
in love; instead we gained an irony that scorched everything
it touched. And I wonder if this irony is the price we paid
for the loss of God. . . . But then I remind myself we are
living creatures—we have religious impulses—we *must*—
and yet into what cracks do these flow in a world without
religion? It is something I think about every day. Sometimes
I think it is the only thing I should be thinking about.

Coupland

Throughout the previous three chapters, I have introduced (1) the set of questions
I am asking in this book, (2) four members of the IVCF, and (3) the ways these
believers communicate among themselves and with non-Christians. By now it
should be clear that IVCF students often feel separated from their non-Christian

peers and professors. Moreover, as I have explained, many IVCF students feel that McMaster privileges the beliefs, values, and worldviews associated with liberalism, pluralism, materialism, and permissivism. According to Reginald Bibby, this evangelical perception is largely correct:

> Education stands out as an institution that not only has been strongly influenced by individualism and relativism but also has done much to legitimize the two themes. Indeed, the mark of a well-educated Canadian is that he or she places supreme importance on the individual while recognizing that truth is relative. To decry individual fulfilment or to claim to have found the truth would be a dead giveaway that one has not graced the halls of higher learning. (1990:71)

This situation marginalizes, alienates, or (to make a verb of an adjective) others evangelical students who generally do not embrace these traditions (or many core elements of these traditions). However, although it might appear that IVCF students would suffer unrelenting and agonizing psychological difficulties during their years at McMaster, the majority of IVCF members do not seem to share such an experience. On the contrary, most IVCF participants I met struck me as no less sane, healthy, contented, and well adjusted than the non-Christian students I have met during the many years I have spent in Canadian universities. In fact, I have found that, with a few exceptions, evangelicals at McMaster seem slightly "happier" than non-Christian students. This obviously unscientific impression is consistent with Frankel and Hewitt's (1994) findings that involvement in religious groups during one's university years is positively correlated with higher levels of physical and psychological "well-being."

This observation raises an obvious question: how do evangelicals retain these relatively high levels of psychological well-being in an institution that not only ignores their values and beliefs but also, according to IVCF students, often promotes "anti-Christian" principles? The main insiders' (or "emic") answer to this question is simply that well-being is a natural by-product of a personal relationship with God (Little 1988:38). A plausible social-scientific answer to this question is not quite as uncomplicated. In the course of interviewing evangelicals, traveling with them, and observing their worship and social interactions, I observed strong evidence of a shared experience which I call by various names: otherness, difference, alienation, and estrangement. While each of these terms has a unique history within the social sciences, I use them more generally to denote the sense of separation these students feel from the non-Christian world.[1]

Although these students recognize their difference and often essential estrangement from their secular peers and professors, with the help of the IVCF, participants have developed creative strategies for managing and transforming otherness. Such strategies enable students to remain loyal to their religious convictions while they participate in McMaster's social and academic life. The underlying sense of otherness has three major forms. The first form is common to most undergraduates, and the two other forms seem to be unique to evangelicals. I will deal with these three types in turn.

It seems plausible to consider non-Christian students and professors to be privileged in an institution that officially favors pluralism and unofficially leaves little or no social space in the classroom for nonliberal, nonpluralistic sensibilities (Bibby 1990; Hammond and Hunter 1984). But evangelical students are not defenseless victims of secularism. Rather, evangelicals' sense of difference has emerged partly as a result of their own participation in a broader process of negotiation between selves (and communities of selves) with unequal access to, or at least different types of, power (Harding 1991).[2] Furthermore, as I have suggested, IVCF members should not be seen as engaged in a futile protest against the decline of their worldview. On the contrary, the chapter seems to help students "maintain difference in a positive sense" (Wuthnow 1989:182).

Throughout my fieldwork periods, many students shared with me stories about the profound feelings of estrangement they experienced when they began classes at McMaster. During an interview, I asked Wendy, a second-year student in religious studies, what her life at McMaster would be like without the IVCF. She replied:

> Oh, I don't think I could have survived Frosh Week without IV. The whole year before I came to Mac, I lived in a completely Christian world. I went to camp in the summers and to a Bible college for a year. And then, when I moved into residence that first year, it was crazy. Okay, listen to this. I was assigned to live in Brandon Hall. So here I am, an innocent Christian girl. The first day I got there, I took the elevators up to my floor and when the doors opened, I saw this big sign that said, "Welcome to Satanic Seventh." I was just *duuhhh*. Now I know that this was the frosh theme for the floor, since I lived on the seventh floor of the res. But back then, it was overwhelming, and then on top of this, people were drinking all the time. The difference between my Christian world and my new residence world is night and day. I was so glad I knew some of the IV people. I'm not even sure I would have stayed at Mac without IV. I would have tried to find other Christians. But probably, without IV, I would have been more of a recluse and studied all the time.[3]

As I have explained in previous chapters, many evangelicals conceive of their relationship with explicitly nonevangelical institutions and individuals as essentially adversarial. However, despite the actual or constructed differences which generate this relationship, there is at least one important area of similarity between Christians and non-Christians. Specifically, most evangelical *and* nonevangelical students I have met at university believe they will face a harsh or at least unpredictable economic climate once they complete their degrees. Thus, while evangelical university students must find some way to cope with being, as Brian said, in "hostile territory," both socially and intellectually, they must also contend with many of the same anxieties other students experience.[4] Before I discuss the unique form of alienation many evangelicals feel in officially secular milieux, I consider the form of estrangement shared by many evangelical and nonevangelical students.

General Estrangement

Whereas a university degree was once a virtual guarantee of a secure postacademic life, this is by no means the case for the majority of the current generation of students (Osberg, Wien, and Grude 1995:200).[5] Many IVCF students tell the same story I could tell: of their parents, twenty or thirty years earlier, confident after the completion of their degrees, concerned simply about which job to accept and where they would like to live, rather than whether they could find work at all, or work in their field, or work in their province or (for some) country. The post-1980s recession, coupled with the fiscal conservatism of federal and provincial governments and major corporations, has greatly decreased the need for many full-time jobs; instead, contract work has replaced these positions. In addition to these changes, the information explosion associated with the Internet has increased the level of technical expertise needed in most entry-level positions (Bridges 1994:4; Osberg, Wien, and Grude 1995:97). Demographers Foot and Stoffman observe that the larger changes we have witnessed in the realms of technology and political economy are strongly correlated with the steady rise of unemployment rates over the last four consecutive decades (1996:68).[6] Predictably, these shifts have had significant effects on the prospects many university students face. In an interview published in the *McMaster Times* magazine, McMaster alumna and Canadian economist Roslyn Kunin gave the following advice to university graduates: "You've got to say good-bye to the old world where you went to McMaster and got a degree and got a nice job with a large organization and were set for the rest of your life. . . . [And] you've got to convince your parents that there is nothing wrong with you" (Kunin in Vowles 1996).

The group of students currently in university is often described by the epithet Generation X. When this term was coined by Douglas Coupland in his 1991 novel of the same name, it referred to my own generation,[7] those born in the late 1950s and 1960s—people whose parents were, by and large, already raising families when the counterculture of the 1960s and 1970s reached its peak. Nevertheless, for a variety of reasons, the term quickly expanded its frame of reference to include those in university during the 1990s. As a result, this term is employed occasionally in this chapter.[8]

Almost all of the IVCF students I have interviewed (as well as most non-IVCF students with whom I have discussed this issue) are nervous about their abilities to succeed in the postuniversity economy. This uneasiness results in their sense of distance from the cultural accretions of middle-class adulthood: mortgages, retirement savings plans, careers, marriage(s), suburban life, pensions, and retirement. Education no longer guarantees anything in the "new world" to which Kunin alludes. Even though demographic data (Foot and Stoffman 1996:23) suggest that the cohort of students currently in university will fare better than Coupland's original Generation X, the technological and economic transformations which characterized the culture of North America when these students (and the original Generation X members) were raised have bequeathed to many of them (us) a sense of anxiety and, in some cases, cynicism about their futures. This pessimism or, to paraphrase Coupland, this scorching irony is manifested in the popular culture of their generation: the suicidal despair of the grunge rock band Nirvana's Kurt Cobain, the wry, caustic wit of *Seinfeld*, the juvenile nihilism of *Beavis and Butthead*; the sarcastic bourgeois humor of *The Simpsons*; and the conspiracy theorism of the aptly named *X Files*.

A word of caution is in order. We might easily find contemporary students who have no misgivings whatsoever about their futures and who would not fit comfortably within the category of Generation X. Despite wholly optimistic undergraduates I have met, however, the serious concerns about the future so well evoked by Kingwell (1996), Coupland (1991), Eddie (1996), and Foot and Stoffman (1996) do seem to be generally characteristic of this generation. Moreover, it seems to me that determining whether contemporary university students are *actually* living in a unique, unprecedented, and inauspicious economic climate is not as relevant as the fact that many evangelical and nonevangelical students alike *perceive* themselves to be faced with unpredictable and perhaps transient occupational opportunities. Like their non-Christian peers, IVCF participants may be considered members of Generation X, but in a distinctly evangelical manner.

Since evangelical students understand themselves to have been born again, I had expected them to be immune to the anxieties of their generation. I discovered, however, that their understanding of the relationship between their faith and their futures is far more ambiguous than I had anticipated. During my conversations with IVCF members, I was often surprised when I encountered some measure of the uneasiness and cynicism typical of the non-Christian students with whom I am personally familiar. Nevertheless, even though many IVCF students expressed skepticism about whether they would find suitable or stable employment in their areas of expertise, I noticed that almost none of them seemed to be distraught about their prospects. When I asked IVCF members why they seemed relatively (relative, that is, to other undergraduates I know) calm about their futures, I discovered that in response to economic uncertainties, students turn to God. Every student I met seems to agree with Steve, who asserted confidently that God has a "perfect will" for his life, which he can choose to obey or not. This perfect will typically encompasses a divinely sanctioned marriage partner, degree program, career choice, and university acceptance, but because God's plan is by definition unknowable, students are reluctant to claim knowledge of its details or its comprehensiveness. Nevertheless, IVCF members profess that whatever happens to them in the future is necessarily part of God's benevolent plan for their lives (Wagner 1990:98).

The best way to illustrate the role of this plan in believers' lives is to consider its place in student discourse. During a small group meeting in the living room of a member's residence room, Cindy, for example, observed: "I mean, look at me. I'm finishing my M.Sc. next year. I may not get the job I want right away, but I'm confident that eventually I will, because I know God has a plan for me. I guess I'd say that I feel a sort of peaceful insecurity about the whole thing." When I asked David, a first-year science student, how he felt about his future, he answered:

"I definitely worry about this—everyone I know does, just because of the insecurity of the future. I have no clue about where I'll be ten years from now. I don't know the future, but I know God has a plan for me. He can take away all of our problems, and I know if I just live according to his will for my life, I won't have to worry."

Nevertheless, IVCF members recognize that some of the choices they make will be contrary to God's plan for their lives. Kelly, a former IVCF member, posited that it "grieves" God that his children do not faithfully seek his plan for their lives (typically through prayer, Bible study, and "fellowshiping" with other Christians) but that God may lead the delinquent back to the path of righteousness. During a conversation one night in Lithuania, Janice, a fourth-year geography student, likened God's response to human mistakes to the process of braiding hair. "When a strand falls out of order, God can find a way to work it back into the braid," she explained.

Participants frequently refer to the tension between their occupational anxiety and their faith in God's plan, but almost all students seem to experience both feelings. During an interview, Lewis, a psychology student, commented:

"Oh yeah, I feel [this general form of alienation]. I think it's just irrational not to think of it. It's only human to worry—like I worry about getting into grad school. But my faith helps a lot, because I believe God has a plan for me. Actually, in Jeremiah it says, 'I have a place for you.' In fact, that's the only part of the Bible I've memorized." Similarly, Frank, a third year kinesiology student, reported, "I don't really have a sense of anxiety about my future because I think God is controlling everything and has a plan for me. But sometimes I forget this and get worried. But with what I want to do with ministry or camp work in the north, this won't be a big problem. But anyway, God's going to work in his time and his way. I'm sure of this."

Many students attribute what non-Christians might consider to be the result of good luck or diligence to a combination of God's plan and their own righteousness. During a moving, tearful conversation about her family's financial troubles, Heather, a third-year English student, said:

I want none of this money thing. I'm interested only in subsistence. God will provide for me. Last summer I knew I had to get a job, like *had* to get a job if you know what I mean. I was really anxious about that, but I prayed and God provided for me. I got a great job teaching a teen-leadership development course. I mean, in these sorts of times I keep remembering something my father said to me: "I've never seen the righteous forsaken." God has always provided for us. My mom's not so trusting. But somehow we always get bailed out.

Finally, students are also aware that their beliefs mitigate against their experiences of estrangement. For example, many of them believe (correctly, as far as I can tell) that they suffer less severe forms of anxiety about their futures than their non-Christian peers (cf. Frankel and Hewitt 1994). Mary, a first-year social science student, admitted, "If I didn't have [a belief in God's plan], I'd probably be a wreck. This definitely underlies my carefreeness at school." As well, Paula, a psychology student, admitted, "I'm spending all this time and money working towards a degree, but for what? I have no clue. My faith helps me cope with this a lot. As a Christian, I think I'm probably less stressed about this than the person sitting beside me in class, though." On the same subject William, a second-year science student, remarked, "Sure I feel worried about my future. Absolutely, one hundred percent. But this all makes me trust in God all the more. My faith helps a lot. I'm sure he led me here and I trust in God, but we are all bombarded by such negative information about our futures. My faith reduces these worries enough that I'm not paranoid or terrified about my future."

Reductionism

Before proceeding, I feel compelled to address the thorny issue of reductionism.[9] As the quotations in the preceding section suggest, many IVCF students seem to suggest that the divine plan allows them to contend better with the uncertainty of their lives. During fieldwork, I heard several variations on the theme that God's plan helps them "to deal with" their economic insecurity. In both IVCF and social-scientific terms, God's plan might therefore be interpreted as a "coping strategy" for managing the concerns that IVCF students have about their futures (Ammerman 1987:192).

However, IVCF members would consider such an interpretation only partly correct. They would recognize in it the self-evident truth that their faith in God's plan makes their lives easier. But they would bristle at what they might infer as the implicit suggestion that the idea of God's plan was somehow consciously or unconsciously invented by them (or their leaders or their tradition) simply to fulfill the essentially psychological task of coming to terms with the vicissitudes of life in an uncertain economy. Furthermore, because I focus on the psychosocial elements of this aspect of IVCF discourse, evangelicals and non-Christian social scientists might even infer that my interpretation implies or presupposes either that there is no God or that God does not have a plan for each of our lives.

Ethnographers are ill equipped to make claims and ill advised to make assumptions about the existence of God or a divine plan. The ethnographer's task is both more limited and more comprehensive: to understand the life-world of the people they study and to translate it into concepts and categories that can be understood by others (Geertz 1994:463). Although the theological implications of the present study may be of interest to evangelicals,[10] my concern is to propose an interpretation of possible nontheological influences on human behavior and social life.

Caution is important in advancing theories that make the convictions one's ethnographic others embrace appear to be delusions oriented essentially at achieving ends fundamentally opposed to those intended by believers. George Marsden argues, "Fundamentalist ideas have long been thought to be 'really' expressions of some other social or class interest. . . . But to reduce beliefs to their social function is to overemphasize a partial truth and so to underestimate the powers of the belief itself" (1982:162). I would defend the theory that belief in God's plan helps IVCF students cope with the complex experience of being, in William's words, "bombarded by such negative information about our futures" in a campus environment they feel is already directly opposed to their faith. This interpretation seems to be supported both by my participation in and observation of IVCF activities and by the scholarly commentary to which I refer throughout this chapter. However, I would qualify my argument by suggesting that, while belief in God's plan is a coping mechanism, such coping is simply one effect and not necessarily the cause or raison d'être of this conviction.

Specific Evangelical Estrangement

In the case of general undergraduate estrangement, students feel alienated from their role in the postuniversity economy. However, characteristic of what I call specific evangelical estrangement is the perception among believers that secular institutional life is no longer welcoming toward traditional conservative Protestant beliefs and values.

As I explained in chapter 1, many evangelicals feel alienated from central elements or the *mentalité* common in secular institutions. This insiders' perspective has also been articulated by scholars.[11] For example, George Rawlyk (1990, 1992, 1996) argues that by the nineteenth century there was a broadly evangelical consensus among Canadians (and more or less explicitly present in major institutions) concerning moral and religious matters. However, although quantitative studies indicate that conservative Protestant participation rates have increased somewhat between the last decade of the nineteenth century and the last decade of the twentieth century, the role of evangelical values and beliefs in public institutions and discourse has been either severely diminished or at least problematized (cf. Ammerman 1990:149). Consequently, although their churches and parachurch organizations are among the strongest manifestations of Protestantism in Canada and the United States, many IVCF students believe that their most firmly held convictions no longer belong at the center of the public institutional dimensions of North American life. Evangelicalism continues to thrive in differentiated (Luhmann 1984) if not disempowered pockets within the broader North American cultural scene (cf. the IVCF's "club" status at McMaster). However, even though evangelicals may justifiably celebrate the contemporary vitality of their tradition, they are acutely aware that the (arguably prevalent) religious and ethical norms of the surrounding culture either ignore or oppose traditional evangelical values. In very few contexts in our culture is the hostility or condescension toward conservative religiosity perceived by evangelicals to be more pronounced than at secular universities such as McMaster.[12] According to these believers, it is at such institutions that the ideology of secularism and, in the words of Clark Pinnock, an evangelical professor at McMaster's Divinity College, the "bias against God" are most explicitly promulgated. Commenting on this phenomenon, Jane, a social work student, said that "No one [at McMaster] will accept us if we say we're Christians. Oh, they'll accept Buddhists and Muslims, and even Jews are okay. But not Christians—*nooooo* way." Moreover, as Brian, a third-year classics student, pointed out in an interview, "Maybe the university is a little more hostile to Christianity than the rest of the world because in university you have people stopping to think and then actually stating their views, whereas in the rest of society people don't usually have to think or talk about their beliefs. In the university, I guess you can discuss God, if you want. But it is also an accepted place to discuss unbelief."

In response to the marginalization of evangelical Christianity on Canadian campuses, a minority of the IVCF's fundamentalists adopt a posture that borders on what might be called righteous resignation (cf. Hammond 1985:221; Berger 1992:43). The vast majority of IVCF members, however, do not espouse such a strict position and prefer to negotiate what I describe as metaphorical "contracts" with their secular surroundings. The specific evangelical estrangement that is the context and inspiration of these negotiations assumes both intellectual and social forms. I will discuss the intellectual form first.

The occasionally adversarial relationship to which I have been referring throughout this book often manifests itself in the form of clashes between evangelical and secular philosophical and scientific principles. Of course, the antagonism generated by these conflicts reflects fundamental divisions between evangelical and nonevangelical worldviews and serves to estrange IVCF members from their secular peers, most of whom, evangelicals believe, share the liberal, pluralistic, and materialist intellectual assumptions that have gained hegemony in the secular academy.

There are several sources of students' intellectually experienced sense of difference. I have discussed some of these issues in this and previous chapters. The most contentious elements of non-Christian teaching and assumptions are evolution, relativism, moral permissivism, and biblical criticism from feminist and atheist perspectives. As we shall see, however, not all IVCF students are directly affected by these issues.

Common contexts in which students experience this form of difference are lectures and conversations in which evolution is taught or assumed as an unassailable fact. While discussing intellectual alienation in general, Carrie remarked that she often gets confused when she listens to one of her professor's lectures about evolution. She commented, "Sometimes I just listen and don't understand how the Creator's plan can explain what my prof is saying. But then I remember what John and Paul said: that Christians are called to believe, not to understand, like it says in John 6:69."[13] During a conversation, Simon echoed Carrie's reliance on faith as an answer to the challenges of evolutionary theory. He remarked:

> When [professors and non-Christian students] start talking to me about evolution,
> I think "this is ridiculous" and immediately barriers go up. But I believe in God
> and the Bible, so I don't worry about them proving me wrong because they can't.
> I totally expect to have problems in university. I mean, university is very human-
> istic, and that's in direct conflict with Christianity. Christians ask "What does
> God want me to do?" whereas non-Christians ask "What do I want to do?" It's
> totally different. (cf. Wagner 1990:91)

Virtually all IVCF students I interviewed describe themselves as creationists. However, many students adopt a conciliatory stance toward students and instructors during conversations about evolution. For example, many students adopt a position similar to the one Lewis takes. "I'm a creationist," he declared in our interview, and then added quickly, "but I don't totally discount evolution. It's a viable theory. But maybe God used evolution to create us." In other words, Lewis reduces evolution to one theory among others, all of which he presupposes must ultimately validate God's creation and sovereignty.[14]

Then again, some (a minority of) IVCF members such as Kirk, an engineering student, are less willing to adopt Lewis's bridging strategy, and prefer to construe the contract Lewis and others have negotiated as a betrayal of the faith. In an attempt to guard creationism from the onslaught of scientism, students such as Kirk are opposed to any form of compromise with the theory of evolution. "In a non-

Christian world," Kirk observed, "our truth is not the one truth, so sometimes we're ashamed and feel dominated by non-Christians. Sometimes Christians are forced to make compromises, like believing in evolution, just because of the pressure of being dominated."[15]

Other students perceive threats to their religious commitments as originating in their academic disciplines. The IVCF social work students, for example, often have very strong opinions about what they view as university-sanctioned moral permissivism. During one conversation, Cathy, a fourth year student, related, "Yeah, sometimes I feel pretty isolated in social work. I don't know how I feel about gay rights, for example, even though [social work students are] supposed to support them. I mean, it upsets me that they don't have the same rights as everyone else, but I also know what God thinks about this issue. And abortion—I believe it's murder, but as a social worker, I can't say that." The liberal moral assumptions inherent in the social work program also frustrate Vanessa, a second year student who asserted, "Social work always really emphasizes how the individual can change everything. But I believe the ultimate hope is with Jesus. This makes things hard, because I have to tell people that they can do everything for themselves, even though I don't believe it."

In response to a question about conflicts between her faith and academic pursuits, Paula, one of only two religious studies students in the McMaster IVCF, commented, "I especially feel this tension in my religious studies classes." She continued her reflection by saying, "It's weird. They just don't want to hear about your personal beliefs, which just takes away from the discussion of religious texts or personalities. They totally deny the personal element, or the issue of the relationship with God. I have nothing against learning about the texts, but there are parts of my faith I can't explain, and I don't like not being able to express something that is so important to my life."[16]

One of the most helpful tools employed in negotiating the IVCF members' metaphorical contracts is what I described earlier as a "semipermeable membrane." In the context of a conversation about her occasional uneasiness in classes, Candace, a third-year English student, expressed some of the same sentiments as Vanessa and Paula when the former referred to the "filter" through which theories and information taught in class must pass before she can internalize them. Candace remarked:

> Sometimes, when I'm reading literature, I think, "Okay, I shouldn't be reading this; it's totally wrong." Like when it has to do with sex. As Christians, we have to filter out this sort of thing from what goes into our minds. Also, the philosophies that the university tends to teach—like being self-sufficient and making people feel the power within themselves. I have to avoid thinking like this by constantly reminding myself that my identity is in Christ. I try to imagine what my life would be like if I was dependent on myself. It scares me. I'm afraid of the thought of being self-sufficient.

Carrie also referred to her intellectual filter during our interview:

> It's a continual battle for me in university. . . . I feel like what I learn in class has to go through a filter of some kind, although the filter is not always that efficient

because sometimes there's so much information coming at you. I think there must be two parts of my brain. . . . Like some of the philosophies they teach us about in class. In one class we learned all about Freud and how all of our motivations come from our libidos. But I think there are other, higher motivations so I file that information on Freud because I know I need to know it, but I just can't accept it.

There are two ways in which IVCF members respond to the threat of cognitive contamination they experience at McMaster.[17] The first strategy involves the blending of ideas from seemingly disparate theoretical realms. As sociologist Robert Wuthnow (1989:149; Berger 1992) argues, most people have a significant and usually unacknowledged propensity to mix or, as anthropologist Ellen Badone (1989:284) suggests, to alternate between religious and scientific worldviews. For example, instead of having to choose between a strictly creationist position or a strictly evolutionist position, many IVCF participants mix these theories, as Lewis's earlier comments reflect. In so doing, students accommodate both the need to remain loyal to their faith and the need to be seen by their secular peers and professors as treating the theory of evolution with the deference expected for generally accepted theories. Such contracts build bridges between Christian and non-Christian students and allow IVCF members to participate in curricular and extracurricular conversations about evolution. By reducing evolution to a divine tool, as Lewis and others do, students can absorb a pivotal element of a threatening intellectual system into a larger creationist paradigm of natural history.[18]

Another evangelical response to intellectual estrangement is to construe this experience as a consequence of the hegemony of an imperious secular ethos. Such an interpretation was promulgated by the charismatic McMaster intellectual Clark Pinnock, a well-known and controversial commentator in conservative North American Protestant circles.[19] At the IVCF's winter retreat in January 1996, Pinnock was the guest speaker. Forty-five McMaster students from various disciplines and stages in their programs attended the retreat, which was held at a Christian camp approximately four hours' drive north of Hamilton. The camp was comfortable and modernized, with separate dining, lounging, and sleeping areas. Although there was plenty of time during the retreat devoted to worship and social and athletic activities, the issues Pinnock discussed clearly formed the intellectual focus of the weekend. Pinnock delivered two animated lectures in the fireplace lounge area of the camp on the second day of the retreat: one in the morning after breakfast and the other in the evening. At the end of each of his sessions, participants broke into small discussion groups. His presentations that weekend confirmed many theories I had been developing about the IVCF's relationship to the secular ethos.[20]

Pinnock lucidly and passionately outlined the nature and causes of evangelical marginalization at a university that directly (as evidenced by the pluralism of its dominant ethos) and indirectly (as evidenced by many professors' and students' critiques of Christianity) embraces a position he describes as "metaphysical naturalism." Pinnock defined this perspective as the assumption that matter is "the cause and answer of all things."[21] His lectures revolved around what he called the powerful and pervasive "bias against God" in contemporary university life. For many students, Pinnock's sessions represented the first opportunity to place their sometimes amorphous experiences of intellectual alienation within a philosophical framework. For example, during a conversation one week after the retreat, Sean, a kinesiology student, had difficulty being specific about the ways in which the secular university ethos was opposed to Christianity. However, he did explain, "When Clark spoke, I realized that, yeah, we are discriminated against."

Pinnock argued, "The fact is that there is no common ground between Christianity and secularism, but there is a common discussion, and I'm just saying that we have the right and the responsibility to get back into it." The "common discussion" between conservative Protestantism and secularism should in theory be permitted and even encouraged in a secular institution such as McMaster. However, Pinnock asserted that, with a few exceptions, such a conversation is not cultivated; when it is, few people seem to be interested. In other words, it is paradoxical that although the university extols the open exchange of ideas, some ideas—especially the evangelical Christian ideas on which McMaster was founded—are rarely discussed. The university's trivialization of evangelical convictions, Pinnock argues, alienates IVCF students from an institution to which they have a right to contribute. "We'd better turn this situation around or it will bury us," he counseled ominously near the end of his first lecture.

In his final lecture, Pinnock explored the ways students might respond to the bias against God at McMaster. He began this lecture by outlining some methods and principles of Christian apologetics[22] so students would be equipped to respond to their peers' and instructors' occasional discrimination. "After you have named and understood the problem, don't stop there. You have the hottest thing going, and you can deal with the bias against you. God has given you minds and hearts for you to do this," he reminded them. Then he cautioned students not to feel overwhelmed by the opposition they experience, and not to wallow in "us-versus-them" rhetoric. However, echoing throughout his presentations was a polemical tone he acknowledged at the end of his lecture: "But I realize I may have contributed to [the oppositional rhetoric] by my talks this weekend."

Pinnock encouraged the forty-five participants at the retreat to conceptualize the alienation they might experience at university as a function of a potent, sophisticated, but not irreversible bias against God, themselves, and their worldview. His remedy for this predicament is twofold. First, he supports Mark Noll's (1994) suggestion that evangelicals should hone their intellectual skills so they know how to respond articulately to the secular bias. Second, believers should appeal to the rights all minority groups enjoy in principle in a pluralistic institution. If evangelicals' attempts to introduce their intellectual perspective into broader conversations within the academy fail, they should employ the same forms of protest favored by other minority groups seeking fair representation.[23]

On the one hand, by exhorting retreat participants to rejoin the "biased" academic discourse through their contributions to the "common discussion in a pluralistic institution," Pinnock intended to evidence and then ultimately bridge the growing gap that estranges conservative Protestants from the secular university. On the other hand, fortress rhetoric predominated in his presentations, both of which were delivered in a passionate and somewhat defensive sermonic style. Although students should try to enter the "common discussion" permitted by pluralism, they were reminded repeatedly that there is actually "no common ground between Christianity and secularism."

Of course, not every IVCF student faces intellectual opposition in his or her classes. Most engineering and commerce students, for example, looked at me blankly when I asked them about the intellectual variety of otherness. Although they are creationists, these students almost never formally confront evolutionary theory in their classes. "I don't feel alienated or anything like that when I'm in classes, because they mostly just focus on science, on how to get things done," Sam responded to this issue.[24]

In fact, not all students who are even directly exposed to challenging ideas such as evolution, atheism, homosexual rights, egalitarianism, or perspectivalism necessarily suffer extensive estrangement. Some students simply treat these theories as elements of the false or, at most, partially true non-Christian teachings with which they must become familiar to succeed at university. These pragmatic students learn and reiterate whatever is required for them to do well in a given course, but their intellectual filters protect them from the atheistic implications of their learning. In these cases, the negotiation or cognitive bargaining which does occur is minimal. Insofar as these students permit such perceived falsehoods to enter or contaminate their minds, they have compromised with the non-Christian ethos of the classroom. However, on the whole, this compromise is a temporary means to an end that requires a minor concession on the part of the student.

Although some IVCF members did not report significant levels of intellectual estrangement, virtually all the students I interviewed reported feeling separated from the secular ethos in another way. This brings us to the second and essentially social form of what I have called specific evangelical estrangement. This second variety of evangelical undergraduate otherness is by far the more common form experienced by IVCF students. While only some of them must ponder on a regular basis contentious theories such as evolution, Freudianism, and Marxism, all students spend a portion of their time at McMaster in the company of non-Christians. Social estrangement refers to the experience of feeling excluded from significant elements of undergraduate socializing, especially those components associated with drinking and sexual activity.

During interviews and casual conversations, all but a small minority of IVCF members revealed strikingly similar experiences of social alienation. Commenting on the differences between herself and her non-Christian peers, Janice admitted, "Sometimes I feel like a goody-goody here. . . . I feel like I can't always be part of the conversations going on around me." Similarly, commenting on his feelings of estrangement, Frank said, "With non-Christians, it's sometimes kinda awkward. I'm very much aware of the differences between us." In fact, for some students, social alienation does not simply separate them from the occasional secular conversation; it inhibits them from participating in almost all non-Christian social activities. Hope, a nursing student from a strict fundamentalist background, shared with me her sense that "I feel cut off, you know, different from non-Christians. Sometimes I just feel like a sissy because I'm not doing the big Thing To Do. I guess that's why I have so few non-Christian friends—because I find it easier to avoid the situation altogether."[25]

Many IVCF students are apprehensive about appearing to reject two major and often related elements of undergraduate socializing: sex and drinking.

Among IVCF students, there is a basic sense of uneasiness with the role of alcohol in the undergraduate culture. For most IVCF students, a critique of the nature and effects of alcohol has been a significant element of their socialization since they were children. During interviews, all but two of the sixty participants expressed the view that drunkenness is immoral. While most of them qualify this conviction by adding that moderate consumption of alcohol is acceptable in certain controlled environments, a vocal minority of fundamentalist students in the group believe that all drinking is "un-Christian."

One night during the May 1996 IVCF mission to Lithuania (intended to foster evangelical university groups), the McMaster team decided to go to Rita's, a relatively expensive restaurant in Vilnius.[26] Attached to this fashionable American-style restaurant is a bar that would be virtually indistinguishable from many trendy "roadhouse" bars in North America. While we were waiting in the bar to be seated at our table, one of the team members and I turned to each other and remarked, almost simultaneously, that we would like to try a Lithuanian beer. A few other members of the team overheard this conversation, and very quickly the issue was being discussed in hushed tones among the whole group. After the two team leaders consulted each of the other team members, they gave us permission to order the drinks. Because all of the "team money" supporting the mission trip came from donations from team members' home churches and families (most of whom would not approve of our alcohol consumption), the team leaders decided that it would not be appropriate for us to buy beer with the team's money.[27] As a result, four of the ten of us in the group ordered drinks and paid for them with our own money.

Once the beer negotiations were completed, one of the women in the group expressed her amazement to Steve, the team member who had proposed ordering the beer: "Wow, I can't believe you drink. I never would have guessed," she exclaimed. The cognitive dissonance she experienced when she learned that a highly respected fellow team member consumes alcohol reflects this woman's fundamentalist upbringing. Steve, by contrast, comes from a non-Christian family without austere anti-alcohol standards. Alcohol is, in many evangelical circles, a problematic symbol of dangerous and forbidden pleasures. Near the end of the Lithuania trip a team member from a Brethren background told the team repeatedly that she was going to "break free" from the strict moral code that she had internalized from her childhood. Her first act of liberation was drinking a beer at another trendy restaurant in Vilnius.

The same tensions I observed regarding alcohol consumption during the Lithuania mission also exist within the IVCF chapter at McMaster. On several occasions, I have observed participants casting aspersions on the moral rectitude of fellow members who consume alcohol. Nevertheless, although divergent views on the issue of drinking occasionally create strains between members, most participants accept these conflicts as tolerable consequences of the intrachapter diversity.

However, a significant degree of social alienation is generated by the differences between the relatively permissive non-Christian attitudes toward alcohol[28] and the abstemious or abstinent policies of IVCF members. During an interview, Hugh, a graduate student, observed, "Conflicts might arise [between himself and non-Christians] if, for example, someone invites me to go out drinking. One night this happened, and I went out with one guy, but decided not to drink. After a while it became obvious to the guy who invited me that I wasn't going to get drunk that night, so he stopped calling me to go out. That was a little sad, but I guess I understand his position."

Peter, a third-year science student, was more unequivocal about his position. He said, "I won't hang out with my non-Christian friends when they're drinking, and this definitely separates me from them. It's hard to be different sometimes. IV helps because it's a place where I have like-minded friends and where drinking is not such a big deal."

The second major source of social otherness for IVCF students pertains to the differences between their virtually unanimous endorsement of premarital sexual abstinence and their non-Christian peers' comparable leniency on the issue.[29] During interviews, I asked students to describe their perspectives on premarital sexual activity. Every student I met embraced abstinence as the only appropriate Christian policy. Because of the discomfort many participants seemed to experience when we discussed sexuality, I was reluctant to ask them about the extent or details of their sexual experiences. Occasionally however, the usually brief conversation on this topic evoked information well beyond the scope of my original and limited questions about their personal standards.

In fact, several students indicated that their relationships are not or have not always been completely chaste. During a conversation with Cindy, a self-defined fundamentalist woman who seemed comfortable discussing the issue of sex, I asked about the limits she set on her physical relations with her partner. "Oh, kissing is okay, but we never do anything horizontal," she replied. Cindy was willing to answer this question, but her tone and posture clearly conveyed that this statement marked the end of that part of our conversation. The other participants who have shared this intimate aspect of their lives with me have adopted some version of Cindy's policy (cf. Wulf, Prentice, Hansum, Ferrar, and Spilka, 1984).

A few members of the group chose to tell me about their sexual experiences before they became Christians. When discussing these events or relationships, participants are usually quite frank. These students typically describe their pre-Christian intimacies as instances of debauchery, bewilderment, or peer pressure. Their universally unfulfilling sexual histories are described as the early and dark chapters within the metanarrative of their eventual salvation (Strozier 1994; chapter 2).

Almost all of the members I interviewed have very strong opinions about their peers' relative promiscuity. A few participants echoed Harriet, a first-year psychology student, who stated bluntly, "Universities are cesspools of STDs and alcohol." Others provided more elaborate answers. For example, in response to my question about social alienation, David, a first-year science student, commented:

> In residence, people's goals are so different. All they want to do on the weekend is get drunk and get laid. I believe moral standards have really changed to whatever is good for the individual. . . . Sometimes it's hard to get my Christian and non-Christian friends to hang out together because my non-Christian friends like to go to clubs and that. And I struggle with this whole club thing, too. Whenever

I go out with them it makes me stumble through lust. I try not to look at girls, but it's hard. I mean, you know what I mean. It's a bar, and there's the music and all the girls and the way they're dressed. I just try to stay focused.

Simon explained that he experiences social alienation when he's watching movies: "If I'm with non-Christians watching a movie and a sexual scene comes on, I won't like it and they will. It's that simple. I mean, I have a fear of God and they don't. I can have a fresh start by asking God for forgiveness, but a non-Christian can't. So, I just usually look away and try not to think about it until the scene is over. But I don't make a big fuss about it or anything."

For many IVCF participants, the anti-Christian lifestyles and moral proclivities of their secular peers are quintessentially localized in the residences. When I asked Steve what sort of a person he thought he would be without IVCF, he replied, "Well, I'd probably be a typical Joe Residence, drinking and having sex all the time." Vanessa also experienced difficulties in her residence. She attributed her social alienation to her moral standards, saying, "I think the fact that I have a fairly narrow worldview in terms of moral behavior separates me from some people. This does create some tension. Like when the girls on my [residence] floor wanted to go to a strip club, I had to say no, and this was a bit awkward at first. But it's not a really negative thing. I actually felt they were missing out, not me."

In response to the social form of specific evangelical otherness, the IVCF implicitly offers itself as an alternative social institution-within-an-institution, with many features that parallel those of the secular student world. Simon, for example, indicated that because of the IVCF, his social estrangement was not acute. "I mean, I'm not lonely, because I have IV friends and I can always talk to God," he commented.[30] Even students who said during our conversations that they experienced little or no estrangement often spoke of the steps they took to avoid these feelings as soon as they arrived at McMaster's residences. For example, Colin, a confident commerce student, remarked that while he was still in high school, he "had heard a lot of stories of how Christians would come from small towns and go to university and be just totally overwhelmed by the life here, especially in the residences. I didn't want that to happen to me, so I looked for a Christian group to join as soon as I got here."

In December 1995, I attended an IVCF party at the IVCF president's "student house" in Westdale, an affluent Hamilton neighborhood where many McMaster students reside. With the following two conspicuous exceptions, the event was indistinguishable from dozens of other undergraduate parties I have attended. First, there was no alcohol at the IVCF party, which meant that as the night wore on, there were no episodes of stumbling, rowdiness, vomiting, or other common alcohol-related behavior. The absence of alcohol also seemed to subdue the conversations I participated in and observed. Second, although I was surprised to hear almost entirely non-Christian dance and grunge music that evening, when the dancing commenced in the living room, dancers did not touch each other. Men and women sometimes danced together or in the same group, but I observed no conventional scenes of dance floor flirtation.

The IVCF offers its members almost daily opportunities to participate in explicitly evangelical social activities. In addition to their weekly events such as large group meetings, small group meetings, Friday lunches, and Friday evening "concerts of prayer,"[31] students can attend special events such as barbecues, dessert fundraisers, progressive dinners, retreat weekends, cost suppers, parties, and semiformal banquets. By participating in these events, evangelicals who are not comfortable in the established non-Christian contexts for undergraduate socializing (bars or parties) can still feel socially engaged in activities that parallel and yet differ from their secular analogues.

By living according to moral principles that represent an implicit critique of prevailing and relatively permissive norms—in short, by "walking the talk," as evangelicals sometimes say—many students believe they are exemplifying the inherently superior Christian lifestyle. During a conversation about the growth and vigor of the McMaster IVCF chapter, Harriet commented that McMaster was caught in a "downward moral spiral." She continued, "When you have a group that's willing to challenge [the 'downward moral spiral'] and to stand against it but not to hide from it or separate from it, this will attract people. The world wants no rules, but like a kid it needs structures. People on my [residence] floor see me as an example, and they need support, and I think IV is like that as a group." Nevertheless, very few IVCF students make obvious public displays of their moral rectitude. In other words, these students are not agitating to have the university return to its explicitly Baptist origins, discussed in chapter 1. Even the subtle negotiation processes I discuss in this work are not veiled attempts to reverse the effects of campus secularization or differentiation. Although many IVCF members might welcome a reenchanting reversal in the nature and purposes of university life, most of these students are more concerned with finding ways of being faithful without being conspicuous or unauthentic (Baxter 1982). In other words, they want to remain others to non-Christians but not to appear to be, so to speak, really other. Moreover, these students' desires simply to be liked by their non-Christian peers should not be overlooked. Not all of their interactions with non-Christians amount to witnessing efforts. Their attempts to edify non-Christians by example are, by and large, discreet and polite, probably because IVCF students are aware that overt or self-righteous efforts would be neither welcomed nor successful.

As if he had anticipated the thesis of this chapter, David, a first-year science student, commented, "IV is an alternative to the social functions and social life of a secular campus. It's a great way to show people that they're missing out on the important things in life by living only for the pleasures of the moment instead of something eternal." As well, readers will recall that at the end of her description of her social otherness, Vanessa commented, "But it's not a really negative thing. I actually felt they were missing out, not me."

I would argue that IVCF members experience an ambiguous sense of difference from their secular peers. My fieldwork with the IVCF suggests that it is inappropriate to assume that all forms of estrangement from a dominant group are necessarily undesirable. In fact, largely because the IVCF (qua alternative institution) facilitates the negotiation of what might be understood as metaphorical contracts with the non-Christian world, the group seems to enable students to transform their other status from a wholly negative to a mainly positive experience. Furthermore, while participants' transformed sense of difference does cultivate personal integrity and corporate solidarity, it does not necessarily permanently estrange IVCF students from their non-Christian peers. On the contrary, because IVCF members employ a gentle form of "friendship evangelism"[32] to spread the gospel (cf. chapter 7), the membrane between the Christian and non-Christian worlds is, as I have suggested, semipermeable.

Participation in ritualized events provides another means of responding to the common evangelical experience of social difference.[33] In the first few pages of this book, I described the IVCF's best attended and best known event, the Church at the John, an evening of worship and singing held in McMaster's largest bar. On the first Sunday evening of every month during the academic year, approximately 550 boisterous students squeeze into the Downstairs John for two and a half hours. Most of the participants are McMaster students, but many are from evangelical youth groups, other universities, and theological institutions in southern Ontario. The event includes prayers, skits, an inspirational message from a guest speaker, and the night's main drawing feature: two forty-five minute sets of energetic folk-rock praise music. There is some variation in the nature and ordering of some of these components, but the underlying structure of the evening remains fixed.

Anthropologist Victor Turner argues that during rituals people move symbolically from one social state to another through a period or condition of "liminality." "Liminal entities," Turner writes, "are neither here nor there; they are betwixt and between the positions assigned and arrayed by law, custom, convention, and ceremonial" (1969:95).[34]

Turner's typology of rituals includes those of "status reversal," in which individuals from low strata of society are allowed for a specified period of time to express dramatically[35] their frustrations at the inherent inequalities of a given social structure (1969:177). During such rituals, socially powerful members of society allow themselves (or are compelled) to assume positions on the social hierarchy much lower than those they occupy before and after the ritual. Turner asserts, "Rituals of status reversal . . . are thought of as bringing social structure and *communitas* into right mutual relation once again" (1969:178).[36]

The Church at the John may be thought of as a ritual of status reversal because it gives the IVCF a prescribed space and time within which it can stage a symbolic coup d'état. After all, as the primary site for the initiation of sexual and drug and alcohol-related activities (cf. Willsie and Reimer 1980), the campus bar is, next to the residences, the most symbolically non-Christian social space in the university. The timing of this ritual (Sunday night) guarantees that the regular occupants of the bar will not be present. Consequently, no individuals representing the dominant campus ethos are actually compelled to assume positions of powerlessness. However, in the smells of smoke and alcohol and in the location and popularity of the bar, the representatives of symbolic domination are metonymically signified. This metonymical presence was manifested clearly at the September 1995 Church at the John, when nearly six hundred participants entered the ritual space through a sticky passageway reeking of an almost overpowering odor of vomit from the previous night's celebrations.

For one evening of every month, the IVCF transforms the Downstairs John into what the chapter's staff worker described as "the church on the world's turf, where nothing is sacred, sort of, but anything can happen." Once the John has been consecrated through prayers at the beginning of the evening,[37] an elaborate ritual of status reversal allows participants to enjoy their temporary, ritually granted hegemony. Such a ritual transformation must be temporary; as Grimes explains, in Turner's paradigm, a ritual "masks social contradictions and enacts them. . . . The symbolic unification which ritual provides is, of course, an ideal one which lies, as it were, on top of very real divisions" (1982:147). The Downstairs John is indeed "turf," contested space that no ritual can permanently deproblematize. However, achieving some form of evangelical *communitas* in such a secular setting allows evangelical undergraduates to claim a symbolic victory over the ethos in which they often feel like "aliens and exiles" (1 Peter 2:11).

Conclusion

Although IVCF participants desire the acceptance of their secular peers, such an aspiration is hardly unequivocal. For example, William lives in one of the McMaster residences. While discussing what he considers the boorish and Dionysian behavior of his neighbors, William remarked, "At [my residence] I just sorta feel like I'd like to belong, but I'd like to belong in my own way." As well, during a conversation about estrangement, Gillian said:

> I know I am separated from other students, but that's because I'm a Christian and am holy and called to act differently. But I don't exactly feel alienated because I don't feel badly about this separation. It's not lonely. It's a growing thing. We are made more holy every day by being separate, but we are in the world and can't therefore alienate other students from us. Even by living in the world, we are purified.

Frank also commented, "Alienation is not really a terrible thing. It reminds us of who we are. We're aliens in this world. I mean, really, this world is not our permanent home." Finally, during a conversation we had following the winter retreat, Lewis asserted, "I don't think Christians should complain about being marginalized from the world, because in this world we are in self-imposed exile. We have to accept what the world will do to us. I don't agree with what Clark [Pinnock] said about the protests and rallies, because we should accept that the world will want to isolate us."

Although most IVCF students I encountered during fieldwork would like to feel more welcome in non-Christian social arenas, they simultaneously cultivate their alienation from non-Christians so they can "belong in [their] own way." Lewis, Frank, and many other believers are truly what Warner calls "elective parochials" (1988), people who *choose* not to conform to the liberal, permissive, secularist dictates of a non-Christian culture. Their enhancement of their own otherness is directed at maintaining boundaries, or what might be better understood as a semipermeable membrane between the evangelical and secular worlds. Although the term "boundaries" seems to connote the "fortress" strategy, the IVCF membrane facilitates a variety of types of evangelical interactions with and responses to the non-Christian world. Whether the site of negotiation is the biology classroom, the residence bedroom, or the campus bar, the IVCF empowers each student to determine the extent to which he or she will accommodate or resist the non-Christian ethos. In short, the contracts which emerge out of this process enable members to conceive of their social alienation as an ambiguous but edifying experience (Wuthnow 1989:182). Thus, the IVCF serves as an excellent example of the way in which, as Warner puts it, "religion mediates difference" (1997a:219).

Among IVCF students, I observed a self-initiated reconstruction of their own otherness. This reinterpretation provides participants with a new and positive way of understanding their difference from their non-Christian peers. Estrangement from their secular peers and professors constitutes proof for the IVCF's fundamentalists that they have not been corrupted by "the world," in effect, proof that the non-Christian world remains alien to them.[38] However, even the relatively liberal evangelicals in the group are aware and appreciative of the edifying dimensions of their intellectual and social separation from the secular ethos. Nevertheless, largely because of the bridge approach to the sometimes troubling contexts of the classroom and the residence, the membrane between IVCF members and non-Christians is semipermeable. Broadly speaking, a combination of fortress and bridge strategies enables students to fulfill three basic needs: to remain loyal to their religious convictions, to protect their sense of difference from non-Christian others, and to participate in McMaster's social and academic life.

In conclusion, IVCF participants are affected by both general and specific forms of otherness. The first form is experienced by evangelical and non-Christian students alike. It stems from the amorphous anxiety many contemporary undergraduates apprehend when they peer over the walls of the university and perceive a society and economy that strike them as unpredictable and unforgiving. In response to this situation, non-Christians and evangelicals sometimes descend into the shapeless anxiety that characterizes Douglas Coupland's Generation X. However, because evangelicals believe that God has a well-organized and loving plan for each of their lives,[39] their worries do not, as William said, render them "paranoid or terrified" about their prospects.

The IVCF participants also describe another major form of alienation, which originates in their separation from what they perceive to be the "anti-Christian" foundations of contemporary secular culture in general and of McMaster in particular. This specific form of otherness may be further subdivided into intellectual and social varieties. In response to these two types of estrangement, members of the McMaster IVCF chapter negotiate complex and dynamic contracts. Such a process provides members of this group with a means of maintaining a fortress to protect their religious integrity, as well as a means of constructing bridges to foster meaningful and constructive interactions with their secular peers and professors.

FIVE

The Role of Women

I will pour out my spirit on all flesh;
your sons and daughters shall prophesy,
your old men shall dream dreams,
and your young men shall see visions.
Even on the male and female slaves,
in those days, I will pour out my spirit.

Joel 2:28

Let a woman learn in silence with full submission. I permit
no woman to teach or to have authority over a man; she
is to keep silent.

1 Timothy 2:11

There is no longer Jew nor Greek, there is no longer slave
or free, there is no longer male and female; for all of you
are one in Christ Jesus.

Galatians 3:28

Whenever I describe the IVCF to non-Christian academic peers, they almost invariably express their astonishment at the fact that at virtually every IVCF event I attend, approximately 70% of the participants are women. Perhaps this level of involvement is not unusual in the world of contemporary Protestantism; after all, in many of the churches IVCF members attend every Sunday, women outnumber men. However, the proportion of women to men is not as high in evangelical churches as it is in the IVCF (Bibby 1987:102; Rawlyk 1996:143). As well, women's roles are usually much more tightly controlled in many if not most evangelical churches than they are in the IVCF. In fact, IVCF participants who attend churches in the Fellowship Baptist, Christian Reformed, and Brethren traditions may never see a woman in the pulpit, or, if women are allowed to speak at the front of the church, they are not usually permitted to become senior pastors or interpret the Bible.[1]

At the IVCF functions I have attended, however, women are in no way restricted in their abilities to lead worship, deliver sermons, organize events, or perform any of the myriad tasks involved in maintaining the group. In fact, the chapter's paid staff worker is a woman, and she tries to ensure that the position of president alternates between a male and a female student every other year. I began to wonder how to make sense of the high level of female participation at every McMaster IVCF event I attended, especially in light of the fact that the scholarly literature on evangelicalism in North America often depicts the tradition as inimical or opposed to the egalitarian or feminist values that are so prevalent at universities.[2] During my research, I found that many, but not all, of the evangelical women I interviewed maintain nonegalitarian views on the role of women. In other words, the common academic depiction of the place of women in evangelicalism seems to be confirmed by my experience, even though I hope to nuance this portrayal somewhat. For example, Denise, a first-year student from a Fellowship Baptist background, commented firmly that she could not accept a woman's preaching or church leadership and then related this to her own family structure, saying, "I mean, I really respect that my mom can submit to my dad's decisions, like it says she should in the Bible." Sheryl, a first-year student with a charismatic (and thus typically more egalitarian) background, distinguished between preaching and leadership. "Okay, I mean, I could accept a woman preacher. I have no problem with that, because the Holy Spirit can show up anywhere, right? But I don't think a woman should be a pastor." Like Denise, Sheryl also linked this belief to her future family setting. "When I get married," Sheryl explained, "I'll accept my husband's decisions. My husband will be the head of the house, like in the Bible. This'll be really hard, because I'm *so* stubborn, but that's definitely what I'll do."

During a conversation about the high numbers of women in the chapter, Buff Cox, the IVCF staff worker, attributed the high level of female attendance to a socialization process that imparts to believers the view that women are naturally inclined or morally obliged to be more publicly religious than men. "Their churches socialize them to believe certain things about what men and women are supposed to do," Cox explained.[3] These students' denominational and familial backgrounds clearly influence their opinions about controversial issues such as the general status of women in their traditions, including their rights to preach or even simply to speak in their churches. However, while church socialization might explain why high numbers of IVCF women attend and help facilitate the group's events, it does not explain the high level of participation and leadership the IVCF allows and, in some cases, expects of women. In fact, given that most IVCF women attend churches which restrict their religious and organizational leadership, one might expect these students to search out analogous auxiliary roles within the IVCF, but quite the opposite seems not only to occur but to be openly encouraged by the group's staff worker and many members of the executive. So, while the effects of IVCF socialization must be kept in mind during any consideration of the role of women in the group, it is only one possible component of a larger interpretation.

Some IVCF members suggested to me that many of the evangelical women active in the group are simply looking for suitable evangelical husbands and are unsatisfied with the courting opportunities available through secular social activities.

However, this explanation incorrectly presupposes that evangelical women are more interested in finding religiously like-minded partners than are evangelical men. My conversations about this topic with IVCF men and women do not support this hypothesis; in general, both men and women from both groups are planning to marry Christians. In other words, this motivation alone does not explain why women so significantly outnumber men at IVCF events.

A more likely explanation for the high levels of female participation in the IVCF may be found in the likelihood that in addition to experiencing the (general) economic and (specific evangelical) psychosocial forms of otherness I described in chapter 4, evangelical women experience an additional form of estrangement. Before I describe this third and uniquely female form of alienation and the IVCF's responses to it, a brief detour into the role of women in evangelicalism will contextualize the issues discussed in this chapter.

Although it is difficult to generalize about a tradition that encompasses such theological and social diversity, it is nonetheless possible to highlight some common themes in conventional evangelical constructions of female gender. There are surely exceptions to this norm,[4] but until the latter stages of the current century, most evangelical women have followed the pattern one might expect from women in male-dominated religious or cultural institutions. That is, evangelical women have generally understood themselves primarily as mothers and wives and only exceptionally as independent career women. As Bendroth observes, historically, "The doctrine of submission, with its heavy emphasis on marriage, assumed that the proper sphere of the Christian woman was the home; outside activities were clearly secondary" (1993:96).

Byle Bruland (1989) and Bendroth (1993) argue that until the 1970s, evangelicalism in North America was not significantly affected by the feminist metamorphoses in definitions of womanhood that began in earnest in the 1960s.[5] Bendroth writes that evangelical history had "provided no strong, public feminine voice or rhetoric of sexual equality. As a result, feminist ideals penetrated [the evangelical] leadership slowly" (1993:120).

With emphases on universal human rights, autonomy, and freedom from structural oppression, the various forms of feminism are quintessentially modern, or perhaps postmodern, social movements.[6] As feminist Byle Bruland argues, for many evangelicals, feminism represents a strong variety of secularizing modernism (1989: 144).[7] Since evangelicalism (and fundamentalism, its less conciliatory sibling) arose at least partly as a form of religious resistance to aspects of modernism (Lawrence 1989), it is not surprising that many evangelicals, including many of those in the IVCF, have been reluctant to embrace the modern ideal of gender equality espoused by the various forms of feminism.

On the basis of his ethnographic work among contemporary American evangelicals, anthropologist Randall Balmer argues that for these Christians, the changing status of women in North American culture is a harbinger, or "bellwether" of our culture's moral decline (1994:59). He writes, "Perhaps nothing has contributed so greatly to fundamentalists' feelings of cultural dislocation than the changing views of women in recent decades" (1994:54). Feminist scholar Karen McCarthy Brown argues that in response to what they perceive as the increasing secularity of our culture and the specific challenges posed by feminism, evangelicals struggle to maintain their patriarchal faith as the "Archimedean point" in a chaotic world (1994: 180).

It is not uncommon for academic commentators to depict the evangelical tradition as a monolith of antifeminism, if not misogyny.[8] However, there are both liberal and conservative movements within evangelicalism as there are within other traditions, such as Islam and Roman Catholicism. Some evangelical liberals are quite comfortable with the equality of women in the church. Those IVCF members who belong to the Baptist Convention of Ontario and Quebec, for example, attend churches which may accept the ordination and leadership of women.[9] Moreover, the exclusion of women from full involvement in evangelical religious life is often problematized directly by IVCF students and their mentors. For example, during one Friday lunch meeting, Joyce Bellous, a self-defined evangelical feminist[10] professor at McMaster Divinity College, discussed Galatians 3:28 and 1 Timothy 2:11, two of the epigrams of this chapter.[11] While commenting on these texts, she argued that "some Christians will use Timothy to say that women are different but equal, but really, that whole idea is a farce. Normally it is used by people who really see women as inferior, or who want to make sure women don't get to share in all of the work of the church."[12] During the meeting, I asked Professor Bellous what she thinks about women who accept the "different but equal" notion. She replied, "Well, I would say that there's no reason women should participate in their own oppression. And during my experiences with groups like this and in churches, I've noticed that women are usually the best enforcers of this idea, even though it is not in their best interests."

Although my conversations with IVCF participants indicate that Bellous's perspective is not representative of the views of the majority of members, her approach does signify emerging issues within the group. While the "different but equal" status of women is still a major element of the contracts IVCF students and other evangelicals negotiate between their faith and feminism, the role of women within conservative Protestantism is gradually becoming a significant and problematic component of IVCF discourse.

Sociologists Stacey and Gerard observe that contemporary "evangelical theology and institutions are serving as remarkably flexible resources for renegotiating gender and family relationships, and not exclusively in reactionary or masculinist directions" (1990:99). Thus, evangelical groups can function as bridges between evangelicalism (as a movement), which is traditionally antifeminist, and feminism, which is traditionally antievangelical. As we shall see, groups such as the IVCF are able to mitigate some elements of the feminist critique of the patriarchal nature of conservative faith. Specifically, these groups permit a more neutral version of the egalitarian values of feminism to be incorporated into evangelical worldviews. Stacey and Gerard (1990) argue that as a result of the bridging strategies of groups such as the IVCF, feminism has had a considerable influence on evangelicalism.[13]

Nevertheless, although the story of women in evangelicalism is not one of simple or unrelenting marginalization, of the sixty IVCF members I interviewed during my fieldwork, only ten attend churches where women are granted full equality. Interestingly, none of these ten mentioned the equality of women as a reason they chose to attend a particular church. Some of these ten students (and many of the fifty others) were completely unaware of their church's official policy on women's roles in the church. So, regardless of the influence feminism is supposed to have had or has actually had on their tradition, more than 80% of the believers in this study attend churches which formally prohibit women from full involvement.

Evangelical university women affirm those aspects of feminism that grant them equal access to education and employment; however, because most forms of feminism are often harshly critical of conservative Christianity, the inclusion of feminist ideals in evangelical contracts has resulted in ambiguous and problematic religious worldviews.

Now let us turn our attention to the third and uniquely female form of otherness to which I alluded earlier. In chapter 4, I described two sorts of estrangement: one affects both evangelicals and nonevangelicals and is fostered by unpredictable economic conditions; the other is characterized by IVCF participants' feelings of dislocation from the sometimes antagonistic or "anti-Christian" ethos of McMaster. The IVCF women, however, must contend with an additional sort of difference, which, for the sake of parallelism, I call "specifically female" alienation.

I would argue that this additional variety of estrangement is partly shared by many non-Christian undergraduate women and partly unique to evangelical women. Earlier, I discussed the fairly recent and problematic role of feminism within evangelicalism, a tradition that strikes many as hostile toward women. However, feminists have argued that the contemporary university is the site of an analogous incongruity, namely, between its formal institutional espousal of egalitarianism and its informal support of masculine hegemony. Specifically, like non-Christian female students, IVCF women must find ways to cope with what some feminists consider the inherent male dominance manifested by educational institutions in which male professors still significantly outnumber female professors. However, the apparent maleness of the North American university system transcends the mere inequality of the male to female ratio among instructors and the conspicuous absence of women authors from course reading lists. A more intractable possible obstacle to egalitarianism, some critics argue, is the maleness of the styles of thinking and interaction expected at universities.

Many feminists have argued that the modern university relies on what Canadian philosopher Lorraine Code (1991) calls an "objectivist" view of the world, which emphasizes abstract and uncontextualized facts and theories.[14] In addition, feminists such as Janice Moulton (1983) suggest that the interaction in contemporary university classrooms manifests what she calls "adversarialism," a communication style based on the confrontation between two essentially aggressive intellectual parties. Underlying feminist critiques of the dominant styles of learning at most universities is the controversial theory that women in our culture are socialized to value relationality and social context rather than individualism and isolated facts. I advance this hypothesis cautiously because this speculation is based on contestable theories about the differences between women and men and needs to be tested more thoroughly. Nevertheless, let us consider some of the evidence for this claim. Psychologists Boverie, Huffman, Philbin, and Meier (1995), as well as Hedges and Nowell (1995), argue that there is considerable congruence between men's culturally conditioned learning styles and university education because both are abstract and competitive; whereas women's comparatively experiential and cooperative styles of learning are not as easily accommodated by the educational institutions most of them attend. Thus both evangelical and non-Christian women may feel alienated by an objectivist and adversarial academic framework which privileges a culturally defined male mode of thinking about the world.

I should note that I have never heard any IVCF and only a few non-IVCF women complain explicitly about their estrangement from the "objectivist" paradigm that some feminists argue undergirds the modern university. However, this paradigm is a relatively recent feminist hypothesis (Code 1991), advanced in philosophical language and publications primarily in the past fifteen years. While Steel, Warner, and Strieber (1992) report that most North American university students are aware and appreciative of the basic tenets of feminism, the specific insight of the philosophical maleness of the contemporary academy may not have filtered down to the average female student. Therefore, I think it is plausible to speculate that evangelical (and nonevangelical) women may, as I have just suggested, *experience* this form of marginalization from their universities without being fully *aware* of it.

Of course, IVCF women may not be simply marginalized (along with some non-IVCF women) by an academic ethos characterized by objectivism and adversarialism. In many ways, the moral permissivism and feminism that are integral components of this institution also disparage the conservative gender roles embraced by most female evangelical students.[15] Many IVCF women experience gender-specific alienation as a function of the disjuncture between their faith, which models conservative gender roles for women, and the university, which at least officially (if not always actually) encourages so-called progressive roles. In sum, while their non-Christian female peers may cope with the first kind of difference, IVCF women may have to shoulder the burden of an additional form of alienation.

In women's studies classes, for example, evangelical women have to endure their non-Christian classmates' allegations that evangelicalism or, for that matter, Christianity itself is oppressive to women. Helen, for example, said:

> My women's studies classes are so violently anti-Christian it's not even funny. In the other classes I'm taking in nursing, people aren't nearly as outspoken. But in women's studies, I really realize my beliefs are different than most peoples.' I don't say much when people are talking [critically about Christianity] because I know from experience that I'll get jumped on. One woman asked me how I could even be a Christian at all. She asked how I could experience the love of a God who oppresses women. I just couldn't think of any answers.

Helen attends a Canadian Reformed church, where women are prohibited not only from preaching but also from voting on issues of church policy and administration, so she is well acquainted with the disempowerment to which her classmate was alluding. Helen's silence in the face of her peer's criticism implies neither agreement nor disagreement with the opinions stated or with the historical record. Rather, caught between the worlds of her traditional faith and her secular education, Helen has decided not to choose either one — *yet*. Opting exclusively for the former is no longer plausible after she has learned about Christianity's complicity in women's inequality. However, limiting herself to a secular worldview is also untenable since it would require her to betray her deepest commitments. Commenting on the capacity of contemporary evangelicalism to respond to this predicament, Stacey and Gerard write:

> Women's turn to evangelicalism represents a search not just for spirituality, but for stability and security in turbulent times; but it is a strategy that refuses to forfeit, and even builds upon, the feminist critique of men and the "traditional" family. Acute "pro-family" and spiritual longings in this period commingle with an uncompleted but far from repudiated feminist revolution. Part of the genius of the postfeminist evangelical strategy is its ability to straddle both sides of this ambivalent divide. (1990:111)

The explicit conflict Helen experienced in her women's studies class is not common among IVCF women, most of whom do not take courses in this department. However, all of the women I interviewed experienced at least some form of the third type of alienation I have introduced in this chapter. As we shall see shortly, in the face of the clash between their faith and the insights and evidence of secular thought, many IVCF women opt for ambiguous solutions like the one Helen has adopted.

The IVCF women and the group as a whole seem to address the third complex female form of otherness I have described in this chapter in at least three ways.

The first response to this alienation is to construe Jesus as a lover.[16] During interviews, female IVCF participants almost unanimously affirmed premarital celibacy as the appropriate Christian stance on sexual activity. In fact, many of them proudly volunteered the information that they are virgins. Remaining chaste in a social milieu that often glorifies sexual activity requires women to take an unpopular stand among their sexually active peers,[17] a stance which produces alienation among these students.

In the perfect, righteous persona of Jesus, however, IVCF women are provided with an acceptable focus for affections that might otherwise be expressed toward men. Psychiatrist Charles Strozier writes that there is "among [evangelical] women a sexualization of their relationship with God; one [woman] spoke of her need to make love to Jesus" (1994: 127). As far as I am concerned, Strozier overstates his case. In contrast, I would describe IVCF affections for Jesus as quasi-erotic. Although IVCF women do not seem to me to be explicitly sexually attracted to Jesus, the passion with which female participants express their love for him strikes me as very reminiscent of the way other women in their age group speak of long-distance human lovers.

The portrait of Jesus as lover is painted in a variety of ways. One of the female guest speakers at the Church at the John used the following image to explain God's loyalty to his followers: "God does not rape our hearts. God is the consummate lover. No, really. I know that sounds strange, but it's true. . . . Do any of you have thoughts in your mind you know you shouldn't have? I know I do, especially for my age. The thing to remember is that amid all this, Jesus is the perfect lover. He's the one who won't let you down."

Participants' quasi-erotic love for Jesus is also expressed in many of the repetitive, yearning songs sung at IVCF events. In "How I Love You," participants sing:

> How I love you,
> you are the one,
> you are the one
> how I love you,
> you are the one,
> God's risen Son,
> you are the one for me

As well, the song "As the Deer Panteth," based on Psalm 42, includes the following lyrics:

> As the deer panteth for the water
> So my soul longs after you.
> You alone are my heart's desire,
> And I long to worship you.
> I want you more than gold or silver
> You alone are the real joy-giver
> And apple of my eye.

Although men also participate in these songs, when IVCF men actually speak of Jesus, they refer to him as judge, father, teacher, mentor, and, least frequently, friend. By contrast, the vision of Jesus as the kind, sensitive recipient and unconditional requiter of love, is most appealing to evangelical women, perhaps because they are socialized to value intimate relationships.

The IVCF offers women spoken and sung opportunities to channel their quasi-erotic energies into the persona of Jesus. In so doing, the group diminishes some of the alienation evangelical women might experience as a function of their commitment to celibacy in a social context characterized by sexual permissiveness. By encouraging women to view Jesus (rather than the men who surround them) as the "consummate lover" and one's "heart's desire," the IVCF offers women an analogous and dealienating alternative to premarital sexual activity.

The second response of IVCF women to their unique form of alienation is what I would call gentle subversion. As I described earlier, most of the women in the IVCF were raised in or attend churches that do not embrace egalitarian gender roles. How can one make sense of the high levels of female leadership in the IVCF when these same women attend churches in which their full participation is not welcome?

Evangelical women enter university with widely divergent opinions about their churches' treatment of women: some support it fully; others harbor misgivings. However, once these women arrive at university, they enter an institution which at least officially disparages traditional evangelical gender roles. For women with some misgivings about their role in the evangelical tradition, arrival at McMaster almost inevitably exacerbates the existing tensions between themselves and their churches. However, those women who are content with their role in their churches may experience the clash between evangelicalism and feminism differently. For example, the shock of being accused by non-Christians of belonging to an oppressive tradition may inspire these women to reject the new secular social context they have just entered and thereby deepen their alienation from their more fully egalitarian peers and the university as a whole. Several of the women I interviewed seemed to have experienced both of these strains at different periods in their educational careers at McMaster.

Although the research is diverse and substantial, many scholars contend that within the highly androcentric conservative Protestant tradition, women can and do find ways to worship meaningfully, to resist the hegemony or domination of their churches' patriarchs, and to participate quietly in real changes within their tradition.[18] Ethnographer Beverly Patterson argues that "where formal structures are restrictive [an evangelical woman] sees and uses informal ones to exert her influence and thus avoids a sense of powerlessness" (1980:77).

If many conservative Protestant women experience some degree of frustration when faced with the limited opportunities their churches offer them, and if these women are aware (to varying degrees) that their secular peers do not support traditional evangelical constructions of gender, then involvement in the IVCF may address both of these problems. Specifically, the IVCF offers many of these students the only opportunities they may ever have to interpret the Bible publicly, lead worship, and participate in religious and organizational leadership. In so doing, the IVCF may resolve evangelical women's rarely expressed and perhaps only latent dissatisfactions with their arguably subordinate positions in their churches. The involvement of women in the chapter may also be interpreted as a symbolic defense against the assumption common among some of their non-Christian peers and professors that evangelicalism is uniformly oppressive toward women. Finally, a small number of IVCF women told me that they hoped their prominent role in the chapter might quietly promote more egalitarian gender roles within the larger evangelical tradition.

If women are attracted to the IVCF partly as a means of struggling for social power within a patriarchal tradition, it is difficult to understand why the men of the IVCF do not protest what is evidently a challenge to their hegemony. During interviews and more casual conversations, IVCF men often openly defend male dominance within their churches as a consequence of a clear and faithful reading of scripture and Christian history. However, regardless of the strength of their convictions about the inappropriateness of female leadership in their churches, not a single IVCF man complained to me about the high profile of women in the chapter. Initially, I surmised that the religious leadership of women in the group might not be resisted by men as a function of their fear of the anticipated response of the staff worker. However, while Cox is a feminist and highly respected by the executive committee and many other members of the chapter, her opinions do not exert determinative or intimidating power over the general membership.[19]

A few days after I reached an impasse on this question, I asked a past IVCF President how he would explain men's (especially fundamentalist men's) apparent openness to female leadership in the group. This issue was obviously one he had considered before because he did not pause to reflect before rolling his eyes and saying, "Oh, I think those guys don't think this is really church. Sure, it's okay for women to do everything at IV, but not at their own churches. This is weird to me, but then that's because I think of what happens at IV as church."[20]

A few men in the IVCF support religious egalitarianism and attend churches that uphold this ideal (the past president belongs to the former but not the latter category). However, if the past president is correct, the chapter's majority of fundamentalist men do not protest the involvement and leadership of women because they perceive prominent IVCF women to be, so to speak, only "playing church." In other words, since these IVCF women do not represent a serious threat to male power within the more formal "church," men do not offer these women any resistance.

The third way in which the IVCF seems to respond to the triple alienation women experience is by allowing ambiguity. During an interview, Mary, a second-year fundamentalist student, and I discussed her views on the role of women in the church. During her first year at university, Mary took a course in McMaster's peace studies program that dealt with liberation theology. "The course made me think that Christianity was totally oppressive. For a while there I was pretty confused." I asked her how she resolved these doubts. She responded:

> Well, I went back and listened to peoples' testimonials. I guess I got away from what Buff calls "Churchianity" and back to the personal aspect of God. Right now I'm kinda struggling with the whole issue of women in the Christian family. I want to know if I should be submissive to my husband like Paul seems to suggest. But I'm a little unsure of all of this. I mean I know what the texts say, so I guess that should be enough, but still, I'm not sure if there are other ways to look at those texts [which seem to support women's subordination]. I'd be happy to find out that I'm deluded, because I really don't want to be submissive to my husband. But I want to know whether I need to take these passages literally. This will tell me what sort of woman I will need to become.[21]

Kelly, another fundamentalist woman, echoed Mary. Kelly said that:

> [The role of women is] a hard topic for me, and I pray about it a lot. I mean, I think I might have some skills in that area [of ministry], but I'm not sure if that necessarily means I should become a pastor. I think I need to study the issue a lot more—to pray about it and to read my Bible and to talk to other Christians about the whole issue. I'm struggling to be faithful to scripture, because I think that's super important. But I also want to be faithful to the gifts God has given me. And I don't think these things have to be [necessarily] opposed. It's hard, Paul.

The IVCF provides evangelical women with a safe place to reflect on the issues raised by challenging academic or social experiences at university. The IVCF women from across the theological and ideological spectrum echo Mary and Kelly's concerns, declaring in a variety of ways that they are unable to fully accept either the traditional roles bequeathed to them by their churches and families or the newer egalitarian feminist roles suggested and embodied by professors and peers at McMaster.

Instead, many IVCF women told me they are "still searching for" or "uncertain about" how they might reconcile their faiths and feminism. By ensuring that the group's leadership, small group offerings, and selection of speakers reflect a diversity of opinion on the role of women in Christianity, the staff worker and executive committee provide questioning women with a secure situation in which to entertain confusing thoughts and feelings about their religious traditions and their secular education.[22] The IVCF thus allows women the liberty of indecision, a four-year period of ambiguity during which the chapter facilitates the "stretching" process inspired by the clashes between feminism and evangelical faith. The undergraduate years are the ideal—and for many perhaps the final—period of their lives for such free reflection. The facilitation of ambiguity may explain some of the IVCF's appeal for McMaster's evangelical women.[23]

Conclusion

The IVCF women seem to experience a unique and complex form of estrangement at McMaster. On the one hand, while I admit that this possibility is speculative at best, women may feel othered by the university as a masculine institution, with its predominantly male professors, reading lists, and objectivist and adversarial modes of operation. This form of alienation may, of course, be shared by evangelical and nonevangelical women alike. On the other hand, IVCF women also describe feeling alienated from the comparatively egalitarian gender roles and permissive sexual norms formally or informally espoused or assumed by their secular peers and professors.

The negotiation of the metaphorical contracts I have described in previous chapters is an ongoing process which occurs so students can resolve or at least diminish the conflicts that arise when they confront their secular peers' views on a range of moral and intellectual issues. Crucial to understanding the disproportionate participation of women in the McMaster IVCF is an appreciation of the contract-facilitating functions of the three responses I outlined. I have argued that the IVCF responds in at least three ways to the unique form of estrangement female members experience. Each of these responses has distinct benefits for believers. First, by construing Jesus as a lover, believers can feel that they do not lack an object for their deepest quasi-erotic affections. Second, by allowing women to participate in religious leadership, the IVCF both facilitates its members' otherwise unfulfilled ambitions and problematizes the non-Christian generalization that evangelicalism subjugates women. And third, by providing a safe social space in which evangelical women can reflect on the competing truth and value claims made by non-Christians, the IVCF may reduce the urgency and anxiety associated with some of its members' uncertainties. Then evangelical women may be able to negotiate the contracts between their faith and feminism (and secularism) more gradually. The allowance of doubt into IVCF discourse on the role of women may also improve the relationships between IVCF members and non-Christians, who might be reassured that their evangelical peers are "not sure about" the role of women in the evangelical tradition. Such a reassurance may mollify non-Christian critics of religion by convincing them that their IVCF friends are not obdurate.

By reducing the estrangement IVCF women experience on the "turf" of the secular university, the three IVCF responses I have described in this chapter contribute positively to the negotiation process I describe throughout this book. These responses represent manifestations of the bridge strategy in that each response seems to decrease the sense of negative otherness evangelical women sometimes experience with respect to their non-Christian peers and professors, but the otherness itself never disappears as a result of these three responses. Rather, it is transformed from a negative experience into a largely positive one. In short, with the help of the IVCF, these women have developed complex, innovative, and empowering strategies that allow them to remain loyal to evangelicalism and, in their words, "stretched" by the liberal educational institutions that more and more of them are deciding to attend.

SIX

Satan and the Spiritual Realm

> For we are not contending against flesh and blood, but
> against the principalities, against the powers, against the
> rulers of this present darkness.
>
> Ephesians 6:12

> Our enemies are not flesh and blood, not our professors
> who give us bad grades because we're Christians, but be-
> ings which are unseen. God, we pray that you and your
> angels will protect us from these enemies.
>
> Frank, from fieldnotes

> Like, when you know something isn't right, but you find
> yourself rationalizing it anyway—for sure this is Satan. Es-
> pecially with lust—that's a good example. Also, with
> doubt. Satan feeds on the doubt that I might have that this
> isn't real spirituality.
>
> Janice, from fieldnotes

Although the prominence of women in the McMaster IVCF challenged my presuppositions about several elements of evangelicalism, the role of Satan in this group's discourse simply bewildered me. Whenever this topic arose during conversations with IVCF students, I became somewhat disoriented. For the first several interviews, I was incredulous and found myself rephrasing the open-ended questions I had posed, seeking more and more details in the answers that were offered to me. I had encountered references to Satan, demons, and angels in most of the scholarly and popular texts I had read before I started fieldwork. However, there is a significant and sometimes categorical difference between what one reads about in the comfort of one's home and what one experiences in the field. In other words, although I was intellectually prepared to encounter Satan, demons, and angels in evangelical discourse, on a deeper level, I was unable to accept that contemporary North American university students would believe in the existence of such entities in quite the way that IVCF students actually do.[1] Eventually, I was able to understand more clearly and without puzzlement what IVCF members mean when they speak of the spiritual realm. In fact, by the end of my fieldwork, I found myself interpreting several unsettling experiences in my own life according to the IVCF's relatively "enchanted" worldview.

Initially, I began investigating this issue by asking students questions about the role of Satan in their lives at McMaster. However, my respondents rarely referred solely to Satan, but rather to a much more elaborate array of nonhuman entities working for and against Satan. In referring to these entities, I use the phrase "spiritual realm" in addition to God, Satan, demons, and angels, partly for the sake of brevity but in addition because I seek to connote by this phrase an entire extrahuman dimension that includes all these figures. Because students talk about the demonic elements of the spiritual realm much more frequently than the angelic elements, this chapter focuses on the former.

The evangelical discourse on the spiritual realm is rooted in both ancient Christianity and recent popular fiction. Biblical scholar Elaine Pagels notes that while the role of Satan was not very pronounced in ancient Judaism (1991:105), the war against Satan and his demon underlings occupies a more central part of the cosmologies of Islam and Christianity (1991:128). In *The Origin of Satan* (1995), Pagels outlines the historical, social, and textual background for the concepts of Satan and demons in early Christian thought. She argues that for centuries, Christians have tended to assume that their social and religious outsiders—enemies and other others—are by definition servants of Satan.[2] The persona of Satan as the usurper of God's sovereignty developed out of apocalyptic Jewish sources and Hebrew Bible texts (1995:179) and was gradually transformed by generations of Christians into the personal and ubiquitous religious figure encountered in the discourse of evangelical groups, such as the IVCF.

It is difficult to determine with confidence why contemporary evangelicals embrace the discourse of the spiritual realm more enthusiastically than their mainline coreligionists. Historian Jeffrey Burton Russell observes that the emphasis on the individual that is typical of Protestantism increased the prominence of Satan. In medieval Europe, one could huddle together with one's community against Satan; after Luther, one had to fight the devil alone (1988:168). This shift from corporate to individual spiritual warfare against Satan may explain why early Protestants seemed to be more preoccupied with their personal religious safety than medieval Catholics.[3] However, it is more difficult to discern the most plausible explanation for the prominence of Satan in contemporary conservative Protestant discourse. The first and most obvious explanation is simply that evangelicals place a much greater emphasis than nonevangelicals on a putatively literal interpretation of the Bible. Because there *are* angels and demons in the Bible (Mk 1:34; 1 Cor 10:20; Rev 9:20; Mt 4:11; Mk 1:13; Rev 7:1), evangelicals steadfastly refuse to turn these ancient entities into sophisticated or vapid modern metaphors for abstract forces of good or evil.

The second source of the evangelical emphasis on the spiritual realm can be traced to two novels. The first is *The Screwtape Letters*, written in 1945 by the renowned Christian intellectual, C. S. Lewis. *The Screwtape Letters* is a collection of letters from a senior demon named Screwtape to his nephew, a junior demon named Wormwood. Although Wormwood occasionally makes some progress in gently leading his human "patient" into perversion and away from God, he is never fully or finally successful, which provokes the ominous wrath of Screwtape, who eventually devours the junior demon. Despite the wide-ranging influence of Lewis's novel, only a small minority of IVCF students made explicit references to *The Screwtape Letters* during our conversations. Moreover, very few IVCF members seemed to be aware of the subtle ways in which Lewis depicts either the junior demon's attempts to delude the man for whose damnation he is responsible or the symbolic nature of the demon's labors.[4]

Very early in my interviews and observations, it became clear to me that the most common influences on or reflections of IVCF members' perspectives on the spiritual realm are Frank E. Peretti's novels, especially *This Present Darkness* (1986), which takes its title from the Ephesians verse quoted at the beginning of this chapter. In *This Present Darkness*, Peretti tells the story of the fictitious American community of Ashton, where Marshall Hogan, an intrepid newspaper owner, and Hank Busche, a stalwart fundamentalist preacher, stumble onto and eventually foil an elaborate Satanic New Age plot to take control of the town.[5] Throughout the novel, the two principal investigators unravel a scheme to eliminate pious and virtuous citizens and to buy most of Ashton's real estate, including its pivotal institution, a university. The aim of this conspiracy is to secure a fortress (interestingly, a secular university) for "the Strongman," a demonically possessed multibillionaire businessman and charismatic New Age leader. Conflicts between the human protagonists are only a part of the story, however; it is obvious that legions of angels and demons are actually impelling the characters and plot.[6]

Almost a third of the students I interviewed mentioned Peretti without being prompted. For example, David echoed many IVCF members' comments when he said, "We all have personal angels, like bodyguards, looking out for us. And we all have demons that attack us spiritually. Especially after reading Peretti's books, I totally believe in angels and demons and the whole spiritual realm." Approximately another third of IVCF participants did not spontaneously mention Peretti but, when asked about him, were all aware of him and quite familiar with the cosmology he depicts. Many of these members indicated that they had read or heard of his books. Other participants commented that although they had not read Peretti's novels, they feel, or have been told by other IVCF members, that they should. However, it is significant that even those who have neither read nor heard of *This Present Darkness* (or Peretti's 1989 sequel, *Piercing the Darkness*) still illustrate their descriptions of the spiritual realm with terms and metaphors strongly reminiscent of his novels.

When discussing the spiritual realm, IVCF students are more likely to cite Peretti than the Bible. In fact, as New Testament scholar Robert Guelich observes, "this particular story, though clearly fictitious on the historical level, has been taken as 'true' or 'real' on a theological level in many circles in the Church today. . . . The novel accurately depicts the nature and means of spiritual warfare as perceived by a number of Christians today. This is so much the case, that the book has frequently come to be known as the 'bible' of spiritual warfare" (1991:57).[7] Part of the reason for the success of *This Present Darkness* is that it provides readers with a more focused narrative depiction of the spiritual realm than they can get through biblical texts (Guelich 1991:37). Moreover, Peretti's novels are set in the contemporary United States, a context obviously more familiar to North Americans and therefore perhaps more plausible than the world of ancient Israel depicted in the Bible. The terms and imagery IVCF participants use to refer to the spiritual realm may ultimately originate in the Bible, but the most recent manifestation of these ancient resources is Peretti's novels. Commenting on the prevalence of spiritual warfare in evangelical discourse, Guelich writes, "What began as a metaphor for the Christian life has become a movement whose expression is found above all in Frank Peretti's novel, *This Present Darkness*. . . . In many ways, though a novel, this book captures the popular understanding of the character of contemporary spiritual warfare" (1991: 34). For example, Howard, a commerce student, said, "Peretti really got people thinking about these sorts of issues. Now, all of a sudden you have people praying against Satan and getting into spiritual warfare and all that." Peretti seems to have gathered together and presented in an easily accessible fictional format preexisting strands of Christian discourse on the spiritual realm. As a result, the spiritual realm has gained an unprecedented prominence in evangelical popular culture since the mid-1980s.[8]

Nevertheless, it is important not to overstate Peretti's significance. As I have suggested, the roots of the contemporary evangelical interest in the spiritual realm are in ancient Jewish sources and the Bible and have been a fixture of Protestant thought for centuries (Guelich 1991; Pagels 1995). The role of Satan in the Bible and Christian history obviously forms part of the unspoken subtext of IVCF students' beliefs about the spiritual realm. For example, in response to my question about the reality of the spiritual realm, Simon, one of the four IVCF members profiled in chapter 2, commented, "I've never really had any real experience with the supernatural, so I can't say what a demon is like, but they're in the Bible, so I know they're out there." Nevertheless, as I have suggested, very few students refer explicitly to the Bible in discussions about the spiritual realm, except perhaps to make allusions to the famous passage in Ephesians.

In this chapter, I explore the fairly narrow range of beliefs shared by almost all IVCF students regarding the ways nonhuman spiritual entities interact with and influence all people, but specifically believers. Then I discuss three of the most common ways Satan is perceived to attack these undergraduates. Finally, I consider four possible interpretations of the IVCF understanding of the spiritual realm. To contextualize the ethnographic material I present, I refer to the cosmology undergirding *This Present Darkness* throughout this chapter.

Before I interpret the role of the spiritual realm among IVCF members, a brief discussion of Peretti's conception of the spiritual realm is in order. Peretti typically depicts angelic warriors as tall, well-built, handsome men who have been summoned from all of the earth's eras and regions, and who bear romantic ancient-sounding names such as Triskal, Guilo, Armoth, Tal, Nathan, and Chimon. Peretti's portraits of angels rely on common stereotypes. Armoth is "the big African whose war cry and fierce countenance had often been enough to send the enemy fleeing before he even assailed them," Chimon is described as "the meek European with the golden hair," and Nathan is portrayed as "the towering Arabian figure who fought fiercely and spoke little" (1986:45). The angels are all armed with swords that glow with a bright white light when drawn for battle. Their wings are "silken, shimmering, nearly transparent membranes" (1986:13) and visible almost only when they take flight.

In contrast, demons are usually depicted as sniveling, black, warty, hideous, and typically diminutive quasi-reptilian creatures with sharp talons and bulging yellow eyes, although some of the senior demons may be much larger and more powerful. However, they may change their appearance to deceive or torment a human being. All of the demons are stealthy, sulfur-exhaling manipulators who bear the names of the evils they promote: Complacency, Deception, Rape, Lust, Jealousy.

On the angelic side of the spiritual realm, there is a strict and unquestioned chain of command, descending from God through several senior angels to Tal the battle chief, to the frontline warriors. On the demonic side of the battle, a similar hierarchy exists: from Satan through a variety of senior demons to Rafar, the demonic battle leader, to a teeming army of demon warriors. A crucial difference between the two spiritual hierarchies is that all members of the Heavenly Host are unflinchingly loyal to their superiors but that the demon Lucius, one of Rafar's immediate inferiors, seeks to undo Rafar's plans to discredit him. Eventually, Lucius's betrayal helps to bring about the triumphant victory of the angelic Host of Heaven.

During interviews and before I read Peretti's novel, I often felt frustrated that participants were unable to specify precisely how beings from the spiritual realm affected human beings. In most cases, students would get flustered when I asked them to clarify this aspect of their cosmologies, and occasionally they would contradict themselves. Sometimes IVCF members would speak of demons or angels as directly implanting thoughts in human minds; at other times, the same people would speak of demons simply "offering" us a variety of sinful thoughts, which we are free to select or reject. Sometimes angels and demons seem quasi-human in their shape and behavior; at other times, they are depicted as more ethereal "forces." Sometimes beings from the spiritual realm appear to inflict physical torment on Christians; in other contexts, IVCF participants claim it is impossible to see demons and angels or for them to have a significant impact on the physical realm except through human agency.

Initially, I attributed the contradictions and intellectual reticence I encountered among IVCF students to the nature of the spiritual realm itself. Because the spiritual realm is, by definition, not fully transparent to humans, I assumed I should not expect students to maintain clear or definitive views on issues pertaining to this realm. Moreover, I supposed, these students are neither trained theologians nor philosophers, so perhaps they are not able to articulate whatever convictions they hold.

I had hoped to find in *This Present Darkness* a well-defined model that described the sort of influence entities from the spiritual realm can bring to bear on humans. What I found instead was much more interesting and ambiguous. In fact, according to Peretti, angels and demons seem to interact with the human realm in *all* the physical and nonphysical ways I have described.[9] In any case, there is a high degree of correspondence between Peretti's portrait of the spiritual realm and IVCF students' depictions. The IVCF students envisage demons both as barely invisible creatures *and* as ethereal forces of evil. Moreover, according to Peretti and IVCF participants, although angels and demons can have actual effects on material objects, their most common means of influencing humans is by suggesting thoughts and feelings to humans in ways both subtle and shrewd. The IVCF participants speak of this mode of compulsion most frequently, telling me stories about how Satan or his demons "made me think" a particular thought or how an angel "told me that was a lie." When I asked participants if Satan (as in the first case) forced a thought into their minds or an angel (as in the second case) literally spoke into their ears, they usually pause and answer that members of the spiritual realm offer or suggest a thought and the individual must decide whether to accept it. However, other students responded that angels or demons could also force a thought into a believer's mind and make it so attractive that the person would be virtually powerless to reject it.

Satan and demons are said to afflict these undergraduates in at least three ways, each of which could easily justify another complete ethnographic study. In the present and more limited context, however, a brief illustration of these modes is appropriate. The first and most common way in which Satan or his demons are thought to assail IVCF students is by "tempting" them. In her response to my question about Satan's tools, Maya, an occupational therapy student, replied, "I want to know more about [demons]. Buff says the devil will get you when you're at your lowest. And for sure, temptation is one of the main ways he tries to get at you."

During conversations with participants, I noticed that women tended to refer to Satanic temptation less frequently than men and that women spoke about it in a general sense, whereas men tended to enumerate instances in which they had been tempted. Moreover, when men provided illustrations of temptation, their narratives almost inevitably concerned specific and contextualized "lustful" thoughts about women. For example, Frank commented:

> Sometimes I'll be just sitting in church and Satan suddenly presents me with lustful thoughts, really clear images out of nowhere. I just have to be strong and I have to rebuke him. You just have to pray and to say no. Yeah, Satan can make me think lustful thoughts—but we have to choose. But the biggest challenge a Christian faces is. . . . Well, let me put it this way: Satan can make something look so good it's almost impossible to say no to it, but you have to say no.

Hugh, a student at McMaster's Divinity College, provided another illustration of Satan's temptations: "Okay, for example, let's say I'm standing on a street. I see a woman and I have a lustful thought about her. So then I turn away from her and there's another woman right there in front of me. Satan probably put her there to tempt me." I asked Hugh whether Satan forced the second woman to walk past him to continue Satan's temptation. "Yeah, sure," he replied, "maybe Satan or one of his demons persuaded her to cross to the other side of the street." I suggested that the woman in question probably believes that she voluntarily chose to cross the street. Hugh answered, "Sure, maybe that's true on one level, but it could also be that Satan or a demon could have whispered something in her ear which she mistakes for her own thoughts."

Later in the conversation I asked Hugh, to describe spiritual warfare. He replied, "Angels and demons are constantly fighting all around me. When something good happens, like when I turn my head away from these two women and avoid the lust, it is almost always with the help of an angel. But I have to exercise my freedom. I could totally ignore or fight the angel." Norman, a student from a strict fundamentalist background, answered the same question by commenting:

> There are all kinds of temptations Satan brings to me. Like there are a lot of beautiful girls on this campus, if you know what I mean. And it's hard to keep my mind pure. Like, if a woman walks by wearing tights or a short skirt, my head will turn, of course. That's from Satan. [People in my denomination] believe there are three ways to be tempted: by Satan, your own sin, and other people. But Satan is the author of all that is evil, although it is a toss-up as to whether it's Satan or ourselves that really causes sin. . . . Peretti's books have been really helpful for understanding this sort of thing.

The second way Satan and his underlings plague IVCF participants is by causing them to be depressed. During interviews and intimate informal conversations, five of the thirty-four IVCF women I interviewed revealed that they suffer from periods of clinical depression that often prevent them from attending classes and leaving their beds or apartments.[10] This figure does not exceed the statistically normal percentage (10–25%) of affected individuals. However, since I did not explicitly ask any of the women I interviewed if they have ever suffered from an affective disorder, it seems reasonable to conclude that I am aware of only a portion of the true numbers of depressed IVCF women. Gail Frankel and W. E. Hewitt (1994) argue that many Canadian undergraduates suffer from depression and that involvement in religious groups during the undergraduate years is positively correlated with physical and psychological well-being. It is difficult to determine if the depressed women in the IVCF contradict Frankel and Hewitt's findings or if, to follow their reasoning, the proportion of IVCF women who suffer from depression suggests that an even greater proportion of non-Christian students actually suffer from this condition than the statistics portray.[11] Normally, IVCF women disclosed their condition in the context of talking generally about what they describe as their "spiritual walk," the current state of their relationship with God. For some IVCF women, being depressed simply complicated this "walk" because it meant they did not spend enough time "doing devotions," the disciplines of reading the Bible or praying.

Four of the five women interpreted their depression as being the result of demonic aggression. One of the clearest manifestations of this attribution came in the form of the Church at the John presentation in January 1996. During her thirty-minute address, Kelly, an international missionary and former member of the McMaster IVCF, referred to Satan at least a dozen times. She also spoke at length of the personal challenges she had encountered during her mission work in Lithuania (cf. chapter 7). One of her main examples was her depression, which she described as an "attack of Satan." In an attempt to illustrate how we can "rebuke Satan in Jesus's name, expose his lies, and break their power," Kelly described the following incident:

> Sometimes the devil uses depression to paralyze me and to keep me from feeling like working and praying. I remember during one such period of time I was on

my knees begging for help from God. And I got very angry. Out loud I rebuked the devil in Jesus's name and forbade the spirit of depression from having a hold on me. Within minutes, I knew that the depression had lifted and I was free from the oppression. (Church at the John presentation, January 1996)[12]

Kelly believes that her condition was the result of Satan's efforts to destroy her ministry with new and potential Christians in the former Soviet Union. Her prayer reflects not only the classic rhetoric of spiritual warfare (as found in the Bible and Peretti's novels) but also evangelical notions of demons as invisible but affecting creatures that are almost literally "on" a person. Almost immediately after her prayer, she felt a weight lifted from her soul, at which point she knew Satan was gone, and she was free to minister to the student members of her group.

During a conversation we had at McMaster, Sheryl, a nineteen-year-old Science student, paused thoughtfully and said that:

> Satan tries to discourage me. Like, I've had to fight a lot of depression recently. In November, I hardly ever got out of bed before noon, and I totally stopped singing. Living in a basement apartment didn't help either. Satan disillusioned me . . . I mean, the depression was an attack of Satan, for sure. When I doubt myself, when I think I'm no good, I know it's a lie from Satan. That's what my mom tells me. She's my hero. She shows me how in the Bible it says all these wonderful things about me. But I know that when my guard isn't up, that's when Satan can get to me.

Gabrielle, one of the IVCF members whose life history I discussed in chapter 2 echoed Sheryl's response to my questions:

> Well, you may have guessed this already, but I'm depressed, and I have insomnia, too. And a temper. Last term, I stopped reading the Bible and attending small group, and I would snap at people for no good reason. Satan is saying, "Yeah, keep feeling like this . . . don't bother getting up or going to school today." I mean, I don't hear voices or anything. But I know these thoughts don't come from God, and they are beyond me. But still, it can be me, I guess, like when I skip classes. But if it's a prolonged state, like when I'm not studying at all [because of depression], it's beyond me, and that's when Satan is motivating me.[13]

The third weapon in Satan's arsenal is deception (Robb 1993:173). In *This Present Darkness*, one of the novel's heroic characters, apparently representing Peretti's views (Maudlin 1989:56), explains that demons appear in many different disguises, depending on the person they are intending to destroy. This character observes:

> To the atheistic scientists [demons] might appear as extraterrestrials . . . ; to evolutionists they might appear as highly evolved beings; to the lonely they might appear as long lost relatives speaking from the other side of the grave; Jungian psychologists consider them "archetypal images" dredged from the collective unconscious of the human race. . . . whatever description or definition fits, whatever shape, whatever form it takes to win a person's confidence and appeal to his vanity, that's the form they take. . . . It's all a con game: Eastern meditation, witchcraft, divination, Science of Mind, psychic healing, holistic education—oh, the list goes on and on—it's all the same thing, nothing but a ruse to take over

people's minds and spirits, even their bodies. . . . Bernice, we are dealing with a conspiracy of spirit entities. (1986:314)

As I have suggested in previous chapters, through their non-Christian peers and courses at McMaster, IVCF students often come into contact with ideas and faith communities that threaten many basic evangelical assumptions about the truth of their faith. For many students, encountering challenging secular ideas either introduces doubt into their lives or capitalizes on the doubt that is already there. As Janice said, "Satan feeds on the doubt that I might have that [evangelical Christianity] isn't real spirituality." Like Janice, many IVCF students consider Satan to be the ultimate author of all their questioning and of the challenging alternatives to evangelical Christianity.

Through his army of demons, Satan is said to trick people into believing all manner of insidious untruths. Although most of the secular ideas by which IVCF students are threatened are derived from pluralism, relativism, inclusivity, and popular culture, the lies about which Peretti is most concerned are those associated with the New Age movement, or what Peretti calls "occultism and Eastern mysticism" (1986:130). During a long bus ride to the annual IVCF winter retreat, I spoke with Carrie about the growing involvement of one of my relatives with the New Age tradition. When I said that I had some serious misgivings about movements called New Age but thought there was some validity in certain elements of the tradition, Carrie stiffened somewhat and stated unequivocally that she disagreed with me. In her view, my relative had been duped by Satan. "The New Age movement is the work of Satan because it tells you there is no God and that you can accomplish everything yourself," Carrie claimed.[14]

During a small group conversation about whether non-Christians might also go to heaven, I asked Oliver, a psychology student, "If God is all-powerful and all-loving, isn't it possible that he is at work in other religions and in the lives of non-Christians?"

Oliver replied immediately, "But God is also a just God, and he gives us a choice to make. The only choice is between God and Satan." Assuming Oliver would agree with the following rhetorical question, I asked, "But, surely all of Judaism or Buddhism is not the work of Satan?" Oliver shrugged his shoulders and responded flippantly, "Why not?" After a brief, tense pause, Cindy, a friend of Oliver's, added, "Yeah, I mean, Satan is called the Great Deceiver, after all" (Rev 12:9; cf. Russell 1988:44). "Right," affirmed Oliver, "he can make so many different religions that are so much like Christianity, but lacking in the aspect of Christ. These other religions are so attractive and so close to the truth that they draw people away from God. I'd call this deception, wouldn't you? And if Satan is the Great Deceiver, well, what does that make those other religions?"[15] After a long pause and a tacit agreement between Oliver, Cindy, and myself, we changed the subject.

The IVCF prayers during spiritual warfare also challenge the deception of demons. During one "concert of prayer," held in a McMaster lounge on a cold night in the winter of 1996, I heard the following prayer: "Fathergod, there is so much deception on this campus. We pray that you will show people that you are the Truth, that the Truth is not in Buddhism or atheism or agnosticism, or in Judaism, or anything else but you, God. And I pray against the lies we are taught in school, like the lie that we come from the apes." As this prayer was spoken, whispered affirmations of "Yes, God" and "Praise Jesus" arose from the group of bowed and seated participants.

Satan also tries to deceive Christians or potential Christians about the strength and support of their religious communities. During a morning meeting near the end of the IVCF mission to Lithuania, Janice remarked, "Sometimes I feel sort of alienated from the rest of the team, but when I feel this way, I just know it's Satan trying to deceive me, and not that the group actually doesn't want me to be a part of it. But it's hard, and I have to remind myself that it is Satan who causes this feeling." In response, other team members affirmed Janice's interpretation by saying, "No way" and "That's not true," when she first confessed her feeling of alienation, and then "For sure," and "Definitely" when she attributed this feeling to Satan's deception.[16]

While Satan's attacks on one's self-esteem often lead to depression, severe attacks can lead to suicidal despair. In the context of counseling a suicidal adolescent girl at an evangelical drop-in center, Harriet, a biology student, informed the girl that Satan was deceiving her about her personal worthiness. The suicidal teenager "kept telling me she heard voices telling her to kill herself. I told her it was Satan trying to trick and oppress her. Satan put those voices into her head, no question. I just can't think of how they'd get there otherwise. Can you?" Harriet reminded the girl that she was a child of God and therefore unconditionally loved by her heavenly father, regardless of what might be happening to her on earth. Harriet wrote several encouraging sentences on a piece of paper, which she instructed the girl to read to herself whenever she started to hear Satan's voice.

Interpretations

One does not have to pay close attention to IVCF discourse to hear direct and indirect references to the spiritual realm, especially to Satan and his demons. Members frequently speak about these entities and engage in spiritual warfare against them not simply because IVCF members believe that demons and Satan exist (a conviction that Rawlyk [1996:112] reports nonevangelical Christians might share). These students also maintain that these denizens of the spiritual realm are actively and almost constantly trying to destroy the faith and bodies of IVCF students, as well as those of their friends and families (convictions that would not be common among "non-Christians," to use IVCF rhetoric). There are at least four possible interpretations of IVCF perceptions of the role of Satan and his demons.

The first and most obvious, of course, is that Satan and demons actually exist. It would not only be reductive but also arrogant to presuppose the nonexistence of some variety of spiritual realm. The sheer invisibility and, even according to Peretti, unpredictability of the spiritual realm means simply that such an alternative sphere of existence cannot be unequivocally verified on empirical grounds. Because angels and demons are intangible and inconstant does not necessarily mean that they do not actually exist or that these entities do not exist in precisely the way described by Peretti and IVCF students. When I asked IVCF participants to tell me about the role of Satan in their lives, none of them appeared to respond to me "as if" such beings existed. On the contrary, they answered my questions as though I had asked them to describe the role of a shadowy, enigmatic uncle in their family. Consequently, one of the ways of interpreting the predominance of Satan and demons in IVCF discourse is simply to argue that these believers have a firm grasp of reality. Demons may, in fact, rouse IVCF members in the middle of the night to afflict them with anxiety attacks and compel women to walk down streets to tempt IVCF men. However, since the present text is a work of social science, it is necessary to consider other and perhaps complementary explanations for the significance of the spiritual realm to IVCF students.

The second alternative to the previous insider's account is to interpret the spiritual realm as an element of IVCF theodicies, or explanations of suffering. As Max Weber (1948:275–282) has observed, a central characteristic of religious systems is the provision and legitimation of theodicies.[17] But a theodicy is only one component of an individual's or a community's "sacred canopy" (Berger 1967; cf. Berger and Luckmann 1966:120), an overarching, socially constructed understanding of reality that explains why all things—welcome and unwelcome—happen. What role might negative elements in the spiritual realm play in IVCF participants' sacred canopy and theodicy?

As noted in chapter 3, all but one of the IVCF members I interviewed believe that God has a comprehensive plan for their lives. According to this perspective, everything that happens to these students must somehow be related to God's plan or to Satan's attempts to foil it. Sociologist Nancy Ammerman discusses the way negatively evaluated experiences are assessed by the Baptists she studied: "When they have no other explanation for their pain, it must be Satan who is persecuting them. Therefore, they do not have to attribute their pain to God" (1987:65). Consequently, believers' lives and worldviews are protected from the vicissitudes of everyday life. Applied to the IVCF, Ammerman's insight seems to explain the plausibility-maintaining function of the spiritual realm.[18]

For example, as Gabrielle said earlier in this chapter, some negative thoughts are "beyond me"; similarly, Harriet also commented that she cannot "think of how [some thoughts] would get there otherwise [than through Satanic influence]," and Maya explained, "All temptations would be from Satan, obviously, since God is all good." Historian Jeffrey Burton Russell argues that such a radical opposition between an entirely good God and a completely evil Satan is rooted in the ancient apocalyptic Judaism, which contributed significantly to the culture and worldview out of which Christianity emerged. Apocalyptic Jews believed that extreme degrees or quantities of evil were more than God would ordain and therefore must be caused by some other spiritual force, a force associated with the figure of Satan found in preexisting biblical texts (Russell 1988:32). Gabrielle, Harriet, and Maya's modern versions of the ancient apocalyptic tendency may also exemplify what Freud called "splitting," the protection of the goodness of a deity (or object or person) by transferring any evil associated with it to another object, in this case, a lesser supernatural force (Russell 1988:245).

The major difficulty IVCF students might encounter in trying to interpret all events they experience in the context of the basic antagonism between God (and God's will) and Satan is that the transcendent actors in this drama are fairly abstract. I would argue that although IVCF participants believe God has a specific benevolent plan for their lives, this plan and the ways God manifests it are remote and often opaque. Ideally, IVCF members maintain intimate relationships with God, but according to believers, God is still the creator of and most potent force in the universe, a role inspiring awe that no degree of intimacy can entirely mitigate. God has a plan for each of us and somehow seeks our cooperation to realize it fully. But this "somehow" may be too ambiguous for evangelicals, who understandably seek clearer, more immediate, and yet angelic explanations for the condition of their lives. Angels thus act as more comprehensible mediators between God's plan for an individual and the individual.

Similarly, from a very young age, evangelicals are told by pastors and peers that Satan opposes God's specific plan for their lives and God's general plan for the universe. However, Satan may also seem too immense and general an enemy for evangelicals, who may prefer to see themselves as the victims of forces either smaller or at least more personal than the ancient and nearly ubiquitous Satan. Just as angels are God's mediators, demons mediate between Satan's (relatively general) efforts to undo God's plans and the specific vulnerabilities of each individual.

Ammerman observes that the conviction that the entire range of human experiences can be reconciled with God's will is more important for the fundamentalists she studied than a "logically consistent theory about evil" (1987:66).[19] The IVCF students similarly place little value on maintaining seamless explanations of evil. Invoking members of the spiritual realm to explain puzzling, painful, or miraculous situations may result in inconsistent interpretations by secular standards. However, for most of the people I interviewed, angels and demons are nonmetaphorical actors in everyday life, so IVCF students have little difficulty integrating the spiritual realm into their understandings of causality. Angels and demons help to make abstract theological explanations about God's will and Satan's opposition more accessible, comprehensible, and, in the most literal sense, imaginable for IVCF students. The dichotomy between the heavenly realm's will for individuals and the demonic sphere's less powerful but undeniable ability to interfere with this plan appears to diminish causative mystery and to leave God's sovereign and purely benevolent will for individuals intact. In short, the references to barely metaphysical enemies may help to explain and contextualize a wide range of theodicical issues.

The third way of understanding the function of Satan in IVCF discourse is to interpret the contemporary persona of the Antichrist as part of a broader evangelical response to the secularization of North American culture and the contemporary university. As I outlined in previous chapters, some theorists[20] maintain that this process has not profoundly decreased personal levels of religiosity, at least as these are measured in terms of theological commitments in Canada or church attendance and theological commitments in the United States. However, in both countries, religion has steadily retreated or been eliminated from major institutions such as education, health care, and the government (Roof 1996:154; Swatos 1983). These recently secularized institutions have been either hostile or indifferent to organized religion and especially, evangelicals tell me, to conservative Christianity.[21] This exclusion of religion from mainstream social institutions is part of the more general process that Max Weber terms "disenchantment."[22]

As I have mentioned in previous chapters, since the late 1970s, conservative Protestantism has returned to the public stage in North America. Some scholars[23] argue that part of the reason for the resurgence of evangelicalism is that these believers are responding (creatively, in great numbers, and with considerable success) to the disenchanting marginalization of explicitly religious concerns from public discourse (Stout 1988) and to what they consider to be an unprecedented values crisis in North America (Marty 1987).[24] Furthermore, the ascendency of the reenchanting experientialism represented by significant elements of contemporary evangelicalism (Cox 1995; cf. Roof 1996:152) is partly a response to the disenchantment or ossification many evangelicals believe is evident within mainstream Christianity.

For the purposes of the present study, the causes of the rise of conservative Protestantism and of the separation between religion and North American institutions are less relevant than evangelical responses to secularization. One of the best contexts in which to observe these responses and Satan's perceived role in them is the contemporary university. As previous chapters have illustrated, IVCF members are acutely aware of the secular character of McMaster University. Turning to Peretti's novel, it is no coincidence that in *This Present Darkness*, the central aim of the demonic forces is to take complete control of Whitmore College, a secular university on which Ashton's economy and culture depend. Writing about Peretti, popular culture scholar Jay Howard observes:

> The foremost battleground for the New Christian Right is the public education system. The stakes are high. To lose this confrontation is to lose the ability to impact children through educational socialization. . . . According to Peretti, the enemy views this battle as part of the ongoing effort to remove the influence of Christians on future generations, a necessary step in the battle to control and mold every segment of society. (1994:196)

The acquisition of Whitmore is a cornerstone of the Strongman's grander scheme to take over the world. Professors at the university are depicted as some of the main conspirators in this plot, promulgating New Age and inclusivist ideas by using "that funny conglomeration of sixty-four dollar words which impress people with your academic prowess but can't get you a paying job" (Peretti 1986:37). Bearing in mind the previous discussion of evangelical attitudes toward feminism, it should come as no surprise that the most dangerous professor in the novel is Juleen Langstrat, a female professor of psychology who specializes in humanism, para-normal phenomena, and the occult.

In *This Present Darkness*, Sandy Hogan, a student at the university and the daughter of one of the protagonists, angrily repudiates her father's attempts to protect her from Langstrat's teachings. Sandy proclaims, "I'm a human being, Daddy, and every human entity—I don't care what or who he or she is—is ultimately subject to a universal scheme and not to the will of any specific individual. . . . And as for me, and what I am learning, and what I am becoming, and where I am going, and what I wish, I say you have no right to infringe on my universe unless I personally grant you that right" (1986:41). Immediately after Sandy's credo, Peretti writes: "Marshall's eyesight was getting blurred by visions of Sandy turned over his knee. Enraged, he had to lash out at somebody, but now he was trying to steer his attacks away from Sandy. He pointed back to [the university] and demanded, 'Did—did [*Langstrat*] teach you that?' " (1986:41). I would argue that Marshall Hogan's defensive reaction is a paradigmatic evangelical (and especially fundamentalist) response to the dark spiritual forces that are believed to use non-Christian institutions to advance narcissistic, permissive, seditious, and demonic New Age ideas.[25] As Hogan bellows his final question, we are reminded that universities such as Whitmore and McMaster represent significant threats to fundamentalists. In this Peretti passage, Sandy may represent misguided or satanically duped non-Christian individuals and institutions. Many believers (at McMaster and in Peretti's novels) might occasionally like to see the secular university, as it were, turned over the metaphorical knee of Christian faith.

In general, the emphasis on angels and demons as invisible or well-concealed actors in the human realm challenges the prevalent materialist conception of causality, according to which all events in the physical world occur as the consequences of prior perceptible physical causes. Spiritual realm discourse also problematizes the Western value of autonomy. Commenting on Peretti's novel, Harvey Cox observes:

> What intrigued me most was the way these supernatural personages, both benevolent and diabolic, make use of human beings to get their respective jobs done. Indeed human beings appeared to have little to do with it. Sometimes the good ones could open themselves to the angelic beings through prayer, but they were also likely to be thwarted by the bad ones conniving with the minions of darkness. (1995:283)

If demons and angels might be responsible for thoughts and behavior and if, in fact (as Cox argues that Peretti presupposes), humans are sometimes ignorant foot soldiers in the real battle between God and Satan, then the predictability of the material universe and the autonomy of human actors are severely compromised.

According to Jeffrey Burton Russell, mainstream liberal Christianity of the present century has "tended to deny or at least ignore the Devil. Many argued that the concept, if it were to be kept at all, should be retained merely as a metaphor for human evil, and the view that Satan exists only as realized in human sin gradually became a liberal dogma" (1988:241). As liberal Protestantism diminished the Devil's role in Christian life, the major modern critics of traditional religion (Marx, Freud, Nietzsche) also problematized the popular belief in radical supernatural evil (Russell 1988:241). The reentry of the spiritual realm into the human sphere of action during what is arguably a considerably disenchanted period in history represents and effects a reenchantment of the world. By increasing the permeability of the membrane between this world and the other world, Peretti has brought demons and angels into the everyday lives and thinking of IVCF members.

The final interpretation of the role of the spiritual realm in IVCF discourse is related directly to the fortress and bridge strategies I have discussed in previous chapters. The fortress approach protects the chapter's members from threatening features of modern life, whereas the bridge strategy seeks to transform or diminish the sense of otherness IVCF students experience in secular institutions.

The IVCF spiritual warfare against Satan, his demons, and the institutions, individuals, and traditions believed to be under the Evil One's domination is a clear manifestation of the fortress strategy. Usually set in the context of group prayers and songs, warfare discourse simply makes public what many individual participants already feel: that evangelicals are members of what Peretti called the "remnant" of loyal "saints," righteous servants of Christ in the midst of "this present darkness." One of the most common contexts in which this strategy is expressed is in the songs sung at IVCF events. For example, in "Above All Else," participants sing:

> You are a mighty warrior
> Dressed in an armour of light
> Crushing the deeds of darkness,
> Lead us on in the fight;
> Through the blood of Jesus,
> Victorious we stand.

As well, "The Battle Belongs to the Lord" includes the following lyrics:

> In heavenly armour we'll enter the land
> The battle belongs to the Lord.
> No weapon that's fashioned against us will stand,
> The battle belongs to the Lord. . . .
> When the Enemy presses in hard, do not fear
> The battle belongs to the Lord.[26]

The sense of living among, if not being besieged by, often demonically cozened infidels[27] contributes to what Martin Marty has described as a form of "tribalism" (1987:316), which unites the group. Anthropologist Susan Harding observes that the "dispensationalist" worldview which undergirds fundamentalist thinking "casts the subjects of 'modern' theories of history, namely, enlightened men and women, as, at best, hapless agents of Satan, at worst, villains with demonic designs. It casts Bible-believing Christians, on the other hand, as temporary victims and the ultimate heroes of history" (1994:63). In short, because spiritual warfare discourse is based on a sharp dualism between the saved and the unsaved, it helps believers to retrench (Berger 1992:43) their sense of superiority (since that is what it amounts to) and to accentuate the fundamental otherness of non-Christians.

However, the fortress-building function of spiritual realm discourse, which Harding so lucidly illustrates, is balanced by a bridging function. This second role of the spiritual realm is reflected in the paradox that IVCF students typically believe that humans have an inviolable responsibility to choose (and will be damned if they do not choose) to enter into a relationship with God, but in the spiritual framework Peretti has helped to build, humans do not really seem to be absolutely responsible for the status of their spiritual, not to mention physical, lives. This paradox is evident in Frank's comment: "Yeah, Satan can *make me think* lustful thoughts — but we have to *choose.* . . . Satan can make something look so good it's almost impossible to say no to it, but you have to say no" (emphasis added).

From a human if not a divine perspective, a person who chooses to reject Christ as the exclusive means of salvation or the guarantor of the good life *and* is also being tormented every day by sulfur-exuding, warty-skinned demons seems to be less culpable for his or her decision than a person who makes the same decision without demonic interference. In other words, a non-Christian may become an unsaved other to evangelicals partly because of powerful unseen forces. This person is therefore deserving of special prayers,[28] an extra portion of tolerance and personal attention. I would argue that spiritual realm discourse is a bridging strategy because it depicts evangelicals *and* nonevangelicals as more or less innocent victims of Satan's shadowy army.[29] Since the lamentable spiritual situations (e.g., being non-Christians, substance abusers, or adulterers) in which non-Christians find themselves are often in significant respects the result of unseen forces, and because evangelicals (thanks to Peretti and a particular reading of the Bible) are so well acquainted with Satan's agenda and methods, IVCF participants feel they have a duty to wage spiritual warfare for the souls of their non-Christian peers at McMaster. This duty entails not simply praying for unbelievers' liberation from Satan and his demons but in addition befriending and sharing the good news with non-Christians.

The role of the spiritual realm in IVCF discourse facilitates two contradictory processes. First, by promulgating the dichotomy between the redeemed (a category in which only angelic members of the spiritual realm and a small fraction of self-proclaimed Christians properly belong) and the unredeemed (a category in which Satan and the rest of an obdurate humanity belong), IVCF students seem intentionally to exacerbate their alienation from non-Christians. However, Satan's second role in evangelical discourse is to inspire Christians to recruit non-Christians to join them in a single army of believers united by common experiences of demonic affliction.

Conclusion

The day after I finished reading *This Present Darkness*, I had a speaking engagement at a local Unitarian church. Although I have spoken at dozens of these kinds of events, as I stepped into the pulpit and began reading my presentation, I felt an almost overwhelming wave of anxiety wash over me. I was almost certain I could hear voices shouting to me, "You can't do this!" "Your voice won't hold out!" "You're about to lose your place!" "Just sit down and shut up!" Somehow I defied these voices, finished reading my text, and sat down.

As soon as I was seated, I began to reflect on this strange and unsettling experience. With Peretti's literary voice and the voices of IVCF participants still echoing in my ears, I probably came as close as a Unitarian can come to believing (as evangelicals might) that I was being attacked by demons. This empathy for IVCF members' fears of demons became predictably less convincing later that day, when my mind returned to its habitual rhythms. But even though I imagine that my experience is probably a consequence of what Harding (1987) describes as the power of fundamentalist rhetoric to draw nonbelievers gradually over the threshold of biblical faith, this memory still makes me pause before accepting invitations to speak in churches.[30]

It would be simplistic and incorrect to argue that the relatively enchanted spiritual framework shared by IVCF students is derived exclusively from Peretti's novels. As Guelich (1991) observes, the spiritual realm and spiritual warfare have long and complex histories within the Judeo-Christian tradition.[31] However, without *This Present Darkness*, it seems unlikely that this realm would have achieved the sort of notoriety and ignominy it now has in IVCF discourse. Furthermore, when IVCF students from more than dozen different denominations talk about and "pray against" elements of the spiritual realm, their spoken and gestural performances are nearly identical and include direct or indirect references to Peretti. Consequently, it is illuminating to treat Peretti's work as emblematic of the views of the overwhelming majority of these evangelicals on Satan and his demons. Using Peretti's novel as a lens through which to view the prominent role of the spiritual realm in IVCF life helps to contextualize some of the elements of evangelical discourse that might strike nonevangelicals as puzzling, to say the least.

In this chapter, I have explored the major ways in which IVCF members perceive and experience the spiritual realm. I have also suggested four possible explanations for the current prominence of the discourse of the spiritual realm in the larger IVCF discursive system. First, one might affirm believers' experiences of the nonmetaphorical reality of the spiritual realm. Second, one might explain the centrality of this discourse as a crucial component of these students' theodicies. Third, one might posit that the spiritual realm helps IVCF members to reenchant academic and social settings, which, as Clark Pinnock maintains, betray a marked "bias against God." Fourth, IVCF students may employ the spiritual realm discourse to distinguish themselves from and simultaneously to ally themselves with their non-Christian peers and professors.

SEVEN

Witnessing at McMaster and Abroad

Go therefore and make disciples of all nations, baptizing them in the name of the Father and of the Son and of the Holy Spirit, and teaching them to obey everything that I have commanded you. And remember, I am with you always, to the end of the age.

Matthew 28:19

I just think we have a responsibility to share what we have with other people. I mean, we have something pretty special: we have eternal life. That's so great. Wouldn't it be selfish if we didn't share it?

Carole, from fieldnotes

We are witnesses to all that he did both in Judea and in Jerusalem. They put him to death by hanging him on a tree; but God raised him on the third day and allowed him to appear, not to all the people but to us who were chosen by God as witnesses, and who ate and drank with him.

Acts 10:39

At a Friday lunch meeting in October 1996, a local fundamentalist pastor spoke passionately to a group of eight IVCF students. The meeting was held, as usual, in the corner of a large multipurpose room in the basement of Divinity College. Several of the students seemed uncomfortable with the young preacher's zealous approach, somewhat out of place in the midafternoon of the week before midterm exams. The preacher exhorted:

Are you excited about your faith? You and you and you [pointing]. I mean, are you really excited that Jesus voluntarily came down to earth and died for each one of your sins? *Your* sins. That's pretty exciting if you ask me. I don't think I deserved it, do you? And now, in this place, how are you sharing your faith? Are you doing all you can to spread your faith in our Lord to the world? Are you sharing your faith with your professors through your papers and with your friends in class? Or do you not believe that the power of God is great enough to protect you? Mac is the most challenging mission field because what is at the forefront of the teaching today will be at the forefront of thinking tomorrow. And some people will tell you that this university is a non-Christian place. But I tell you that this is true, but not completely true. Actually, this university is a pagan place. So, again, what did Paul do? He went to the world of the lost people and did not expect them to come to him. Are you doing this? Are you going to the world of the lost people all around you or are you waiting for them to come to you? . . . And don't forget: you are disciples of Jesus Christ cleverly disguised as students who have to go to the world of the lost people and not expect them to come to you. It's like people here don't know they're lost. It's like convincing a sick person they're sick. But we have to do it.

This pastor leads a small Fellowship Baptist church in downtown Hamilton and has several contacts with members of the IVCF. Although his form of quasi-revivalist fundamentalism is not representative of mainstream evangelicalism or the McMaster IVCF, his message does reflect some basic evangelical approaches to the non-Christian "others" with whom IVCF participants live during their years at university. In various ways, these cleverly concealed disciples of Christ are exhorted to make the McMaster campus their "mission field" in which to witness to spiritually "lost" and "sick" unbelievers.

In this chapter, I describe and discuss the practice of witnessing to two different and largely non-Christian groups: university students in Hamilton and Lithuania, where the IVCF sent teams of student missionaries each spring for five years until 1996. After I provide an outline of these two mission fields, I describe various witnessing strategies. Finally, I explore the following central witnessing issues: the emphasis on the emotional component of faith, IVCF witnesses' understandings of themselves during witnessing, and their faith in the comprehensive nature of God's will.

This chapter is a detailed ethnographic account of neither the group's mission to Lithuania nor the Lithuanian students' reception of the mission team. Rather, the IVCF's Lithuania and McMaster witnessing endeavors represent case studies in basic witnessing strategies and problems. Throughout this chapter, I tend to emphasize Lithuanian examples because throughout the previous chapters I have discussed issues related to IVCF students in the McMaster setting and have not explored the Lithuanian witnessing context in detail.

The word "witnessing" refers to the process of sharing the salvific good news of Christ's life, death, and resurrection with non-Christians. When one "witnesses," one is claiming to have had an experience of the personal and divine reality of Christ. Although Christ's sacred status can be partly discerned through studying the Bible, this truth is apprehended most clearly through one's personal relationship with Christ, a crucial prerequisite for evangelical faith. Consequently, the goal of witnessing is to facilitate the nonbeliever's entry into an intimate relationship with Jesus Christ (Burridge 1991:4). Of course, as I have suggested throughout previous chapters, believers strive to change not just individual lives; in so doing, they also want to reshape the broader culture so that it more clearly embodies their beliefs and values.[1]

Christian missionary endeavors have been widely disparaged by commentators who believe that relatively affluent, white, Westernized Christians have compelled or encouraged natives to adopt lifeways that are inconsistent with their physical or social surroundings.[2] Nevertheless, just as early and relatively objectifying ethnography has been replaced or complemented by contemporary or postmodern ethnography,[3] the imperious and unabashedly ethnocentric Protestant missionary style of the nineteenth and early twentieth centuries has also, for the most part, been slowly supplanted by an approach to one's "mission field" that is more respectful of the lifeways of the non-Christian "other."[4] Perhaps the ability of evangelism to respond to growing critiques of its imperious history explains the fact that there are more missionaries in the 1990s than at any other time in history (Burridge 1991:x). Nevertheless, as we shall see, even the most sensitive evangelist must, in the end, believe and proclaim that he or she knows something of vital interest to the relatively unenlightened non-Christian listener.

Although Protestant evangelistic or missionary work is often situated in less developed countries, it has a long and noteworthy history in North America. In fact, evangelism has played a major role in the establishment of Christianity in Canada specifically, as well as in North America generally.[5] Moreover, historian Michael Gauvreau writes that in nineteenth-century Canada the influence of Protestant evangelism was not limited to the religious culture of the country; it made a significant impression on nonreligious institutions as well (1991:58). Eighteenth-and nineteenth-century evangelists were sufficiently successful at establishing churches, encouraging conversions, and influencing the societies in which they witnessed that by the end of the nineteenth century evangelical Protestantism had become embedded in Canadian and North American life (Gauvreau 1994:220). Until the early part of the present century, therefore, evangelicals felt at home in North America, a continent characterized by what George Rawlyk (1992:298; cf. Noll 1992:547) described as a broadly evangelical consensus on morality, the divinity of Jesus, and the reliability of the Bible.

However, within the first half of the twentieth century, the evangelical "consensus" to which Rawlyk refers had deteriorated.[6] This change led evangelicals to perceive North America as, in one IVCF member's words, "hostile territory." As such, this increasingly secular domain became slightly repositioned in evangelical discourse as a site in need of more concentrated evangelistic efforts. Thus, when IVCF participants and other evangelicals I have met talk about "mission fields," they are as likely to refer to McMaster University and North America in general as they are to Africa or Asia. As I have outlined, domestic witnessing is not a twentieth-century invention. But since the major institutions in North America have become arguably more disenchanted in the last part of the twentieth century than ever before (Swatos 1983), the culture as a whole is perceived by many of the believers I have interviewed as fundamentally and stubbornly inimical to evangelical beliefs and values (Rawlyk 1996:12). This antagonism, of course, sets the stage for evangelists.

Although the IVCF's annual mission to Lithuania is in many ways a traditional missionary project, the group's day-to-day witnessing to their non-Christian peers at

McMaster is not categorically different from the group's work in Lithuania. Both (usually local) witnessing and (usually international) missionary work involve interactions with non-Christians, in the hope that these others are converted.[7] Evangelical witnesses, regardless of their geographical locations, seek in some way to obey Jesus' Great Commission (Mt 28:19).[8] Consequently, in this chapter I often use the concepts of witnessing and mission work interchangeably.

The McMaster mission field comprises approximately 14,000 students in a southwestern Ontario city of 317,000 people. All students and faculty are, in a manner of speaking, witnessing "targets." A small minority of IVCF students tell me they witness to their professors and teaching assistants directly by discussing evangelical issues in their assignments or classroom contexts. However, most IVCF participants are content to witness to their educators by quietly exemplifying Christian virtues such as kindness or honesty.

In September 1995, I enrolled in one of the thirteen IVCF small groups organized for the 1995–96 academic year. Small groups meet usually once a week throughout the academic year to discuss a variety of issues.[9] Because I was interested in learning about witnessing, I registered for the small group planning to study Paul Little's *How to Give Away Your Faith* (1988), a popular text replete with practical advice to help evangelicals witness to non-Christians.[10]

Lithuania is the other context in which I observed IVCF witnessing. Lithuania (approximate population: 3.7 million) is bordered by Poland, Latvia, and Byelorussia. Its capital city is Vilnius (approximate population: 590,000), and its annual per capita income in the mid-1990s is roughly $3,000 (US). For a variety of reasons, it was one of the last European countries to be Christianized by the Roman Catholic church.[11] Christianity was officially adopted as the Baltic state's religion in 1384, but was not accepted at a popular level for several centuries. The worship of pagan deities continued for centuries and was gradually replaced by or incorporated syncretically into Catholicism. Even after decades of Soviet-style communism, Catholicism is still by far the largest religious movement in contemporary Lithuania.[12]

Presently, Lithuania is struggling to Westernize its economy and government, both of which were decimated by the withdrawal of Soviet financial aid (following the country's 1991 liberation) and the reluctance of Westerners to invest in the country after it achieved independence. Specifically, I spoke with several resentful Lithuanians who believe the Americans betrayed them by failing to support the post-Soviet Lithuanian economy. Although the Lithuanians I met are often skeptical about the information they receive about Western countries,[13] they still have a passion for Western, especially American, commodities. The nearly ubiquitous Western-style advertising along the elegant main streets of Vilnius now eclipses the vestiges of Soviet-style marketing. Perhaps symbolic of the economic model that is rapidly gaining ascendancy in Lithuania, the country's first two McDonald's restaurants were scheduled to open a week after the mission team left the country at the end of May 1996. Shaking his head, Shawn, a long-term International Fellowship of Evangelical Students missionary, pointed to a bag of potato chips in the hands of a Lithuanian man and said to me, "Look at that. You put an American flag on something, even if it's made in China or Lithuania, and it'll sell out like that. I hate it."

Several commentators have suggested plausibly that the rise of conservative Protestantism (and especially fundamentalism) in North America is a manifestation of these Christians' opposition to significant elements of modern society.[14] Perhaps the recent interest of some Lithuanians in North American evangelicalism is related to this general pattern. After all, Lithuania has just entered the contemporary world, characterized by advanced technology, consumerism, democracy, pluralism, and economic globalism. Many Lithuanians told me and other team members that they feel uneasy about their role in the individualistic, competitive market economy that typifies Western capitalism.[15] In fact, because Lithuanians have not entered the world of advanced (or perhaps "late") capitalism gradually, as North Americans have (at least relative to Lithuanians), Lithuanians' sense of dislocation from the economic, social, and moral conventions of the modern world system may be more severe than that of Western evangelicals.[16]

Because evangelicalism presents its adherents with a coherent and meaningful worldview, it is possible that the incipient attraction of some Lithuanians to evangelicalism reflects their quest for a Western-style "sacred canopy" (Berger 1967) with which to protect themselves from the uncertainties associated with their inexorable movement toward a Western-style economy. However, the form of Christianity conveyed by IVCF students may offer Lithuanians more than just a protective metanarrative about their new place in the grand (Western capitalist) scheme of things. One might argue that the evangelical emphases on personal righteousness and the development of the believer's salvific personal relationship with Jesus, contribute— perhaps by default—to the general evangelical lack of interest in economic issues. At the very least, the highly individualistic nature of most forms of conservative Protestantism might facilitate the spread of capitalism in the former Soviet Union and the acculturation process of its citizens. So, North American evangelicalism may offer Lithuanians a worldview which (perhaps unintentionally) does not encourage a critique of the underlying principles of democracy and capitalism (Fields 1991). Such a critique (more common, for example, in liberation theology [Berryman 1987]) might undermine Lithuanian Christians' emerging procapitalist (or perhaps protocapitalist) worldviews. In short, the members of the IVCF mission team did not explicitly promote what Timur Kuran describes as "fundamentalist economics" (1993:289; cf. Brouwer, Gifford, and Rose 1996; Iannaccone 1993), unless by this term one means a focus on the individual's religious experiences and choices and the concomitant deprivileging of rigorous socioeconomic analysis.

In 1991, a friend of Buff Cox suggested that the McMaster group send a contingent of students to witness to Lithuanian students. Although Cox was reluctant at first, she prayed about this possibility and eventually became convinced that "this is what God wanted me to do" (cf. Wagner 1990:180). Cox committed the McMaster chapter to sending teams of student missionaries to Lithuania for one month annually for five years, beginning in May 1992. The McMaster team went to Lithuania under the auspices of the International Fellowship of Evangelical Students (IFES), the international umbrella organization to which Canada's IVCF belongs.

Cox knew the 1996 group of seven students would be smaller than the previous four missions, which had attracted between nine and twenty-four students. Therefore, she was understandably cautious about the effects an outsider's presence might have on the team and on Lithuanians. Because Cox and I had developed a very positive rapport since I began conducting my fieldwork in 1994, and I had already interviewed all of the team members, however, she agreed to let me accompany the team, provided the two long-term missionaries living in Lithuania agreed. After I had exchanged several letters over electronic mail with the two missionaries, approval for my participation in the final mission to Lithuania was secured.

The IVCF team's mission was to help cultivate the nascent evangelical groups that have arisen on Lithuanian campuses since the disintegration of the Soviet Union in 1991. Western European and North American (but mainly American) evangelical and fundamentalist mission organizations have devoted a tremendous amount of energy and money to evangelize the people of the former Soviet Union. As far as some residents of the former Soviet Union are concerned, some of the North American missionaries have treated these Baltic non-Christians (of course, almost all of them would probably have described themselves as Catholics) in a condescending manner (Finley 1991; Thorogood 1993). In contrast, throughout the orientation sessions for the mission, Cox emphasized that team members should be cognizant of the tendency of Western Christians to patronize Lithuanians, to misrepresent Christianity, and, likely, to frustrate the goal of drawing people into the evangelical fold. The IVCF witnesses were advised to operate in a "learner" or "servant" mode and to maintain an "open mind" during their missionary efforts.

The IVCF members often refer to their form of witnessing as "friendship evangelism," the practice of sharing the gospel in the context of sincere friendships. This form of witnessing is also based on the assumption that the non-Christian's conversion should not be a condition of the friendship. The IVCF's form of friendship evangelism is an evangelical adaptation of what Jongeneel and Van Engelen (1995) describe as "dialogue theology."[17] Broadly speaking, this approach advocates a mode of witnessing that emphasizes the conversation between the witness and the non-Christian rather than the consequences of this interaction.[18]

Although IVCF missionaries formed relationships with Lithuanian students in the hope that the latter would "come to Christ," IVCF team members did not seem to consider their Lithuanian conversational partners to be passive auditors. In fact, Canadian participants remarked frequently that they felt they were learning more about what it means to be a Christian from recently converted Lithuanians than they felt they were able to teach these new believers. The IVCF members' interactions with Lithuanians were intended to initiate a context for evangelism and therefore had to convey the message of the necessity of a personal relationship with Christ. Ultimately, of course, witnesses must also begin to convince nonbelievers of their essential spiritual deficiency. Nevertheless, these conversations also challenged, edified, and, according to IVCF rhetoric, "stretched" the missionaries themselves.[19]

The *Lietuvos Krikščionių Studentų Bendrija* (LKSB), or Lithuanian Christian Student Fellowship, is the Lithuanian analogue of the IVCF. The LKSB has chapters in Vilnius, Klaipeda, Kaunus, and Panavegys. Its active membership is approximately eighty students. Previous McMaster team leaders have chosen to spend their time differently, but the 1996 leaders decided to send the team to Panavegys (approximate population: 100,000) for the first week and Vilnius for the next two weeks.

During the last ten days, the team facilitated a Bible camp, enjoyed a five-day vacation in St. Petersburg, and returned to Vilnius and Panavegys to throw farewell parties for the students they had met during the month.

The group from McMaster consisted of seven students and myself. All of the team members have appeared at least once during the previous chapters, and three of them were featured at length in chapter 2. Janice, a former IVCF executive member and recent McMaster graduate in geography, was the team leader. Steve, another former executive member and a recent science graduate, controlled the team's finances. The other members were Simon, a geography student; Oliver, a psychology student, Denise, a first-year student, Jocelyn, a social work student; and Gabrielle, a second-year English student. Simon and Oliver were both invited to join the executive within the next two years. The team was organized according to a strict hierarchy. Before the team left Canada, all members had to accept Janice's leadership, agreeing to follow her orders even if we did not like them or they seemed irrational. As is the case whenever an IVCF consensus is of great significance to the group, our formal acceptance of Janice's authority was signified at an orientation meeting with a group prayer to bless her leadership. Steve, the next oldest member of the team, supported Janice's decisions and made executive decisions when she was absent. Although the team was structured hierarchically, the leaders were never domineering. Usually successful attempts were made to achieve consensus on most decisions; when this was not possible, Janice's or Steve's decisions were considered final.

Two long-term IFES missionaries (Shawn and Kelly), also former McMaster students, had already been in Lithuania for approximately two years each. They joined the core group of seven team members, meaning the team almost always consisted of ten North Americans including myself. Kelly served as Janice's coleader, a logical designation in that Kelly speaks fluent Lithuanian. Shawn, also bilingual and a resident of Vilnius, helped to plan events and prevent the team from getting lost.

My participation in and observation of the mission team's efforts inaugurated a new phase in my fieldwork with the IVCF. Previously, my contact with the chapter's members had been productive and intimate; however, with the exception of the winter retreat, I still returned to my own home every night. Living and traveling for a month with nine group members in the sometimes trying social and physical surroundings of a very poor country provided me with a new perspective on the way IVCF students live, worship, and communicate with each other and non-Christian others. Stripping participants of the familiar luxuries of North American life permitted (and perhaps forced) them to express their commitments and personalities in a lucid and occasionally stark manner.

In Panavegys and Vilnius, we were housed in spartan and poorly maintained university residences. In Vilnius, we had no hot water for the two weeks we were there, and we did our laundry, dishes, and daily ablutions in the same sink.[20] In both cities, my room adjoined or was adjacent to the "boys' room," where Steve, Simon, and Oliver slept. This proximate yet separated arrangement was ideal; it allowed me to spend the majority of my time with the team and yet gave me a private place to write my fieldnotes.

Although there was some variation, a typical day in Lithuania was organized in the following manner. After breakfast, the team would spend approximately forty-five minutes doing devotions (Bible study[21] and singing). Then we would take a bus or walk to one of the university campuses, where I was responsible for guarding team members' belongings as the team split into groups of two or three to "do prayer walks,"[22] which lasted approximately forty-five minutes. After the prayer walks, the team would reconvene and wait until the area they had chosen[23] began to fill with people.

The team would then perform two or more of the five dramas they had learned before they left Canada.[24] Set to American music, these dramas were mostly pantomimes that depicted human vanity in the face of God's love and power, our dependence on God's forgiveness, and human sinfulness. Because most of the audience members were probably unable to understand the words in the songs, after the dramas either Kelly or one of the Lithuanian evangelicals would explain the dramas' plots and morals and the purpose of the team's presence in Lithuania. After this explanation, one of the Canadian team members would stand beside a translator and share his or her "testimony," the story of how he or she became a Christian (cf. Ingram 1986). Then team members would walk into the audience and talk to the Lithuanian students, with more or less difficulty, depending on whether the Lithuanian students in question spoke English and whether translators were available. The team members handed out tracts in Lithuanian and English, which included brief testimonies, a brief account of God's love, phone numbers of the evangelical student leaders in their city, a schedule of the IVCF team's activities that week, and an open invitation to the Bible camp at which the team members hoped people might commit their lives to Christ. Kelly usually stood behind the book table on which Lithuanian Bibles and Lithuanian and (translated) English evangelical texts were displayed. She handed out the texts and tracts and chatted with curious Lithuanian students.

After these performances and conversations were completed, the team would go for lunch, frequently inviting and paying for Lithuanian students to join them. Then a brief period of free time followed lunch, but most often the team would return to the residence and begin planning for the evening's or the next day's events. After a modest and hurried dinner (almost invariably bread, cheese, and pickles), the group would host an evening event: a Bible study, a worship event, a "Canadian culture night," a "question night," or sometimes a social event. After the evening activities, the team returned to the residence for a "debriefing" session (which lasted between half an hour and two hours)[25] in which members discussed their impressions of and concerns about the day's events. Debriefing was followed by a prayer session.[26] The day's official events usually ended around midnight, after which people would often stay awake for an hour or more talking casually.

Witnessing may be understood as an attempt to encourage a person to abandon his or her "frame" or paradigm of personal meaning and to adopt the evangelical frame instead (Goffman 1974; Ingram 1989). It is also a rhetorical art form analogous in some ways to political or didactic rhetoric. As in the contexts of politics or teaching, there are no simple procedures friendship evangelists can follow to contribute to or effect another person's salvation. In the end, the potential convert must make the final decision. However, as in all rhetorical domains, there are conventions of interaction which, when observed, make the missionary and his or her message more acceptable.

Two IVCF texts provide insights into the conventions adopted by or at least suggested to IVCF witnesses. One of these texts is *How to Give Away Your Faith* (1988) by Paul Little. This book was employed by an IVCF Small Group devoted to witnessing. The other text is a duo-tang of photocopied materials on witnessing that was compiled by former IVCF Lithuania missionary leader Steve Cox (Buff Cox's husband) from various sources and distributed to the Lithuania mission team a few weeks before we left Canada. Witnessing strategies fall into two basic categories: those pertaining to body language and those related to interpersonal interactions. Most of these practices are fairly obvious and also apply to successful non-witnessing interactions. What follows is a brief list and description of witnessing strategies.

The body language most helpful for sharing the gospel with non-Christians includes displaying good listening skills, making eye contact, maintaining an open posture, and waiting for the other person to finish speaking before beginning.

The interpersonal skills specific to the context of witnessing are being informed, being enthusiastic, contacting others socially, establishing common ground, arousing interest, taking initiative, not giving the person more information than he or she can absorb, not condemning, emphasizing the central message of Christ's incarnation and resurrection, confronting the person directly, using the casual touch, having a good joke ready, praying in public, avoiding "in" vocabulary, expressing love, following up, discussing sin experientially,[27] being relaxed, being verbal, being polite, being confident, being positive, being bold, and being led by the spirit.[28]

These witnessing strategies and the ways they might be applied in Lithuania were discussed at length during the orientation sessions held in the months before the mission. As well, they are occasionally mentioned at large group meetings in the context of presentations and prayers about witnessing on campus. However, most of these suggestions are already IVCF evangelistic conventions. Ironically, one of the clearest indications of the existence of implicit guidelines for acceptable witnessing came during the chapter's 1996 winter retreat, where I encountered a woman whose approach to me was diametrically opposed to the common IVCF method of witnessing.

One evening as I sipped hot chocolate in front of the fireplace in the lounge building at the Ontario resort where the retreat was being held, I was approached by a first-year student named Sandy who had heard about my study. Initially, she came across as gentle and timid. After asking me a few questions about my research, she asked me about my own faith and whether my encounters with Christians had challenged any of my beliefs. I explained Unitarianism to her briefly and offered her some examples of ways my own faith had been "stretched" by my interactions with the IVCF. Then she began to criticize my religious tradition, asking sweetly, "Yeah, you talk about love, but how can someone love fully, or even live fully without Christ? I just think that's impossible." After a few more questions about Unitarianism, she said flatly, "Well, it says in the Bible that only Christians will go to heaven. What do you say to that?" I was stunned by this interchange, mainly because it was completely unlike the dozens of courteous discussions IVCF members had intentionally initiated in an effort to encourage me to convert. In an attempt not to spoil what had so far been a fruitful and relaxing retreat, I had to suppress my academic and personal defensive instincts during this conversation. After approximately fifteen minutes of this conversation, I gently changed the subject and left the room.

By the time I completed my fieldwork in May 1996, I had been engaged in a hundred or more conversations in which an IVCF member (and sometimes several at once) witnessed to me. The previous anecdote relates the only time in the three years I have been associated with the group that someone has adopted an aggressive, patronizing, and condemnatory tone with me. The day after this incident, I learned that Sandy had been involved with the group for only two weeks. Clearly, her approach struck me as incongruous in that setting because she had not been enculturated in IVCF witnessing conventions. Ingram describes a equally inconsistent episode of "spiritual bullying" by a member of the Campus Crusade for Christ, concluding that "such behaviour was rare in the Crusade and always came from a novice or staff trainee" (1989:22).

The McMaster IVCF neither explicitly teaches the strategies outlined in the Little and Cox texts nor requires that all participants employ them. Obviously, many students arrive at university with their own styles of relating to non-Christians already entrenched in their personalities. However, through small and large group meetings that deal with witnessing and most commonly through casual IVCF conversations, newer members quickly learn that they are expected to utilize a nonconfrontational and dialogical style of witnessing.

The following discussion of three aspects of the witnessing I observed should provide readers with a contextualized sense of this practice. The first issue to explore is the auxiliary role played in IVCF witnessing by the intellectual component of Christianity. At the winter retreat, Clark Pinnock, a professor at McMaster's Divinity College, emphasized the need to "find a reason for our hope." He was paraphrasing 1 Peter 3:15: "Always be ready to make your defence to anyone who demands from you an accounting for the hope that is in you." In chapter 4, I discussed the winter retreat as a site for the philosophical clarification and crystallization of many students' vague sense of alienation from McMaster's secular ethos. But in addition to bringing the "bias against God" into an extremely sharp focus, Pinnock also explored in great detail the logical basis of basic Christian theology as well as its intellectual superiority to all other (but especially secularist or, in his words, "metaphysical naturalist") worldviews.

Although Pinnock and Cox emphasize a balance between the emotional and the intellectual components of witnessing, IVCF students opt overwhelmingly to stress the former element.[29] For example, one afternoon the team decided to take the train with a group of approximately fifteen Lithuanian (mostly LKSB) students to visit the medieval castle of Trakai, once the seat of power in Lithuania. On the train I sat across from Oliver, who was speaking with an articulate Lithuanian non-Christian woman who was interested in the LKSB and Christianity in general.[30] During their conversation, this woman asked Oliver the following question: "I have a friend who believes that all religions have the same ultimate purpose. You know, they are here to help us with the same things. I think I believe that, too. I mean, there are so many cultures in the world. How can there be only one religion that is right for all of them? That doesn't make sense to me." Oliver, a compassionate and sensitive man, replied softly, "I believe there is only one right way. But I haven't really studied any of the other religions. I guess maybe I should." As far as I know, Oliver has not embarked on a study of other religions since he returned to Canada. But, as we shall see, that is beside the point: he does not feel that such an investigation *could* detract from the truth or cogency of his faith. Another anecdote should illustrate this conviction.

A few days after the trip to Trakkai, the team held a meeting to discuss the question evening, which was scheduled for the next night. The purpose of this evening was to provide a forum for potential Christians to ask more established IVCF and LKSB members questions about issues such as the existence of suffering, creationism, and the truth claims of other religions. When the issue of discussing other world religions arose during the planning session, almost everyone admitted their ignorance. Kelly suggested that if a team member was asked a question about other religions, he or she could answer that the essential difference between non-Christian faiths and Christianity is that "other faiths emphasized what you can do to be a good person or to win God's favor, while Christianity emphasizes God's grace entirely." As she finished this sentence, she turned to me, perhaps as an "expert" in religious studies, and remarked, "That's probably an exaggeration, I know. But it's true, isn't it?" After I replied that I thought this view misrepresented non-Christian religions, we discussed the potential analogues for God's grace in other religions.

We had only two and a half hours to plan this event, and I observed immediately after we commenced that most of the team members were nervous. "What am I going to say if someone asks me about fossils or Hinduism?" Gabrielle asked, adding, "What do I know about that stuff?" Jocelyn agreed and offered an alternative to the evening's agenda: "Look, I just don't feel comfortable trying to answer all those questions. That's not really my thing, you know? Why don't we just talk about God's grace in the world instead? Then maybe we could sing or pray, sort of like a large group meeting. I'd feel better about that." Although two other team members supported Jocelyn's suggestions, the team leaders said they felt committed to the original plan for the evening. Eventually, Janice assigned a topic to each member of the team and told them to spend some time praying and thinking about how they would deal with questions that might arise.

The next evening, only twelve Lithuanians (most of them LKSB members) joined the fairly apprehensive IVCF team in the classroom booked for this occasion. One of the Lithuanians present was an extremely articulate bilingual agnostic woman named Danya. During the evening, Denise claimed that it is impossible to lead a moral life without a belief in God. In response, Danya recited a litany of human rights abuses committed in the name of Christianity throughout history and demanded to know how Denise would respond to these travesties. Denise answered (or avoided answering, depending on one's interpretation) Danya's question by replying, "Well, I see what you're saying, but I don't think it's really our place to judge other people." When Danya asked about the possibility of reincarnation and the experiences of children who recognize adults they have never met, Jocelyn answered (or evaded), "Well, that's an interesting question, Danya. All I can say to it is that we should all read the Bible and find out what it has to say about these questions, because there can't be more than one Truth." Then, addressing Simon, Danya argued that the biblical (Genesis 1:26) account of the human "dominion over" animals has contributed to environmental degradation. Simon seemed dumbfounded. After a long pause, he said he believed that because the first two chapters of Genesis suggest humans are made in the image of God, and that God brought the animals before Adam to receive their names, "animals are here for us. In fact, I think the whole earth would not have been made if it was not for humans." This comment evidently aggravated Danya, who continued to pursue Simon. Simon, for his part, gave no indication that he was interested in discussing the scientific or ethical implications of his statement.

These two anecdotes illustrate that the style of witnessing typical of McMaster's IVCF does not emphasize the intellectual foundations of Christian faith. By this characterization, I do not mean that IVCF participants do not believe their faith is intellectually compelling, but rather that they are either not able or not inclined to explain their faith in the intellectual terms expected by and acceptable to many non-Christians.

In *The Scandal of the Evangelical Mind*, evangelical scholar Mark Noll argues that contemporary evangelicalism favors "conversion to the exclusion of gradual growth in grace, the immediate experience of the Holy Spirit instead of the contemplation of God in the created realm, the prizing of popular [evangelical] wisdom over against the pronouncements of the authorities" (1994:32). Noll characterizes as a "scandal" the fact that for many evangelicals and nonevangelicals, the designation "evangelical intellectual" seems almost oxymoronic.[31] Noll refers primarily to evangelical academics and their tendencies to avoid the religious questions raised within their disciplines. However, his insights also help us understand the role of the intellectual elements of Christianity in IVCF friendship evangelism. Neither the students who tried to "lead me to Christ" during fieldwork nor those I observed witnessing in Lithuania emphasized the historical veracity of or philosophical proofs for the existence of God or any other elements of their shared beliefs. Although all witnessing presupposes that witnesses have to some degree systematized their beliefs formally (Ingram 1986), I found that these systems were rarely discussed by team members and were often neither philosophically sophisticated nor well considered.

Witnessing is intended, at least ultimately, to encourage the listener to convert or, in Ingram's (1989) words, to enter into an alternative "frame" in which to understand and experience the world. But conversion is not dependent mainly on the use of eloquent theological argumentation to convince non-Christians to accept a predominantly intellectual worldview. On the contrary, one's full acceptance of an evangelical's witnessing message (in other words, one's conversion) is characterized mostly by a fundamental reorganization of one's whole being rather than simply one's mind.[32] In other words, IVCF students do not emphasize the intellectual substructure of Christianity because their own experiences of faith and conversion are characterized primarily by the profound emotional and existential support they perceive from God and their community.[33]

The second witnessing issue I will consider is the role of God's will in the IVCF's evangelistic discourse. In previous chapters, I described God's will as a frequently invoked explanation for all manner of human experiences and social realities. I argued that IVCF members' anxieties about their economic prospects do not paralyze most students because they are certain that, regardless of the vicissitudes of the economy, God has a plan for their lives. For IVCF students, the will of God seems to function as a useful explanatory principle, invoked both to acknowledge gratefully the ultimate divine origin of some apparently explicable event (e.g., when a fund-raising project is as successful as the planners had hoped) and to decipher the true origin or meaning of some apparently inexplicable event (e.g., when seven hundred participants attend the Church at the John).

Since these students believe that God constantly wills that humans enter into a relationship with him, believers interpret—perhaps *must* interpret—events in their relationships with non-Christians as fulfilling some role in this plan. For example, Cindy explained to our small group that her grandfather had recently suffered a stroke. She was clearly disturbed by his suffering and its role in God's plan. "I prayed to God, and he doesn't answer my prayers. I just don't understand his plan," she said. However, Cindy continued, "Sometimes it's hard to remember that he does have a plan for us. I guess that the bright side of this whole thing is that it gives me a chance to witness to my dad, to let him know that Jesus can support him during all these problems."[34]

In Lithuania, God's will was frequently employed to explain experiences for which nonreligious explanations might have challenged the sovereignty or benevolence of God. One afternoon at a university campus in Vilnius, one of the group's dramas was interrupted abruptly by an irate Lithuanian university administrator who had not received the appropriate documentation to confirm that the group was allowed to perform in the building. Half an hour after the commotion ended and the large assembled audience dispersed, Kelly interpreted the apparent failure positively: "Who knows? Maybe God didn't want us to continue to do dramas there. But think of how much attention we got because of that scene. Look how many people we had at the book table. That was amazing, wasn't it? He definitely works in mysterious ways." Team members appeared to accept Kelly's interpretation. When we were alone a few moments later, I asked Denise how she knew that what appeared to be a fiasco from a performative perspective was actually a part of God's plan for their day. She shrugged her shoulders and replied, "I don't know, it just is," later explaining that "it says he has a plan for us in the Bible, so this must have been part of his plan."

That night I did not feel well, so I stayed at the Vilnius residence while the group went off to lead another Bible study session. When the group returned to the residence, they were effervescent. Denise poked me playfully in the shoulder. "Hey, hey, you. This is for you who thinks God doesn't have a plan for everything. Wooooo hooooo! He so totally does it's not even funny. You should have been there tonight. It was awesome. It totally rocked. Just try to tell me God doesn't have a plan, man." After several other people had gaily celebrated God's mysterious ways, I pressed them for a description of the evening. Apparently there was a misunderstanding that evening, because before the team could unlock the university classroom they thought they had reserved, an Irish woman approached the door and informed the team that she uses that room every Tuesday evening to teach her students English. However, when the instructor learned that the team spoke English and was prepared to perform dramas and discuss English (biblical) texts, she allowed them to lead her class. She introduced the team and left soon thereafter, leaving the Canadians with, as several of them put it, "a captive audience" of Lithuanian students. The team performed all of their dramas and led an animated Bible study; as well, they answered questions about Canada. I asked the members of the team who were explaining the evening's wondrous events if it would be possible to interpret what happened as the result of coincidence or even a lazy or overworked teacher who wanted to enjoy a beautiful spring evening. The group members paused and looked at me, puzzled, it appeared, that I was not immediately convinced by their interpretation of the evening's events. "No way," several of them answered confidently.

For the first three weeks of the mission, team members placed great emphasis in their witnessing and prayers on the conversions they anticipated happening at the weekend Bible camp near the end of the month. However, by the end of the Bible camp and mission as a whole, no one had committed to Christ.[35] This apparent numerical failure seemed to disappoint most team members, even though they tried to construe (for my benefit and their own, I imagine) the lack of conversions positively, as being part of God's plan for the Lithuanians.[36] "We planted some seeds, for sure," Oliver commented. Steve echoed Oliver's sentiment, asserting:

> You know, I was never that into the whole numbers thing, or with the whole way the Bible camp was organized around the big moment of commitment. I'm just glad that I had a chance to spend some time really talking with Lithuanians. I know we all planted some seeds this weekend; now we have to wait and see what happens next. I'm definitely going to keep in contact with the people I met here and see if I can help them get to know Christ that way.

The immediate and unequivocal consensus among the mission team that all events, even people *not* becoming Christians, are manifestations of God's plan for their individual lives or the team's fortunes, was also characteristic of IVCF participants at McMaster. Regardless of whether the mission team or individual witnesses in Canada meet with apathy or intolerance in their endeavors, all events in which they find themselves are (and, again, perhaps must be) somehow authored or lovingly overseen by God (cf. Wagner 1990:182).

The final issue is the role of witnessing in the negotiation of otherness, or the maintenance of boundaries between the Christian and non-Christian worlds. Witnessing in both the McMaster and the Lithuanian contexts requires students to venture out of what is for many of them a comfortable IVCF or Canadian evangelical cocoon. As is probably the case for all inherently stressful practices, witnessing situations can be particularly revelatory of a person's self-understanding and indirectly of his or her understanding of the other to whom he or she is witnessing. During my fieldwork with the IVCF witnesses in Hamilton and Lithuania, two elements of their self-understanding were especially evident.

First, I observed that students identified to a great extent with the experiences of Christ's apostles. Since, as noted in chapter 4, these students often experience some form of estrangement from their non-Christian peers and professors, such a self-understanding should not be surprising. As Larry, for example, expressed it, "I don't think Christians should complain about being marginalized from the world, because in this world we are in self-imposed exile. We have to accept what the world will do to us. . . . [and] that the world will want to isolate us. We should try to share what we have with others; but if they don't want to hear it we can't do much about it." Echoing Larry's comments, Barbara, a second-year science student, observed, that "in the Bible it says 'Blessed are you who are persecuted in my name.' This makes me feel better, for sure." In another interview, Gillian commented that she does not consider her alienation from her non-Christian peers to be an undesirable state, "because I'm a Christian and am holy and called to act differently."

When an IVCF student approaches a non-Christian in the adjacent residence room at McMaster and attempts to engage this student in conversation leading first to friendship and then (the former student hopes) to conversion, on some level the IVCF student understands himself or herself as obeying the Great Commission, quoted at the beginning of this chapter. The anger, rejection, and indifference the friendship evangelists may receive from the unbeliever are interpreted as the price of being a latter-day apostle. By making public what in North American culture is usually a private matter, Ingram argues that the witness has broken some of our culture's implicit rules of civility and privacy (1989:20).[37] The witness has stepped outside what IVCF students call their "Christian comfort zone" and has risked the ridicule of non-Christian peers. However, possibly because of the gentleness of the form of evangelism espoused by the IVCF, students' witnessing efforts almost never result in complete ostracization from non-Christian peer groups.[38] McMaster witnesses might therefore be called "occasional apostles": their forays into witnessing are, for most of them, exceptions to the normal course of their student lives.[39]

In Lithuania, by contrast, team members were well aware that they were being observed not only by me (qua ethnographer and, as important, qua non-Christian whose conversion many of them thought to be immanent) but also by Lithuanian students. This awareness shifted the apostolic self-understanding to the foreground. During morning devotions on the Gospel according to Luke two days after the team arrived, Kelly prayed: "God, please help us to remember that we're all like little apostles out there. What we're bringing these people, well, without it they really are living in the shadow of death." Kelly's comments were echoed frequently by team members throughout the month in Lithuania.

The mission to Lithuania required apostolic fortitude for several reasons. First, our physical surroundings and new diets were, as I mentioned, significantly less appealing than those to which most team members were accustomed. Second, the congested residence rooms in which we lived meant that the interpersonal difficulties that emerge among any small group of travelers went largely unresolved, although attempts were made to ameliorate the tensions. Third, three of the Canadian participants are members of visible minorities (two Indo-Canadians, one African-Canadian). Although the staff worker tried to prepare the team for the stares and double takes we would encounter in Panavegys and Vilnius, no amount of advance orientation could disarm such blunt demonstrations of racism and xenophobia. There were several difficult racist incidents during the month.[40] By the middle of the mission Oliver, the African Canadian team member, had become discouraged by the almost daily reminders of his racial otherness. However, as he described in a debrief session one night, "For the last while I've just been really bummed about the whole race issue. All those guys dropping the 'N-bombs' [calling him and his two teammates 'niggers'] and all the stares were just starting to make me just want to get out of this place. But then Steve came over to me one day and gave me a biblical verse—from Second Peter—and I read it and wow, that just totally put things into perspective. So now I'm okay."[41] The team members' identification with Christ's emissaries fortified them as they commenced and continued what was for all of them their most challenging witnessing experience.

The apostolic designation was not applied solely to themselves. The team often used this language to praise the committed and enthusiastic work accomplished by the LKSB leaders. Reflecting the modern dialogical form of witnessing, one afternoon during lunch, Steve said reverently, "I'm just so blown away by Yvanna and Donata. Yeah, like *I* came here to teach them something. *As if.* They're just amazing. I love them. Those two are like twentieth-century Pauls. They're so fearless it's amazing."

Another facet of the team members' apostolic self-understanding involves the role of Satan. In the previous chapter, I discussed the prominence of Satan and his demons in IVCF discourse and noted that these characters from the spiritual realm are not spoken of or noticed every day. However, in Lithuania, all team members made frequent references to the work of the devil. For the first week in Lithuania, I was puzzled by the heightened prominence of anti-Satan rhetoric used in the group's devotions, prayers, and conversations. Moreover, I noticed that the group was never as animated during their prayers as when they "prayed against" Satan.

The first morning after we arrived, several team members felt slightly ill or had not slept the night before. Amid whispered murmurs of "Yes" and "Yes, Jesus," Janice prayed, "Satan, we bind you from this campus and this team. . . . God, we thank you for giving us the power to crush serpents and scorpions, and Satan we bind you. Because of Christ you cannot affect us here. Even though some of us may get sick, or feel tired, we know we have God protecting us and that in his name we can rebuke you, Satan." A variety of this prayer was offered almost every day. Sometimes the prayers were oriented toward protecting the Lithuanian evangelicals, as when Steve prayed, "God, I just pray that the Evil One would not attach himself onto Yvanna and Donata."

But even more frequently the prayers were directed at preventing Satan from damaging the team's mission, health, and intragroup dynamics. On the third day of the mission, Steve asked me what I thought about spiritual warfare. Since Steve was the past president of the IVCF, he and I had worked together throughout the previous academic year. I knew that I could not evade his questions or give him only a partial or sanitized answer: he would notice and feel patronized. Consequently, I told him that the rhetoric of spiritual warfare was one of the most baffling elements of IVCF life for me and that it was very difficult for me to "get inside of" this sensibility.[42] I explained that I thought that the prominence of the spiritual realm in the Lithuanian context reflected the need for order in a time of chaos. In other words, in places and times of cultural dislocation when the plausibility of one's worldview is threatened (Berger and Luckmann 1966), means of diminishing disorder and inexplicability are crucial.[43] Thus, I suggested Satan was being employed by the group to symbolize and concretize the amorphous sense of anxiety and disorientation they were experiencing as they tried to come to terms with their new (albeit brief) lives in Lithuania.[44] Unfortunately, as soon as I had finished explaining my interpretation, Steve and I had to discontinue our conversation when another team member joined us.

One evening when the whole team was talking about the differences between Christianity in North America and Lithuania, I asked them how they would explain the sharp increase in the number of references to Satan and demons during their prayers in Lithuania. Did their frequent references and allusions to the spiritual realm suggest that there were more demons in Lithuania or that the team was being "attacked" more often here? Janice replied, "No, it's not that. There are demons everywhere, and Satan is at work everywhere, attacking us in a lot of ways. I think we're just more aware of his activities here because we're trying to live out our faiths and to think about them every day, whereas in Canada, it's just, you know, not as conscious a thing every day."

Janice's answer seems to confirm my hypothesis. Although her explanation presupposes the existence of the spiritual realm and my interpretation does not, Janice and I agree that because of the new circumstances in which these IVCF members found themselves, Satan's efforts are more conspicuous to them.[45]

Conclusion

Witnessing brings several elements of evangelicalism into focus. I would argue that the following three conclusions follow from my observation of and participation in the IVCF's witnessing efforts. First, during witnessing, the intellectual component of the faith of these students is regularly subordinated to the experiential and emotional elements, mainly because these latter emphases reflect what the witnesses value in their own religious experiences and what they assume potential converts will also value. Second, in (especially international) witnessing contexts, the Pauline vision of non-Christians as "lost" and the more modern (Perettiesque) sense of witnesses as Satanically "attacked" become more prevalent and perhaps necessary elements of these evangelicals' self-presentations and apostolic self-understandings. Third, the frequent references to God's will and Satan's attacks seem to represent creative responses to the anxiety, disorientation, and culture shock witnesses experience in witnessing situations both in Lithuania and (albeit very differently) at McMaster.

Witnessing represents one of the major negotiation contexts for the evangelical contracts with the secular "turf" described in previous chapters. Moreover, by requiring the believer to distinguish quite formally between self and others and to position himself or herself in the role of the disseminator of truth, witnessing contributes significantly to IVCF students' distinct self-understandings, as well as to the definition of their others. Witnesses by definition adopt a position of spiritual superiority (Harding 1987:171) from which to coax non-Christians out of the "shadow of death," to quote Kelly. Consequently, witnessing requires adopting (to varying degrees) a paternalistic approach to one's others. Although nonbelievers often find this dimension of conservative Protestantism distasteful, for evangelicals, witnessing is based on God's clear directive to bring the gospel to all the nations of the earth.

In Lithuania, this paternalism (much more established than the newer dialogical method) was exemplified in a range of ethnographic encounters: from the team member who said she was determined to help Lithuanians but (three weeks after we arrived in Lithuania) did not know that communism was the political system in place in Russia before the fall of the Soviet Union; to the team members who would often describe Lithuanians as "Catholics, not Christians", to the team members who discredited all other world religions without knowing anything about them.

During fieldwork, I experienced many examples of mild condescension, as many IVCF participants took me aside and in various ways expressed their concern for the ultimate fate and current state of my soul. After what I thought was the end of several interviews at McMaster, students would begin to get ready to leave my office, then pause and settle back into their chairs and begin to transform the interview into a witnessing opportunity. To this end, they would ask me pointed questions about my own tradition and what I thought would happen to me once I died. In Lithuania, team members (often several at the same time) would draw me into conversations late at night, apparently to explain some element of Christian truth, or to disabuse me of some erroneous belief. In the context of one of these conversations, Kelly explained a common witnessing metaphor to (and certainly for) me. "Look, I guess I just see myself as a beggar who has found some free food. Now I'm trying to tell all the other beggars where they can find the food."[46] By this time in the mission, the team had accepted me as a member of the group, and I had developed strong friendships with several participants. Therefore, I felt I could be honest with them. I replied, "Well, that sounds great. But it seems to me that you're doing more than this. Actually, it seems more like you're trying to tell people who are full that they aren't. Actually, it's even more than this. You're telling people who are eating other food that it is actually the worst kind of poison, though very good tasting poison." Several members shook their heads, looked at me compassionately, and replied that I had missed the point of the metaphor. Maybe I had. Unfortunately, as is often the case in ethnography, the conversation was cut short by another event, so we could not discuss this issue further.

While I think my representation of the essentially paternalistic relationship between witnesses and non-Christians is fair, it only partially captures evangelical aims. During my fieldwork, I also witnessed undeniably laudable elements of these missionaries' interactions with and responses to non-Christians. For example, on several occasions when the team was performing dramas or sharing testimonies at Lithuanian universities, members of the audience would mock the performers, laughing at or mimicking the teams' movements or turning their backs on the performance. Perhaps even more challenging for the team were the occasions when no one seemed even remotely interested in the presentation. On these sorts of occasions, the team simply continued to present their dramas and testimonies, refusing to let a hostile or sometimes nearly nonexistent audience thwart their witnessing. During these difficult performances, I often watched the team with amazement and wondered whether I would be strong enough to withstand such lack of interest and coarse impudence.

The IVCF members' attempts to witness to me became increasingly tolerable and eventually humbling once I felt the sincerity of their concern and the depth of their faith commitments. While participants had shared with me their motivations for witnessing in Lithuania weeks before we left Canada, somehow experiencing their earnestness personally allowed me to know, and later to describe, their intentions more "thickly" (Geertz 1973). For these evangelicals, the firm belief in the righteousness of their convictions empowers them to travel thousands of kilometers to endure the occasional indifference and hostility of those they seek to enlighten. They may believe that the Lithuanians, like myself and other non-Christians, are "lost" or "sick," but I have seen IVCF students weep for the desolate living conditions of the Lithuanians and have been touched by their prayers and concern for me.

Throughout this book, I have discussed the way the IVCF is able to foster the combination of fortress and bridge approaches to non-Christians and the non-Christian ethos in general. I have suggested in previous chapters that these strategies facilitate the negotiation of metaphorical "contracts" between Christians and the non-Christian world. Because witnessing often involves the intentional interaction of a believer *qua* believer with the nonbeliever *qua* non-believer (Hammond and Hunter 1984), it represents the most explicit example of the negotiation of these contracts. More to the point, because friendship evangelism by definition requires the believer to engage the non-Christian in a nonconfrontational manner, it seems to represent a clear example of a bridge strategy, aimed at diminishing the distance that separates Christians from non-Christians.

However, this appearance may be misleading for two reasons. In chapter 1, Hammond and Hunter were quoted as pointing out that "to be surrounded by secularists not only elicits a siege mentality apparently; by opening up missionary opportunities, it also provides the occasion to hone and renew [the witness's] faith" (1984:232). Similarly, Nancy Ammerman writes, "As the believer is evangelizing, she is, on the one hand, drawn into increasing encounters outside the protected environment of the home and congregation. On the other hand, the very nature of the encounter reinforces her sense of distinctiveness. As she seeks to convince another of the need to be saved, she is reassured of her own salvation" (1994:163). So, while witnessing seems to be a bridge from the Christian to the non-Christian world, this bridge is designed to function in two ways. First, it reaffirms a believer's saved status; the conversation with the nonbelieving other is at least partly an act of self-creation, the employment of the non-Christian as an aid in constructing one's Christian (and thus different) self. Second, the bridge is intended to lead converts directly back to the evangelical fortress I have described elsewhere. Once the evangelical "frame" "intrudes" in a non-Christian's life (Ingram 1989), the new believer gradually becomes increasingly critical of certain (permissive, secular, pluralistic) elements of contemporary culture. In fact, some new believers (e.g., Oscar in this study) are nearly consumed by the need to repudiate and destroy the paradigm that once gave their lives meaning. After their conversion, after crossing the bridge, recently saved individuals often find themselves on the opposite side of a wide chasm that divides them from non-Christians. Obviously, this increases the believer's alienation from non-Christians.

Nevertheless, friendship evangelism does have two bridging consequences that Hammond and Hunter (1984) and Ammerman (1994) neglect. First, even when intentional witnesses fail to draw their non-Christian peers closer to Christ, their friendships with nonbelievers remain. In fact, the vast majority of these Christians' interactions with non-Christians are not explicitly (as far as both Christian and non-Christian are consciously aware) oriented toward the nonbeliever's conversion. These friendships seem to ameliorate the estrangement IVCF students sometimes feel from their non-Christian peers. The second bridging function of witnessing is related to the purpose of evangelism. Specifically, as I indicated earlier, among the witnesses I have studied, the ultimate goal of friendship evangelism is to draw everyone over the bridge and into the fortress of evangelical faith. However, if everyone was to enter the fortress, eventually it would cease to function as a bastion of Christianity against a culture of non-Christian others. None of the evangelicals I have met before, during, or after my fieldwork are confident that such complete evangelization is realistic or immanent; in fact, most are highly doubtful. Nevertheless, the conversion of all non-Christians is, for most believers within the IVCF as well as within the broader evangelical community, an ideal (Rawlyk 1996:123), which seems, in the grand scheme of God's plan (cf. Mt 28:19), to reflect a bridge rather than a fortress strategy.

In short, the IVCF's style of witnessing contributes to contracts in which the fortress and bridge strategies coexist. As previous chapters have also demonstrated, in a variety of ways, the McMaster IVCF promotes a delicate balance between protecting the faith from the corruptions of what some members consider an anti-Christian world and offering the faith to the vast majority of needy nonbelievers.

Conclusion

For the Lord's sake accept the authority of every human institution, whether of the emperor as supreme, or of the governors, as sent by him to punish those who do wrong and to praise those who do right. For it is God's will that by doing right you should silence the ignorance of the foolish. As servants of God, live as free people, yet do not use your freedom as a pretext for evil. Honour everyone. Love the family of believers. Fear God. Honour the Emperor.

Peter 2:13–17

In *The Struggle for America's Soul: Evangelicals, Liberals, and Secularism* (1989), Robert Wuthnow summarizes the support for the conventional notion that university education and religiosity are incommensurate in some fundamental way: "Virtually all surveys and polls, whether of the general public, college students, church members, or clergy, show inverse relations between exposure to higher education and adherence to core religious tenets, such as the existence of God, the divinity of Christ, the divine inspiration of the Bible, life after death, religious conversion, and the necessity of faith in Christ for salvation" (1989:145).[1] Given the congruity of the surveys and polls to which Wuthnow refers, how can one explain either the sheer size of the McMaster IVCF chapter or its success at facilitating the retention of its members' faith commitments? On the surface, it seems reasonable to expect that a religious group devoted to markedly conservative ideas and values would not flourish at a secular university. Since precisely this is happening at McMaster, we are left with three possible explanations. First, one could argue that these two hundred evangelicals are totally unaffected by the secularizing effects[2] university education is supposed by some scholars to have on believers. This hypothesis is obviously untenable, because students consistently speak of their frustrations about the secular ethos of the campus. Second, one could suggest, following Hammond and Hunter (1984:233), that these believers inhabit a well-fortified "Christian ghetto," the natural consequence of living among so many nonbelievers.

I have suggested throughout this text that IVCF members do, indeed, have access to an evangelical fortress that protects them and their besieged subculture from certain elements of secularism. However, this interpretation overlooks another major source of the group's strength: that in a variety of ways the IVCF facilitates constructive interaction between its members and non-Christians, interaction that is not oriented primarily toward witnessing. The third and, I would argue, most plausible explanation of the vitality of the McMaster IVCF is that this group helps its members to mediate difference (Warner 1997a:219). In other words, the IVCF provides its members with a framework within which to negotiate contracts between its members' evangelical convictions and the university's broadly liberal and pluralistic conventions.

When asked to provide illustrations of university experiences they perceive as cognitively threatening or contaminating, IVCF students commonly mention listening to lectures about scriptural authorship, human evolution, feminism, the age of the earth, critiques of religion, and the moral neutrality or potential biological bases of homosexuality. However, as I have outlined throughout this book, it is not primarily in the realm of ideas that secular educational institutions and evangelicalism are most opposed. For IVCF students such as Harriet, who refers to McMaster as a "cesspool of STDs and drinking," the sexual promiscuity, alcohol consumption, and moral relativism associated with the non-Christian student ethos (especially the residence ethos) often generate or underscore the most serious disjunctions between themselves and their non-Christian peers. During my fieldwork, I met a small number of IVCF members who reported almost no tension between their religious convictions and their formal academic experiences (often in engineering, kinesiology or commerce programs); but virtually all students reported strains between their evangelical moral commitments and the comparatively permissive moral standards of non-Christian students. Whether IVCF students are motivated mainly by intellectual challenges to their beliefs or by moral aversion to the behavior of their non-Christian peers, all members of the IVCF seem to have negotiated some form of a metaphorical contract with McMaster's dominant non-Christian ethos. I argue that such contracts are designed to forge practical compromises between the requirements of evangelical faith and those of the new academic and social settings in which IVCF students are embedded.

In this book, I have explored both the tensions that arise between IVCF members and non-Christians and the ways IVCF students and the group as a whole respond to these tensions. I have attributed the management of the threatening elements in IVCF students' academic and social milieux to a "selectively permeable membrane" suspended between the evangelical and non-Christian worlds. I chose this metaphor because it seems to represent quite accurately an interpretive screen employed by the group's members to distinguish themselves from the rest of campus.[3] But other metaphors might work equally well to explain this process. For example, during an interview, Carrie, a prominent member of the group, echoed what several other students said or implied. In response to a question about whether she experienced any tension between her education and her faith, she replied, "It's a continual battle for me in university. In my psychology classes, of course, they don't teach according to Christianity. I feel like what I learn in class has to go through a filter of some kind, although the filter is not always that efficient because sometimes there's so much information coming at you. I think there must be two parts of my brain." When I asked her if she could describe a situation in which her filter is operative, she referred to "some of the philosophies they teach us about in class. In one class we learned all about Freud and how all of our motivations come from our libidos. But I think there are other, higher motivations; so I file that information on Freud because I know I need to know it; but I just can't accept it."

The purpose of Carrie's filter is to control the potential influences of subversive ideas and values; and the IVCF-supported membrane between herself and the non-Christian campus accomplishes exactly this task.[4] Moreover, this filter may be understood as the tool of two distinct evangelical approaches to relating to non-Christian students and institutions. As I have suggested in previous chapters, the fortress and bridge strategies are ideal types and therefore do not exist so purely in practice. Because both of these strategies are often expressed simultaneously, it is sometimes difficult to discern two distinct approaches. However, I would argue that at least in the phenomenon I am studying, both ideal types are at work beneath the sometimes confusing surface of social relations and personal contracts.

The fortress strategy is most evident when an evangelical employs a constricted form of this filter to impose barriers between himself or herself on the one hand and secular peers and situations on the other. In such a situation, the membrane functions to protect evangelicals from threatening elements of the secular educational ethos, such as relativism, evolution, promiscuity, and alcohol consumption. For example, IVCF members commonly construe themselves as God's allies in the ongoing battle between angels and demons. By casting non-Christian individuals and institutions in the roles of unwitting pawns in Satan's battle against God, IVCF students can feel justified as they retreat behind the walls of their fortress and consequently separate themselves from their hell-bound non-Christian peers.

The fortress strategy is also manifested by the two main evangelical interpretations of biological evolution I observed during my fieldwork. To disarm the cognitively threatening materialist element inherent in evolutionary theory, those who espouse the first interpretation of evolution reduce it to, in the words of dozens of IVCF students, "*just* a theory," after which students can continue to embrace a putatively literal version of the biblical account of creation. The second approach to evolution is to subsume the theory and its evidence under a larger creationist interpretation. In other words, students may accept that the earth is billions of years old, and that evolution did happen, but they usually hasten to add that evolution did not occur among *Homo sapiens*, and that God (rather than natural selection) has simply used evolution to make the sort of world we have. In this way, God's sovereignty and the believers themselves are unchallenged, since everything remains under God's aegis.[5]

The metaphorical filter I have described regulates which non-Christian ideas and experiences flow *into* an evangelical's world. In addition, it regulates the sorts of interactions IVCF students are encouraged to have with the non-Christian world. In other words, the membrane in question is selectively permeable in both directions. For example, when faced with what they perceive as cognitively or morally threatening situations, IVCF members are reluctant to relate either at all or at least in a casual way with non-Christian students or ideas. For example, approximately half of the students I interviewed are morally opposed to drinking at bars, and some of these students are opposed to drinking in any context. Other relatively liberal members indicated that while they consider purposely getting drunk immoral, they are not opposed to having one or perhaps two drinks at a bar. However, for all the students I interviewed, the amounts, purposes, and contexts of one's alcohol consumption are tightly circumscribed. Drinking to get drunk is the least acceptable option, and total abstinence is the most acceptable option, with most students' opinions approximating the latter option. Most students did not pause before answering my question about alcohol consumption, suggesting that they had already formulated personal policies on this problematic issue. Their resolute (although somewhat diverse) positions on alcohol consumption reflect not only the complexity of this issue but also the varying degrees of permeability that the membrane I have described can assume.

Similarly, these Christians' interactions with the non-Christian world are also problematized and restricted in cognitively dangerous situations like discussions about evolution and other contentious intellectual issues. During interviews, IVCF students described a complex array of inhibitions surrounding the ways they relate to non-Christian ideas and individuals. In most cases, when a peer or professor criticizes Christianity or challenges some aspect of evangelical orthodoxy in class, students choose to remain silent because they are afraid of being punished either academically (by comparatively materialist professors and teaching assistants) or socially (by non-Christian classmates who might be startled or alienated by evangelical beliefs).[6] The secular university classroom is an environment that typically privileges or presupposes if not always what Clark Pinnock calls a "bias against God," then at least a general indifference to the possibility of God's relevance to most academic matters. The IVCF students indicate that they experience at McMaster the hegemony of the assumption that personal faith is not germane to most of the social or intellectual issues explored in their classes. It is not surprising, therefore, that these students usually choose to exclude their religious convictions from academic settings.

When students do choose to introduce into classroom discourse evangelical convictions regarding the age of the earth, the second coming of Christ, or God's establishment of absolute moral truths, they do so in a very cautious manner.[7] These rare assertions often assume the form of witnessing or apologetics, discursive forms that rely on specialized rhetorical practices aimed at disabusing and/or converting nonbelievers. Gabrielle, a former student of mine in a biomedical ethics course, felt sufficiently protected by my presence in the classroom to tell the class about her biblically based negative evaluation of homosexuality. "You saw what happened," she said in an interview. "I was just attacked. That experience was really frightening. I just jumped in with two feet and prayed that God would give me the words. I just wanted to let the group know that not everyone was thinking the same way as they were." I was able to restrain her classmates' responses to her views; but this experience reminded both of us of the privilege enjoyed by liberal values at McMaster.[8]

While the filtering process associated with the fortress strategy neutralizes or, to use Gauvreau's metaphor, tames the more threatening features of secular education and a liberal ethos, the IVCF's selectively permeable membrane also functions according to a more positive strategy. I have called this second approach to the secular ethos the bridge strategy to connote the linkage of previously separated terrains.

In situations of minimal or nonexistent cognitive or moral danger (during a linguistics or engineering lecture or the registration process), IVCF students might discern almost no differences between themselves and their non-Christian peers. Some students (mainly those in engineering, commerce, and kinesiology programs) seemed confused when I asked if they ever felt uncomfortable in their classes because of their religious convictions. "No, not really. I'm in engineering, so we pretty much just study how to make things work. Religion isn't really an issue in my classes," one student replied, chuckling. In fact, most of the evangelicals I interviewed do not spend the majority of their days paralyzed by the hegemony of McMaster's secular ethos. In the majority of their social interactions, explicitly religious matters are rarely at the forefront of IVCF members' minds; nor is alienation a by-product of the majority of their experiences with non-Christian individuals and institutions. In terms of the metaphors I have been using, for most students much of the time, the holes in the filter are open wide and the bridge is well traveled in both directions.

The best way to comprehend the bridge strategy is to observe its simultaneous deployment with the fortress strategy. In situations of moderate or significant cognitive or moral danger, the bridge strategy is a crucial means of diminishing estrangement. One of the ways this strategy can ameliorate relations between evangelicals and non-Christians is by cooperating in the eventual transformation (or, to extend Berger's metaphor, decontamination) of dangerous ideas or values. In other words, it is often, and possibly usually, the case that the bridge strategy works in conjunction with the fortress strategy. For example, after evolution is reduced to one of many theories or a theory commensurate with creationism, students are able to assimilate it intellectually as such, without the apprehension that might otherwise accompany its consideration. Thus, both fortress and bridge strategies seem to be operative: the fortress strategy repudiates what several IVCF participants call the "anti-Christian" dimensions inherent in the theory of biological evolution, and the bridge strategy allows students to accept the transformed idea.[9]

The next bridging movement allows evangelicals to narrow the gap sometimes separating them from secular individuals, or from the secular ethos in general. For example, since evolutionary theory arguably forms part of the intellectual assumptions many people bring with them to university, being able to use this theory in academic and social settings reduces the estrangement that might arise between IVCF members and non-Christians as a function of believers' ignorance of the theory. Many of the IVCF students I interviewed were able to talk about evolution in an informed manner; but none of them accepted any of the atheistic implications of evolutionary theory.[10] This ability to speak intelligently about evolution also has the effect of facilitating these students' academic success, since professors expect them to be able to attain a familiarity with the theory. Consequently, for IVCF members, the scientific literacy yielded by the transformation, integration, and employment of this problematic theory has welcome disalienating consequences.[11]

The simultaneous or sequential expression of fortress and bridge strategies is also evident in the function of the spiritual realm in IVCF discourse. As I described earlier, construing non-Christians as the defenseless victims of and sometimes agents for Satan accentuates the difference between believers and nonbelievers. However, by maintaining that all humans are victims of the same demonic forces, the distinction between Christians and non-Christians is somewhat mitigated.

Another instance of the collaboration between the fortress and bridge strategies is manifested in the role of a particular strand of popular youth culture among IVCF members.[12] Consider the influence of *Seinfeld* and *Friends*, two of the most popular situation comedies on prime time television and (in the mid-1990s) the centerpieces of the National Broadcasting Corporation's popular Thursday night offerings. In the days and weeks following an episode, I have heard my own (mainly non-Christian) students as well as IVCF members imitating the characters' dialogue, gestures, and quips, suggesting strongly that these students' verbal rhythms and vernacular are either reinforced or generated by the discursive conventions normalized by the casts of these television programs.[13]

The IVCF students' participation in the popular culture of their generation seems unproblematic until one considers the moral messages implicit and explicit in the lifestyles of these television characters. None of the characters in either *Seinfeld* or *Friends* lives the sort of life or celebrates the kind of values embraced by most IVCF students. For example, none of the characters is married, and all of them drink and engage in casual sex. In fact, probably half the dialogue on these two shows is explicitly or implicitly sex-related. Moreover, none of the characters shows even the slightest interest in religion. In fact, when a character's sphere of concern does reach beyond his or her private interests, it rarely extends beyond the material prosperity or sexual conquests of his or her own small group.

I have discussed the ways an IVCF member can participate in a conversation about evolution by drawing the theory through a filter and reducing it to an erroneous or incomplete and therefore cognitively unthreatening theory. It seems likely that a similar filtering process is also occurring with respect to television programs. The restrictive porousness of this membrane may strain out some of the more troubling elements of popular programs like *Seinfeld* and *Friends* in order to allow inoffensive elements such as verbal inflections and some jokes to be assimilated into evangelical discourse without simultaneously betraying believers' convictions.[14] This process not only increases students' cultural literacy but also may normalize their relations with non-Christian students. If IVCF students can become conversant in the popular culture of their generation, then they are more likely to be accepted into a non-Christian's intimate social sphere.[15] One of the advantages of being able to converse freely with their non-Christian peers is, of course, that it makes the religious convictions (promoted either through explicit witnessing or by example) of these "occasional apostles" more palatable and less exotic for non-Christians.[16]

Largely because the IVCF chapter is capable of addressing if not always satisfying the social and spiritual needs of both its fundamentalist majority and its liberal minority, a coherent group ethos is maintained amid considerable theological and ideological differences. The fundamentalists in the group might prefer to employ the fortress strategy to preserve what Frank Peretti (1986:349) calls "the remnant" of loyal Christians, and these members would rather the chapter did not experiment so much with female leadership and liberal worship styles, materials, and messages. However, the fundamentalists in the IVCF are evidently willing to allow the liberals in the group, including the staff worker and most of the executive committee members, to set the more moderate tone of the chapter.[17] Although the fundamentalists in the IVCF find the fortress strategy more in keeping with their own predispositions, most of the liberals I interviewed also employ the fortress strategy when they find themselves in situations of significant cognitive or moral danger. And while liberals have a tendency to favor the bridge approach to the non-Christian world, fundamentalists often make nonpatronizing bridging overtures to non-Christians (including myself). In other words, it would be inaccurate to argue that the fortress strategy is rooted exclusively in the fundamentalist side of the chapter and the bridge strategy exclusively in the liberal side. It is even inappropriate to suggest that there are two distinct factions. In fact, with a few significant exceptions, most members of the IVCF (and the conservative Protestants I have met outside this group) combine elements of the fundamentalist and liberal evangelical worldviews and fortress and bridge strategies, even though most participants have a (sometimes only slight) preference for one of these approaches. Most previous studies of evangelicals[18] have tended to emphasize the way these believers employ fortress strategies to distinguish themselves from their non-Christian peers. These studies have greatly deepened our understanding of these groups. However, it seems to me that this conventional focus has told only part of the story of these groups' interactions with the non-Christian world.

The evangelical tradition in which almost all of the group's participants were raised includes rich theological and moral resources that have engendered both strategies for relating to the non-Christian world. I would suggest that, for the most part, twentieth-century North American evangelicalism has (with varying degrees of success) employed both approaches in an attempt to preserve what many believers perceive to be a besieged gospel *and* to ensure that they are on good terms with their non-Christian neighbors. What is interesting about the McMaster IVCF chapter is its success at striking a delicate balance between two impulses that are at the heart of evangelicalism. Both strategies and the selectively permeable membrane which facilitates them allow evangelical students to sustain and even cultivate their faiths during the impressionable years spent within an institution which is often both intellectually and morally inhospitable to their convictions.

The contract metaphor I have employed throughout this study connotes both the negotiated and the dynamic qualities of the compromises made by IVCF members: negotiated because difficult and contentious; dynamic because ongoing and revocable. These contracts are necessarily negotiated by each individual, but the group facilitates this mediation by offering its members patient moral support when women are struggling with their roles, rousing admonitions by guest speakers to avoid excessive compromises, models of durable contracts through the testimonies of older members, shelter from and access to the contentious "turf" of campus life, dramatic images of their diabolical enemies, and witnessing opportunities to traverse the gulf sometimes separating the evangelical and non-Christian communities.

Commenting on the state of social-scientific research on evangelicalism, ten years ago Robert Wuthnow wrote that "ethnographic research should be a high priority. We need to hear evangelical church members speaking in their own words to learn how they construct reality, how they confront the secular society" (1989: 171). The present work is one response to Wuthnow's appeal. This project represents the only comprehensive social-scientific study of any chapter of the Inter-Varsity Christian Fellowship in North America. In fact, as far as I can tell, this project is the first full-length academic study of *any* contemporary evangelical university student group. As such, this work provides insights into the ways members of a conservative Protestant campus group speak, pray, worship, organize themselves, and understand their relations with the larger secular institution in which they are located. More broadly, this ethnography also represents a case study in the nature of evangelicalism in North America and among a generation whose religious inclinations are, as one would expect, just beginning to be studied.

I studied the McMaster IVCF not only to understand the group itself but also to use the group as a case study in the survival of religious groups in essentially secular environments. My interpretation of this phenomenon in this time and place emphasizes the continual negotiation of contracts facilitated by a filter that is deployed according to fortress and bridge strategies. I realize that the metaphors I have chosen to interpret the McMaster IVCF are drawn from multiple conceptual domains. Although combining the imagery of architecture, biology, and commerce may be unwieldy at times, these assorted concepts still strike me as the most suitable aids for explaining this group.[19] In short, the members of this group (and perhaps other evangelicals) are able to maintain their religious identities in a secular environment because they sustain and employ an elaborate psychosocial construct that enables them to manage, transform, and sometimes diminish the otherness they experience when they confront non-Christian worldviews, values, and individuals. As William suggested in chapter 4, the IVCF helps him to belong, but in his own way. In her ethnography of American evangelical elementary and high schools, Melinda Wagner argued, "If the Christian walk is going to endure in American society, it must be walked in the American way" (1990:136). As I have suggested throughout this book, IVCF students have definitely made the kinds of compromises Wagner documents in her book and implies are necessary in her prediction. However, I do not think that the secular world has the power Wagner's projection suggests. William can—and has—chosen to walk his Christian walk in his own way. Of course, his way will correspond closely to his peers' ways, just as it will be heavily influenced by the ways of the surrounding North American society. Still, he has found a way to make his walk distinctly his own and not simply an expression of a hegemonic North American society.

Nancy Ammerman argues that the rise of conservative Protestant groups should be understood positively as a validation and defense of a "culturally coherent way of life" (1987:193). Similarly, anthropologist Susan Harding defends her conservative informants and their communities from the "otherness" imposed on them by academics who often parody fundamentalists as "aberrant, usually backwards, hoodwinked versions of modern subjects" (1991:374). As well, in *The Fundamentalisms Project*, sociologists Robert Wuthnow and Matthew Lawson write that interpreting fundamentalism "as a kind of cultural criticism, rather than dismissing it as a form of mental retardation, allows its creativity and vitality to be recognized" (1994:42).[20] Furthermore, in his ethnography of a group of Appalachian Baptists, Jeff Todd Titon (1988) concludes that fundamentalists do not create pathetic delusions to protest the death of their way of life. Rather, like nonevangelical believers of virtually all kinds, these evangelicals creatively adjust and apply their preexisting traditions to their life circumstances.[21] These scholars offer crucial corrective insights for both scholarly and popular perspectives on evangelicalism. The individuals whose voices I have woven throughout this text and the complex group dynamics I have delineated further validate the perspective that evangelicals are not illiterate hillbillies,[22] nor are the coping and survival strategies employed by these believers purely reactionary or desperate responses to the dominant culture of contemporary North America.

The negotiating process so central to the paradigm I am proposing helps IVCF members forge new relationships with non-Christian individuals and institutions. The transformation of threatening experiences reduces both the cognitive and social discomfort evangelicals sometimes feel on secular campuses and the alienation this discomfort sometimes creates between these students and their non-Christian peers (or the university ethos in general). As the instigators of this transformative process, the students in this ethnography emerge as religious and cultural innovators. Or, to borrow a term from Lévi-Strauss (1966; cf. Wagner 1990), these students can be understood as *bricoleurs*, as people who work with the symbolic materials and tools at hand to create something new. By focusing on evangelicals' creativity in the face of the perceived hegemony of the secular ethos, not only do we gain a more nuanced view of the resistance of marginalized groups but also we begin to see these Christians as the multidimensional and imaginative people they are. At the very least, an emphasis on evangelicals' enthusiastic and creative responses to perceived marginalization might help us understand why evangelical church and parachurch groups show no signs of disintegration and are almost the only sector of contemporary North American Christianity sustaining and even increasing its membership (Bibby 1993:6; Rawlyk 1996). Finally, a subtler vision of these believers might also challenge the profound condescension I have encountered when discussing evangelicals with liberal Christians, academics, and friends.

I suspect that analogous metaphorical membranes exist between most other evangelical groups and their surroundings and that to forge acceptable contracts, individuals in these groups participate in the ongoing contraction and expansion of the membrane's perforations. It also seems plausible to suggest that similar dynamics (involving fortress and bridge strategies, a membrane, and contracts) are at work in the relationship between other religious groups and their nonsupportive or antagonistic environments (for example, Muslims and Orthodox Jews in secular institutions). And finally, I would argue that the general dynamics I have outlined are also pertinent for the study of nonreligious groups experiencing the opposition of (and thus similarly "othered" by) some dominant group (for example, African Americans living in predominantly white suburbs or women in predominantly male corporations). Consequently, the approach explained in this text should allow us to understand a variety of examples of the interpenetration of tribalism (fortress building) and globalization (bridge building) that characterizes North American life today (Ammerman 1997:214; cf. Barber 1996).

My interpretation of the IVCF may also help to explain the evangelical proclivity for combining elements of apparently contradictory worldviews in their contracts. The IVCF participants represent a relatively learned subculture within the broader evangelical population. Consequently, one would expect to find among these students a fairly high degree of awareness of the contracts they are negotiating. However, I have found that these students often blend elements of the secular and evangelical worldviews without extensive reflection on this mixing. This tendency often leads to the coexistence of contradictory ideas and values within an individual's contract.[23] The negotiation process draws into one's contract seemingly disparate elements largely because this process normally occurs sporadically, with a compromise on the issue of alcohol one month, and then resistance to compromise on the issue of women in the ministry the next week, followed by a reconsideration of one's position on evolution two weeks later, and so forth. There are certain beliefs (such as the supremacy of God and the importance of a personal relationship with Jesus) that are nonnegotiable (cf. Wagner 1990:207), but there a great many other beliefs and values on which IVCF *bricoleurs* are willing to compromise, often in a piece-meal fashion. Consequently, although students are conscious of the tension between themselves as Christians and the (sometimes "anti-Christian") secular ethos, they are rarely aware of the larger contract that the dynamic process of negotiation necessarily produces.[24] Students' lack of formal awareness of the larger agreement they are mediating does not detract from the creativity I mentioned. Nor does it distinguish them from non-Christians or academics. Few of us ever think of the larger themes, tendencies, or contracts in our lives on a self-conscious level. As Laurence Iannaccone writes, "From time to time, academics must pinch themselves to recall that most people are not terribly concerned with nor constrained by logical consistency" (1993:361). I do not think it is helpful or fair to expect of evangelicals a degree of self-awareness and consistency we do not expect of nonevangelicals. Nevertheless, since the secular university mandate reflects the priorities of the non-Christian majority, evangelical contracts with this institution may sometimes strike observers as awkward, anachronistic, or at least conspicuous. However, I would argue that even non-Christians (in both the evangelical and social-scientific senses) harbor convictions and assumptions that are in significant tension if not completely contradictory, such as the value of motherhood and the upward career mobility of women or the value of environmental protection and the pursuit of material wealth. I would suggest that to sustain these essentially contradictory beliefs and values, we all make "awkward, anachronistic, or at least conspicuous" contracts with the institutions in which we participate.

Another way to explain the sometimes confusing content of evangelical contracts may be implied in chapter 5. As I explained in that chapter, many evangelical women employ what ethnographer T. M. Luhrmann calls a "strategy of ambivalence" (1989:341) during their years at McMaster.[25] Such a strategy allows these women to maintain feminist and fundamentalist values simultaneously while not fully embracing either. The postponement of what might be called intracontract conflict resolution may decrease the tensions produced by the problematic elements in many of these women's contracts. This period of uncertainty seems to correspond to what Victor Turner (1969) calls a "liminal" period, during which believers are suspended betwixt and between social roles. Turner suggests that alternative, uncertain, or ambiguous values and roles may be adopted during liminal periods, but he does not include in his definition a clear indication of the duration of liminality. I suggest that liminality might persist for the entire period of a student's three or four years at McMaster and might allow students to tolerate the seemingly untenable comingling of conflicting ideas and values in their contracts.[26]

In the final paragraph of the final volume of the groundbreaking *Fundamentalisms Project*, Gabriel A. Almond, Emmanuel Sivan, and R. Scott Appleby write:

> Fundamentalisms are caught in a debilitating paradox. As long as they remain fixed in the enclave culture and mentality that nurture them, fundamentalists are fated to be no more than disruptive and relatively influential dissenting minorities; yet once they exit the enclave, mentally or otherwise, they find that their fundamentalist religious ardour quickly yields to the pragmatic, compromising strategies of a world not to their liking—the impure, very real world outside the enclave. (1995:504)

At least in the context of North American Protestant fundamentalism, this paradox is not actually a true paradox, if by this word one means pejoratively to denote a frustrating and unresolvable contradiction. In practice, believers regularly, and it seems often simultaneously, exist in their "enclave" (or fortress) and in what R. Stephen Warner calls the glorious impurity (1997a:234) of contemporary society. This paradox—I would call it a dynamic tension—is far from debilitating. Rather, it is capable of facilitating new and robust forms of conservative belief and practice.[27] Combining the demands of boundary maintenance with those of participation in secular institutions is challenging and in some instances aggravating. However, thanks in part to a myriad of alternative institutions such as the IVCF, evangelicals engage (more or less successfully) in this process of negotiation virtually every day.

In the tradition of postmodern ethnography, I would like to conclude this study by reintroducing Ruth, one of the individuals who inspired this study. More specifically, I would like to consider the contract she has negotiated. Ruth is a graduate student in psychology and has been active in the McMaster IVCF for five years. She has served on the chapter's most prestigious committees and has been friends with all of its presidents and Buff Cox, its staff worker. Nurtured by the IVCF structure and ethos, Ruth has taken advantage of many opportunities to contemplate and formalize the contract between her faith and her academic responsibilities. Her age, maturity, and proximity to the center of the IVCF, as well as her prominent career within the chapter, mean that she is not representative of most of the chapter's members. However, in many ways, the contract Ruth has negotiated between her faith and her scientific responsibilities exemplifies a McMaster IVCF ideal.

Ruth entered McMaster as a fairly naive fundamentalist from a rural Brethren background and has maintained many traditional conservative Christian beliefs and values.[28] Although she originally joined the IVCF because she was apprehensive about what she called the "very secular" nature of the university, she no longer relies on the group as a "haven or a shelter for Christians. I wouldn't make excuses for this function. But I want to motivate people not to be so afraid of secularism." Her faith is now regularly "stretched," perhaps neither more nor less than when she arrived, but at a more intellectual level. In response to my question about whether she experiences tension between her faith and her education, Ruth said:

> As I grow academically, I have to think hard, but I always try to fit it into my spirituality. In school, I am eager to learn what is being presented. I don't want to be close-minded. But I don't want to separate my science and my Christianity. I strive to bring it all together.
>
> Sometimes I need to accept that there's a real difference between me and non-Christians. I need to think through my bias. But sometimes I'm going to stick with my bias. Like with creationism—I believe in it, but also that the earth might actually be billions of years old. I won't budge from that. I'll get my M.Sc., but I will have had to live with the tension.

Ruth is uneasy about the commensurability of her scientific endeavors and non-Christian friends, on the one hand, and her faith and IVCF friends on the other. She "won't budge from" certain components of the contract she has negotiated between her scientific and religious commitments. In other words, in some cases she will opt to remain what Warner calls an "elective parochial" (1988), one who chooses to embrace ideas and values somewhat (and sometimes significantly) at odds with the liberal, secular society in which she lives. Like other IVCF participants, she is engaged (in her case, quite consciously) in an ongoing negotiation process aimed at reconciling these issues. Few IVCF participants are as aware as Ruth is of the "bias" she describes; few have constructed as elaborate a contract as Ruth's. Like Ruth, few of the IVCF members I met consider themselves finally successful at "bringing it all together." Nevertheless, Ruth and the other participants with whom I lived for a year and a half are compelled and often content to "live with the tension" of being children of God in a Godless institution.

Notes

NOTE TO PREFACE

1. To limit the scope of this book, "North America" refers to Canada and the United States. In other words, this book will not discuss Mexico.

NOTES TO CHAPTER ONE

1. Early each year the chapter publishes a "chat sheet" which lists members' names, student numbers, departmental affiliations, and telephone numbers. The chat sheet for 1995–96, the academic year I was most involved with the group, included two hundred students. There were people who chose not, or who were not able, to have their names appear on this sheet. Since there is no formal procedure for becoming an IVCF member, throughout this book, a "member" denotes anyone who by frequent association or self-definition so identifies himself or herself.

2. For the most current information on the IVCF, see the IVCF Canada's Website: www.ivcf.ca/index.shtml. The American IVCF Website address is: www.gospelcom.net/iv/. The McMaster IVCF Website address is: www.ivcf.ca/index.shtml.

3. The only real names used in this book are those of the following religious and academic professionals associated with the IVCF: Elizabeth "Buff" Cox, Clark Pinnock, and Joyce Bellous.

4. The executive committee includes the following positions: president, clubs administrator, large group coordinator, Church at the John coordinator, Church at the

John worship leader, outreach coordinator, small group coordinator, treasurer, and IVCF staff worker.

5. These figures refer to the churches in which students received the majority of their religious education. Very often, their families left these churches for reasons ranging from doctrinal disagreements to occupational resettlement (cf. Bibby and Brinkerhoff 1973). I was surprised to discover that many of the students in my sample were raised in the United Church of Canada, a tradition normally associated with theological, moral, and ideological liberalism. However, the families of almost all of these members left their churches as a result of what they perceived as the United Church's excessively permissive stance on the role of women and the ordination of homosexuals.

6. The questions were purposely open-ended and often elicited answers and conversations I could not have predicted. Quite often, the participant and I would discuss the possible meanings of the question itself at length before he or she offered an answer. The questions were: How and why did you become involved with the McMaster IVCF? Is there tension between your school world and your IVCF world? Is there any tension between your IVCF friends and non-IVCF friends? What role do you see IVCF playing on campus? Why do you think this chapter is growing? What would your university life be like without the IVCF? What do you think of the references to Satan and battle imagery in the songs and addresses at IVCF events? Would you describe yourself as "alienated" from non-Christian students or from McMaster University itself?

7. In Ontario, generally speaking, on both an individual and corporate level, "Fellowship" Baptists are more theologically and morally conservative than "Convention" Baptists.

8. See Cox (1995) and Neitz (1987) for discussions of these movements.

9. See Badone (1989), Balmer (1989), Danforth (1982, 1989), Geertz (1973, 1994), Klassen (1994), Narayan (1989), Rosaldo (1989), Tedlock (1983) and Titon (1988).

10. Although this book might be considered an example of "interpretive," "experimental," or even "postmodern" ethnography, I am least comfortable with the last description, unless by postmodern one means simply to imply the attempt to allow the other's voice to be heard often and clearly and the effort to foreground the conditional and partial (Clifford 1986) nature of my interpretations of IVCF life.

11. In Brian Morris's (1987) lengthy bibliography of anthropological studies of religion, all but two were situated in non-Western locales.

12. See Ammerman (1990), Badone (1989), Balmer (1989), Davidman (1991), Klassen (1994), Peacock and Tyson (1989), Peshkin (1986), and Titon (1988).

13. In her critique of postmodernism, anthropologist Margery Wolf writes that postmodernists "suggest that we are in crisis . . . because we have claimed an authority that does not exist, told truths that are only partial, and (mis)represented an Other that conceals the construction of the Other by an invisible anthropological Self. [Postmodernists'] solutions to these problems, however, do not include better ways of doing fieldwork, but different (better?) ways of writing ethnographies" (1992:136).

14. Unitarian Universalism (or simply Unitarianism) grew out of the Protestant Reformation. After centuries of development in Europe, the tradition began attracting adherents among liberal intellectuals and cultural leaders in the northeastern United States. Until the middle of the twentieth century, most Unitarians would have understood themselves as liberal Protestants. In general, contemporary Unitarians are no longer required and no longer tend to believe in the divine or unique nature of Jesus. Instead, Unitarians share a respect and enthusiasm for each individual's responsible search for religious meaning. The tradition is now noncreedal, theologically eclectic,

and religiously liberal. For an introduction to Unitarian Universalism, see Buehrens and Church (1989).

15. Of course, the prejudices I once held are hardly unique to Unitarians. I have found that these condescending presuppositions are very popular among liberal Christian, atheist, Roman Catholic, Buddhist, Jewish, academic, and nonacademic colleagues and friends. Many people from such backgrounds rolled their eyes when I told them that I took the religious organization and aspirations of evangelicals seriously. After I told him about my project, one liberal United Church minister sneered and asked, "But aren't you just going to end up justifying these people?" Other peers and professors worried aloud that I was at risk of "going native" or, to use evangelical rhetoric, accepting Jesus Christ as my Lord and personal savior.

16. In chapter 3 (on rhetoric), I discuss the way IVCF students, like many other evangelicals, restrict the term "Christian" to people who have "a personal relationship with Christ," a criterion which often excludes approximately 80% of people who consider themselves Christians. Only a few of the members with whom I spoke seemed uncomfortable with the exclusivity of this term.

17. See Bruce (1982) for an account of the relationship between the SCM and the IVCF.

18. For a similar discussion of this term, see the definition propounded by George Rawlyk, Mark Noll, and David Bebbington, three of the leading scholars of evangelicalism, in their edited volume, *Evangelicalism: Comparative Studies of Popular Protestantism in North America, the British Isles, and Beyond: 1700–1900* (1994:6).

19. Rawlyk (1996) found an emphasis on a personal relationship with Christ to be characteristic of the evangelicals represented in the comprehensive 1993 Angus Reid poll on religion in Canada.

20. See the five volumes of the *Fundamentalisms Project: Fundamentalisms Observed* (1991), *Fundamentalisms and Society* (1993), *Fundamentalisms and the State* (1993), *Accounting for Fundamentalisms* (1994), and *Fundamentalisms Comprehended* (1995), all of which were coedited by Martin E. Marty and R. Scott Appleby. The first volume is an especially helpful discussion of the varieties of fundamentalism and a good justification for the neologism "fundamentalisms." See also Marty and Appleby (1991).

21. Instead of speaking in terms of modernism (a loose and sometimes misleading concept), I focus on what Lawrence would consider some of the various manifestations (see brief list in this sentence) of modernism (1989).

22. See Peshkin (1986) and Wagner (1990) for ethnographic explorations of American fundamentalist schools. Peshkin is more convinced than Wagner that these private elementary and high schools are able to remain fully separate from the non-Christian world.

23. Canadian evangelicalism has its roots in a combination of Scottish common sense philosophy (the theory that all truth is obtainable through the use of uncomplicated observation), Baconianism, Calvinism, the philosophy of the Enlightenment (Gauvreau 1991), and American conservative Protestantism. Eventually, the Canadian forms of evangelicalism differentiated themselves from their European and American progenitors. For historical accounts of the Canadian tradition, see Rawlyk, Bebbington, and Noll (1994); Rawlyk (1990); Gauvreau (1991); and Stackhouse (1993).

24. This debate involved differences of opinion about evolution, new approaches to interpreting the Bible, and the appropriate posture to adopt in one's relations with "the world" (Marsden 1991; Wuthnow 1989).

25. Further comparative research would be required to determine if this lack of interest in politics distinguishes IVCF members from their secular peers. Their apoli-

ticism does, however, distinguish them from American evangelicals. After all, in the United States, conservative evangelicalism has become significantly allied with the Republican party. See Cox (1987), Simpson (1994, 1983), and Wilcox (1992).

26. This conclusion is based on three sources. First, during interviews, I asked respondents both whether they would consider themselves fundamentalists and what this term meant to them. Second, we also discussed their opinions about "the modern world." Third, Buff Cox, the chapter's staff worker, also confirmed that most members could be accurately described as fundamentalists.

27. Capitals in original. This Statement of Purpose is published by IVCF Canada on its website: www.ivcf.ca/index/shtml. See also www.ivcf.ca. For commentary on the slightly different 1968 version of this statement, see Stackhouse (1993:104).

28. During two years of fieldwork with the IVCF, I met only one Roman Catholic and no students from Orthodox backgrounds. Furthermore, the Roman Catholic woman referred to herself as "a Christian, but a cultural Catholic." This distinction is explored in the penultimate chapter. See Stackhouse (1993:138–142) for a historical account of the issue of the role of Catholics in the IVCF membership and national executive.

29. Space does not permit an account of the evolution of the notion of secularization from Auguste Comte to the present era. See Berger (1967), Bibby (1993), Bruce (1992), and Dobbelaere (1981, 1984).

30. See Berger (1992:36), Finke (1992:155), Finke and Stark (1992), and Wuthnow (1988).

31. Hunter suggests that in response to the prevalent cultural pluralism in North America, evangelicalism has diminished its public reliance on inflammatory concepts such as sin, hell, exclusivism, and final judgment and adopted a conciliatory posture toward non-Christians. Moreover, Hunter asserts that as a concession to the trend toward subjectivism in the culture at large, evangelicalism has focused on the emotional needs and psychospiritual growth of its members, a trend which distances the movement from its ascetic and doctrinal roots (1985:160). See Wagner (1990) for another discussion of these kinds of compromises.

32. "Secularism" refers to the more rigid, ideological form of secularization. "Secularization" describes the retreat of religion from the public or personal spheres. Secularism involves the active attempt to exclude religion from public life (Wilson 1992: 209).

33. See Gauvreau (1991), J. Grant (1988), McKillop (1979, 1994), Rawlyk (1990, 1992, 1994), and Stackhouse (1993).

34. McKillop defines "higher criticism" as "the quest for the historical Jesus and for a critical understanding of the biblical record" (1994:204).

35. Similarly, George Marsden links the secularization of American Protestant universities to the rise—again, culminating in the early part of the present century—of pluralism and a broadly defined liberal Christianity, which came to be equated with civilization itself (Marsden Longfield 1992:9–45).

36. Such an interpretation seems especially false, given the fact that the IVCF has grown from forty members in 1988 to two hundred in 1997.

37. McMaster University Act of Incorporation, 1887.

38. The change exemplified at McMaster is also evident in the world outside the university's gates, a world in which, as philosopher Jeffrey Stout observes, "belief in the existence of a specific sort of God and in certain aspects of a vision of the good cease to function as a presupposition of our moral discourse with each other" (1988:79).

39. Berger contends that most people in a pluralistic society experience some degree

of "cognitive contamination," the questioning of one's beliefs in light of exposure to other religious and secular perspectives. There are three possible responses to this contamination. One can "bargain" with the new worldview and selectively accept certain new cognitive components. One can "surrender" entirely to the new perspective and abandon one's existing worldview. Finally, in the face of cognitive contamination, one can "retrench" in two ways: defensively, by building a fortress to protect one's world and one's community; and offensively, through aggressive attempts to conquer the outside world and remake it according to some traditional religious model (1992:39–43). It seems to me that Berger's metaphors are quite helpful for understanding both the Canadian and American religious scenes.

40. Bibby points out (1993) that this proportion has not changed significantly since the 1871 census. For a consideration of the differences between Bibby's lower and Rawlyk's higher figures, see Rawlyk (1996:224).

41. Moreover, Bibby and Brinkerhoff report that Project Canada's 1990 comparison of Canadians' "original" versus "current" affiliation indicates that while 400,000 people had joined mainline Protestant churches, 425,000 joined evangelical churches (1994:278). In other words, Bibby and Brinkerhoff point out, while the net gain is only 25,000 people in favor of evangelical churches, the real significance of these figures is that 8% (or 16% according to Rawlyk) of the population is competing with the vast majority of mainline Christian churches and claiming a numerically small but proportionately large victory. When Bibby and Brinkerhoff project this trend forward, they predict that in approximately twenty years, the total "market share" for evangelicals will exceed that of mainline Protestants and will be closing in rapidly on the Roman Catholics (1994:278). This new trend is of personal interest to Bibby, who is an evangelical himself and whose intellectual energies appear to be turning more openly toward defragmenting religious traditions (1993).

42. About 50% of evangelicals are what Bibby calls active members, 30% marginal members, and 20% inactive members. The figures for the mainline Protestant churches are reversed: 20% are active, 30% marginal, and 50% inactive (1993:173).

43. As a result of the small total numbers of evangelicals in Canada, the evangelical successes at retaining active members have not profoundly affected the generally decreasing levels of overall Canadian church attendance. Bibby observes that before the 1950s, approximately 60% of Canadians worshiped publicly; by the 1950s, this number had dropped to 50%; in the 1970s, the number dropped again to 33%; and in the 1990s, only about 20% of Canadians worship regularly (1993:4).

44. For quantitative data on the religious beliefs and degree of involvement of Canada's young adults, see Rawlyk (1996:49–116) and Bibby (1993:95–114).

45. Clubs such as the Gay/Lesbian/Bisexual Association, the IVCF, and the Muslim Students Association receive the same level of financial support from the McMaster Students Union; and all clubs are entitled to staff display tables during the annual Clubsfest at the beginning of each academic year.

46. Such increased marginalization might be inspired by the shortage of meeting space in a potentially overcrowded university or the cessation of the basic funding all clubs receive.

47. The contracts forged by IVCF members seem to evidence what Steve Bruce (1988) and Clyde Wilcox (1992) describe as "the politics of lifestyle defense." According to this interpretation, participation in the IVCF is not just a protest against or lament over secularism. Rather, IVCF membership is primarily an intentional positive strategy for sustaining the evangelical subculture. Berger and Luckmann would describe these contracts as examples of the legitimation of symbolic (and perhaps actual) universes.

Such legitimation efforts are hardly unique to evangelicals or even to minority groups. Berger and Luckmann write:

> Specific procedures of universe-maintenance become necessary when the symbolic universe has become a *problem*. As long as this is not the case, the symbolic universe is self-maintaining, that is, self-legitimating by the sheer facticity of its objective existence in the society in question. One may conceive of a society in which this would be possible. Such a society would be a harmonious, perfectly functioning "system." Actually, no such society exists. . . . Every symbolic universe is incipiently problematic. The question, then, is the *degree* to which it has become problematic. (1966:123)

48. The modern university is to many people epitomized by its scientific methodology and its concomitant reductionism, evolutionism, and materialism. The IVCF members are not primarily opposed to science per se. Only a small number of IVCF participants are aware of the implicitly (and perhaps explicitly) secularizing effects or challenging elements of the scientific method (G. Grant 1986). For most participants, the only intellectually threatening feature of their education is evolutionary theory. Moreover, most IVCF students are in faculties (e.g., engineering, commerce, kinesiology, English) in which the opposition between their faith and the theory of evolution rarely manifests itself explicitly. Even students in explicitly scientific departments report only minimal levels of intellectual conflict between their faith and their academic pursuits. This academic armistice is achieved through their belief that science is the disciplined study of a natural world created (according to some, fewer than six thousand years ago) in every detail by God. The opposition of IVCF students is directed primarily at the liberalism that is another major feature of the modern secular university. More specifically, IVCF students identify the moral laxity of their peers, the relativism of their professors, and the university's sometimes "anti-Christian" climate as the main sources of their otherness. For example, during an interview in December 1995, one woman said that "the university sets up rules that mean that basically we can't discriminate against anyone except Christians."

49. It should be noted, however, that each IVCF chapter is unique as a function of its membership, its staff worker, and the institutional context in which it exists. Hammond and Hunter's survey sample of ten universities and colleges included only one non-Christian institution. The IVCF at that institution may have emphasized what I call the fortress strategy.

50. While Berger's metaphors are helpful, I find that his focus on the "cognitive" element of bargaining and retrenching cannot adequately convey the emotional, spiritual, and communal dimensions of IVCF members' negotiations. I prefer the fortress, bridge, and contract metaphors because they are less limiting.

NOTES TO CHAPTER TWO

1. Since the first scholarly use of the life history method in the early part of the present century (Thomas and Znaniecki 1918), this approach has become an important but not widely used social-scientific research tool. It has also been the subject of critical appraisal. See Klassen (1994); Langness and Frank (1985); Linde (1993), Mandelbaum (1973), Rosenwald (1992), and Watson and Watson-Franke (1985).

2. Peshkin's *God's Choice: The Total World of a Fundamentalist School* (1986) includes four student life histories. Peshkin's life histories reveal that even his strictly

fundamentalist students exert a degree of autonomy in the process of self-definition. Nevertheless, the students in Peshkin's study are significantly more concerned than IVCF students about doctrinal conformity.

3. Mandelbaum emphasizes the role of "dimensions," "turnings," and "adaptations" in a person's life history. By "dimensions," Mandelbaum means "experiences that stem from a similar base and are linked in their effects on the person's subsequent actions" (1973:180). Mandelbaum's dimensions include the cultural, biological, psychosocial, and social (1973:180). "Turnings" denote the "major transitions, that the person has made . . . [in which] a person takes on a new set of roles, enters into fresh relations with a new set of people, and acquires a new self-definition" (1973:181). Finally, he describes an "adaptation" as a "built-in process" through which individuals alter some of their "established patterns of behaviour to cope with new conditions. Each person *changes* his ways in order to maintain *continuity*, whether of group participation or social expectation or self-image or simply survival" (1973:181). My interpretations of these four life histories focus mainly on the place of turnings and adaptations in these students' personal and religious narratives.

4. For example, it became clear to me that several students used our interviews to lead me, a "non-Christian," to convert. Even those who did not appear to be witnessing to me during interviews were certainly aware of my own religious convictions. It is unlikely that this awareness would not have affected the telling of their stories.

5. Linguist Charlotte Linde argues that the inevitable and always significant influence of the researcher on the subject's self-report casts aspersions on the scientific rigor of the life history (1993:47). However, I think one can argue that by highlighting the interpenetration of researcher and subject and the concomitant conditions this places on the final text or interview, ethnographers are, ideally at least, emphasizing a variety of analytical influence that regrettably remains veiled in most social-scientific studies. Ethnographic uses of the life history thus best capture what Linde calls the "structurally and interpretively open" nature of the stories which constitute a life (1993:31), even if these histories are always interested, always collaborative. However, the classical social-scientific warnings against the excesses of subjectivity ought still to remind the ethnographer not to abandon any attempt to convey at least a less mediated portrait of a person. Nevertheless, I am mindful of folklorist Kirshenblatt-Gimblett's observation that "presenting the text as a quotation by a researcher is, among other things, a technique for lending to that text the imprimatur of scholarship" (1989:131). Linde (1993) distinguishes between the life history method associated with ethnography and what she considers the more scientific life story approach favoured by sociolinguists. Her insights into the creation of coherence in and among life stories are illuminating for ethnographers working in life histories. However, her treatment of these stories and their tellers might seem overly detached to many ethnographers. For example, in Linde's (1993) acknowledgments section, she reserves her deepest appreciation for "the people who told me something of their lives and whose stories are treated here dispassionately as objects for analysis."

6. As in previous and subsequent chapters, information such as an individual's name, distinguishing physical attributes, and place of residence has been altered. In Steve's life history, this policy had to be bent, if not broken, because his presidency (1995–96) was both a crucial element of his personal development and a fact that makes his real identity obvious to many people. Steve was aware and accepting of this situation.

7. "We know that all things work together for good for those who love God, who are called according to his purpose" (Romans 8:28).

8. The young earth hypothesis is the fundamentalist assertion that the earth is not older than ten thousand years. See Morris and Parker (1982:252) for a discussion of the scientific evidence supporting this theory.

9. This issue is addressed in chapter 5, on the role of women in the IVCF.

10. The sociological term "career" refers to a person's movement through the role expectations and systems of prestige associated with a particular institution. Thus, each person I interviewed had a "career" within the IVCF. Gabrielle's life history, for example, relates the early peaking and then fairly sudden diminishment of her career within the chapter.

11. Gabrielle's perception of Cox's actual power to limit her IVCF career may or may not be appropriate. At the very least, Gabrielle's interpretation may explain why, earlier in her narrative, she seemed to identify the IVCF with Cox when she said, "Highbury is more liberal than the Gospel Hall, but not as liberal as Buff," rather than ". . . not as liberal as the IVCF."

12. During my fieldwork, I was a regular participant in and observer of a small group devoted to exploring the phenomenon of witnessing on campus. At one of these meetings, Cindy, a graduate student member of the chapter, said, "This morning as I was driving to school I was listening to Chuck Swindol on the radio, and he said, 'If you can't remember exactly when you became a Christian, then you probably aren't one.' That totally makes sense to me." One afternoon in Panavezys, Lithuania, Jocelyn, one of the members of the Lithuania mission team, told another team member that she does not remember the moment she became a Christian. The other team member then asked Jocelyn, "I don't mean to be critical or anything, but isn't that like saying that your parents make you Christian?" After a short, pregnant pause, Jocelyn replied tersely, "That's just one of the things that makes us different, I guess." The tension implicit in this conversation was not resolved during the trip.

13. Simon commented, "I see my personality as a gift from God. I don't want to say 'gift,' because that sounds so, I don't know, bold. But really, I think I am pretty personable and that I have to use this to make people who are new to IV feel comfortable. Now I'm totally comfortable at IV, but I want to remember how difficult it can be to fit in there sometimes."

14. It is possible that Steve chose to emphasize the historical authenticity of the Bible in his life history for my benefit. He may have assumed that because I am a scholar of religious studies, if he could persuade me to appreciate the veracity of these biblical accounts, then I would be encouraged to become a Christian. However, it seems to me that as he began to answer my question about how he had authenticated the events in the Bible, he became suddenly (or perhaps subconsciously) worried that my academic background (which actually includes only a limited familiarity with the historical issues he was addressing) would enable or incline me to question his assertions. Thus, his disorientation when faced with this question might be the result either (a) of concern that I might try to refute his commitments or (b) of his troubling recognition of the fideistic basis for these commitments.

15. See Harding for a discussion of the way fundamentalist rhetoric allows people to "make leaps of imagination across centuries, likening what happened to Jesus to what they experience today" (Harding 1994:153).

16. As I discuss in chapter 5 on women in the IVCF, deferring resolution of this issue is a common IVCF strategy.

17. Also evident in two of these narratives is the role of sexual activity and sexual violence within (respectively) Carole's and Gabrielle's life histories. The prominent role of sex in these two narratives may reflect a reason people are attracted to evangelicalism:

it provides other-worldly forgiveness and discipline for one's sexual excesses and comfort for one's sexual woundedness. Two men (Oliver and Lewis, whom I introduce in subsequent chapters) also spoke of traumatic sexual experiences as inspirations to become or continue to be Christians.

18. Ethnographer Susan Harding (1987; 1990; 1992) illustrates both what she describes as the biblical rhythm (1987) underlying evangelical styles of communicating the gospel and the biblical subtext and motifs evident in evangelical narratives. Because biblical stories have played a role in most IVCF members' lives, biblical themes emerge frequently in these students' life histories and my own conversations with them. Although the Bible is not the focus of this book, readers may be able to discern the connection between these students' comments and issues and stories rooted in the Bible.

19. Strozier's use of the word "fundamentalist" is very broad and would include almost every IVCF student I have met.

20. The crisis periods that often produce these internal bifurcations are not unique to evangelicals. On the contrary, as Lewis Rambo argues (1993), such predicaments are commonly associated with a wide variety of religious conversions and spiritual development.

21. During the two years I have known Steve, I have heard his "testimony," or story of his conversion, eight or nine times. I have heard two distinct versions. In one version, Steve emphasizes the active role of the Holy Spirit in directing him toward a certainty that God loves him and life has meaning. However, on other occasions, Steve tells another story in which he describes himself as a searcher who was not satisfied with the uncritical materialism of his non-Christian peers. Then Steve meets an evangelical friend who supplies convincing philosophical answers to virtually all of Steve's questions. Neither God nor the Holy Spirit is actively involved in this narrative. Rather, it is by the rational strength of his friend's answers that Steve decides to become a Christian. During a long and intimate conversation in Lithuania, I brought up the difference between these two stories. Steve explained that the exclusion of the Holy Spirit in the second version was purely accidental. However, the styles and contents of the stories are quite different, possibly suggesting that Steve may alter his testimony depending on the size and religious affiliations of his audience.

22. For many students, this second assertion could also be made from an emic or outsider's perspective, in that these members would agree that conversion also inevitably strengthens or at least clarifies one's relationships with all individuals and institutions.

23. See Behar (1993:19) for a discussion of the way life history ethnographers "snip" and "sew together" elements of an individual's life so they can be understood and heard as never before.

24. See Crapanzano (1980:139) for a discussion of this reflexive element of fieldwork. He writes: "Fieldwork must be understood within its temporal dimensions as a process of continual discovery and self-discovery. There is considerable truth in Paul Ricoeur's involuted definition . . . of the hermeneutic as 'the comprehension of self by the detour of the comprehension of the other.'"

NOTES TO CHAPTER THREE

1. See Sutton (1980) for an account of the role of speech, chant, and song in a Southern Baptist church.

2. "Outing" refers to the act of exposing another person's homosexual orientation without this person's consent. "Fly" means beautiful or sexy within the context of African

American youth culture. "Away" is a term Islanders use to refer to all places except Prince Edward Island.

3. For example, in an effort to problematize the conventional understandings of fundamentalists as simple-minded hillbillies, anthropologist Susan Harding writes, "Fundamentalists create themselves through their own cultural practices, but not exactly as they please. They are also constituted by modern discursive practices, an apparatus of thought that presents itself in the form of popular 'stereotypes,' media 'images,' and academic 'knowledge' " (1991:373). See Kapchan (1995:482) for a consideration of the ambiguous role of genre in performances. See Hanks (1987) for a study of the way colonial Mayans blended the discursive genres characteristic of Mayan and Spanish cultures. Such a process may be understood as a mixture of two sets of dramatic role expectations and narrative themes, the combination of two plays on one stage.

4. Jean Comaroff makes an analogous observation with respect to the "implicit" counterhegemonic discourses she studied in South Africa (1985:261).

5. Anthropologist Melinda Wagner argues that the use of this kind of rhetoric indicates that conservative Christians want "to sacralize the secular" (1990:104). Wagner's student participants were involved in an officially Christian institution, so her study differs significantly from mine. However, her observations about the ways evangelical students introduce traditional Christian language and customs into settings in which such forms would not normally be found are definitely helpful for understanding similar processes in the IVCF. Wagner explains that this form of rhetoric and the discursive traditions behind it also underline the human dependence on God (1990:201).

6. Evangelical author Paul Little quotes linguist Eugene Nida as describing these terms and practices as "Protestant Latin" (Nida in Little 1988:82).

7. Tedlock also discusses the criteria of the proper use of gestures, onomatopoeia, and the linking of the story to the context of its telling (1983:166).

8. According to ethnographer Jeff Todd Titon, the language unique to a particular religious group consists not merely of a body of knowledge about God but a body of lore (1988:205). Through learning lore, one acquires "know-how": one learns not simply about the nature of God but primarily about *how to get and stay in a relationship* with God. To extend the previous theatrical imagery above, one acquires rhetoric not simply to know *about* one's fellow performers or the divine playwright but to know *how* to relate to them. By using the rhetoric of a religious group earnestly and correctly, one, by definition, "draws closer to God." As Titon suggests, "to know this language is to know God" (1988:205).

9. For example, IVCF members differ with respect to their views on speaking in tongues, the role of women in the church and home, the status of other religions, drinking, the date of Christ's return, and the age of the earth. Sometimes these differences create significant tensions within the group. One former member told me that he "just couldn't handle the way they talked about Satan and homosexuals." Another member, Ron, a first-year student who is unsure if he wants to remain a part of the group, said, "Sometimes I get really frustrated with IV people. Sometimes I think they're all a bunch of hypocrites—you know, they say one thing and do another. If I leave, it'll be because of that."

10. However, there remain some unresolved differences of opinion with respect to worship styles. Some IVCF participants (for example, those influenced by the charismatic movement) raise their hands in the air and close their eyes during worship, while others (especially those from [noncharismatic] fundamentalist churches) have told me they are not comfortable with this practice.

11. Specifically, she belongs to the minority of IVCF students who could not re-member the specific time of their conversions.

12. See folklorist Elaine Lawless's article for a discussion of the nearly uniform and "formulaic" rhetorical performances of the Pentecostals she studied (1988:13).

13. I have never, for example, witnessed any IVCF member being "slain in the spirit," an experience which often involves falling down, convulsing, laughing, making animal sounds, or speaking in tongues. This behavior is associated with Pentecostal and neo-Pentecostal (or charismatic) groups such as the Toronto Airport Christian Fellow-ship. In Lithuania, I observed speaking in tongues at close range when I was alone with four Lithuanian evangelical students who broke into tongues in the middle of a unison Lithuanian prayer. Frankly, I was terrified until I realized what was happening—and even then I could not seem to regain my composure or return to my proverbial eth-nographic comfort zone. Contemporary Pentecostalism has its historical roots in Cali-fornia. See Harvey Cox (1995) for a history of this phenomenon. Cox argues that episodes of speaking in tongues, or glossolalia, represent the failure of ordinary spoken language to express ecstatic experience (1995:91). Glossolalia expresses the "language of the heart," the language beyond language (1995:120). Since the rise of the "Toronto Blessing," the gift of tongues has become a topic of debate among IVCF students. Several members of the IVCF (not all of whom would consider themselves charismatic) have experienced this gift of the Holy Spirit; this gift, however, is not given (or is not accepted) at IVCF events. Although I know that a few of the group leaders regularly pray in tongues, this fact is not widely known in the chapter. Glossolalia would be considered another form of IVCF rhetoric if not for the secrecy which surrounds its (probably limited) practice in the group. Speaking in tongues is still so controversial that it is kept at the margins of IVCF rhetoric.

14. Turner's *communitas*, an "unstructured . . . and relatively undifferentiated . . . community . . . of equal individuals" (1969:96), is also most clearly manifested during sung worship.

15. Writing about M. C. Hammer's music, Christian educators N. Lynn Westfield and Harold Dean Trulear suggest that Hammer's music "substitutes an individualistic form of self-transcendence for knowledge of God. . . . The aim of the form of spirituality represented by Hammer is to affirm the individual" (1994:221).

16. Two immediate limitations arise in attempting to use Harding's model in the present study. First, her focus is on the rhetoric associated with the attempt to convert or "witness to" non-Christians. Thus, one would expect the rhetoric she studies to reflect the goal-oriented missionary context of its deployment. However, the rhetoric she de-scribes is also evident among postconversion IVCF participants. The second possible limit to the usefulness of Harding's model for this study is that her work concerns a thoroughly fundamentalist group, whereas the IVCF includes both fundamentalists and evangelicals. However, members of these two wings of the IVCF are sufficiently similar in their religious outlook and use of language that Harding's insights can be applied to the group as a whole.

17. Related to the study of rhetoric is the analysis of the narratives and myths groups use to "tell their stories." Donald Heinz writes that the American "New Christian Right," the decentralized movement of conservative activist evangelicals and fundamentalists, is engaged in establishing a "counter mythology" to what they see as the prevailing nar-rative of "secular humanism" (1983:133).

18. These concepts and terms may also be too philosophically dense to be used as regular elements of intra- or extra-IVCF rhetoric. Thus, these terms are of little explicit rhetorical "use" to students who are, on the whole, not interested in theology as such.

For example, the Friday lunch meetings feature usually academic speakers who address a variety of theological and moral topics. Of all regular IVCF events, these meetings attract the smallest number of participants.

19. Note the similarities between Lewis's account and those of Gabrielle and Carole in chapter 2. For all three students, traumatic sexual experiences played major roles in their becoming Christians.

20. In many formal IVCF group settings, it is common to have at least one occasion in which the members of the group have an opportunity to share their testimonies. I witnessed several of these occasions. See chapters 2 and 7 for other discussions of testimonies.

21. The figures for the United States are roughly the same, although participation and membership rates are higher. The total number of people who could reasonably be called evangelicals or fundamentalists is also approximately two to three times higher in the Unites States. See Berger (1992); Finke (1992); Finke and Stark (1992); Roof (1996); Wuthnow (1988).

22. The common denominators among this small number of interviewees are that they are women and that they are ideologically liberal. There may be more people who are reluctant to use this term. I did not ask this question in my interviews but rather waited to hear if the participants would indicate explicitly or implicitly that they were uncomfortable with the word.

23. Stackhouse describes the difficult debates on the issue of whether Roman Catholics could be members of the IVCF and, if so, whether they could serve on the staff (1993:138–142). The decisions of the national IVCF board of directors "maintained the traditional Protestant evangelical character of IVCF" and made it clear that Catholics were not welcome to serve as staff members (1993:142). However, because the IVCF has historically always welcomed as student members anyone in agreement with its Basis of Faith and Statement of Purposes (which are not explicitly anti-Catholic), in principle, Catholic students may join the movement.

24. I asked Steve if he thought that IVCF members lived two lives, one in the secular ethos and the other in the evangelical one. He replied, "I wouldn't really say it was two lives. I'd say one life in two worlds." This division is the focus of chapter 4, on difference.

25. The necessarily privatized role to which religion is relegated as a result of the evangelical desire to live peacefully among non-Christians is consistent with Bibby's findings (1990, 1993).

26. An indication of the influence of substitutionary rhetoric (and of the IVCF) is the fact that three weeks after arriving in Lithuania, I started to use these alternative profanities as natural components of my own speech. This experience seems to support Harding's (1987) argument that evangelical rhetoric insinuates itself into one's subliminal mind.

27. Despite virtually unanimous objection to profanity, there is, as one might expect, some diversity of positions on the righteousness of the invented substitutes. Recently I posed the following question to Steve, who uses these alternative words regularly: "It's so obvious what you really mean when you say 'Frig you, man.' Why don't you just say it?" He replied, "I see what you mean, but I don't know . . . I just know it's different." In response to the same question, Jane, however, was more direct. "Yeah, I know. That's why I even try to avoid using words like 'chuck,' because whenever I hear the word 'chuck,' I can't help but think of that other word." See Peshkin (1986:206) for a discussion of a related conversation.

28. However, the concept of the kingdom of God continues to be the source of debates among these evangelicals. During one large group meeting, participants were

divided into three smaller groups to discuss the references to the kingdom of God in the Bible to determine, in part, whether the kingdom is something that was accomplished by Christ's life or that will come into being in the future. Near the end of this discussion, one participant said, "So what's the answer? No, seriously, there are enough of us here and we're smart enough and the Bible can't say two things at the same time. We should be able to come up with an answer to this question tonight." The group was unable to come to a consensus on the issue, but most of the members were willing to accept or at least unwilling to deny the president's suggestion that the kingdom might be both fully transcendent and immanent and that it might even include non-Christians in some way. There are, however, IVCF members who strongly reject this form of inclusivism and would limit their interpretations of children of God and kingdom of God to Christians.

29. See Tedlock for a discussion of Zuni speech patterns that set certain statements apart from others (1983:178–193).

NOTES TO CHAPTER FOUR

1. Nevertheless, let me explain some of these terms. The term "estrangement" is self-explanatory. The notions of difference and otherness have become increasingly significant elements of academic discourse since the rise of postmodernism in the humanities and social sciences in the 1970s. Both terms connote the deep awareness evangelicals have of the fissure between themselves and non-Christians. On the philosophical and social scientific notions of otherness and difference, see Baxter (1982), Clifford and Marcus (1986), Geertz (1994), Harding (1991), Levinas (1969), Simpson (1996), and Wilmsen and McAllister (1996). The other word I employ to connote otherness is "alienation," a term with a rich and convoluted history. The term appears most commonly in the context of Marxist analyses of modern societies in which workers are said to be alienated from nature, the means of production, their fellow workers, their products, and finally, themselves (Baum 1975; Marx 1956). Although this ethnography is not Marxist in orientation, there is in Marx's concept of "alienation" the germ of the contemporary non-Marxist use of the term. The way I employ the word "alienation" lacks the Marxist focus on political economy and the Hegelian focus on the synthetic overcoming of alienation (Baxter 1982:115) but borrows from Marx the more rudimentary notion of separateness. Although the concept of alienation is still laden with Marxist connotations, I use the term alongside "difference" and "otherness" to denote a general sense of separateness. Thus modified, the term captures the essence of many IVCF students' comments about their experiences of otherness at McMaster.

2. On the postmodern redefinition of power, see Foucault (1990:92).

3. Some non-Christian undergraduates also feel diminished in relation to the university, which appears to be a large, seemingly unsympathetic and immutable institution. See Hallen (1983) for a discussion of the alienation derived from the disharmony between the egalitarian rhetoric of education and the authoritarian structures of academic life.

4. Other interpreters of evangelicalism have commented on this phenomenon. Harvey Cox argues that most scholars of Pentecostalism missed the "double-barrelled disillusionment" that these evangelicals experienced: disenchantment about the failures of science, progress, and modern culture, as well as the shortcomings of traditional religion (1995:104). Karen McCarthy Brown writes that evangelicals are under a "double attack" from the "general stress of our time" and the "direct challenges to their faith" in the form of higher criticism and evolution (1994:179). Finally, in response to the question

of why fundamentalism has become so visible and belligerent, Martin Marty suggests that the movement is a response to the mixed offerings of modernity and the values crisis in America (1987:316), the first of which correlates with what I call "general estrangement" and the second with the main source of evangelicals' criticism of modern culture.

5. The only consistent expression of occupational optimism comes from IVCF engineering students or from students who intend eventually to take over thriving family businesses.

6. At the end of 1996, the overall Canadian unemployment rate for youth aged fifteen to twenty-four was 16.1% (Government of Canada 1997). For an alternative account of the changes Foot and Stoffman describe, see Bridges (1994). For an overview of the larger economic forces behind our tumultuous era, see Galbraith (1992).

7. In fact, the group this term designates is technically a "cohort" and not a complete generation.

8. There are significant differences between Coupland's original Generation X and the baby boomers' children in university in the 1990s (Foot and Stoffman 1996:22). Younger members of the current catchall Generation X were warned from an early age that their lives would be difficult, that they would have to market themselves and be highly adaptable. Most of the members of Coupland's original Generation X were raised without such encouragements to entrepreneurialism, largely because an education at that point was still perceived as a guarantee of future success. For a fictional profile of the world of the younger siblings of the original Generation X members, see Coupland's *Shampoo Planet* (1993).

9. On the social-scientific tendency to reduce others to exotic stereotypes—in short, to ignore the "voice" (Clifford 1986) of the other—see Fabian (1983), Marcus and Fischer (1986), and Said (1978).

10. For believers, my analysis might help answer questions such as whether God exists, whether the Holy Spirit is responsible for the growth and vitality of the McMaster IVCF, whether students are in fact drawing closer to God as a result of the IVCF, and whether Satan is actually engaged in trying to undermine the group's members' faith.

11. Wilcox's study (1992) of the causes of support for the "new Christian right" (NCR) in the United States represents one exception to this general theme. He argues that alienation is not a source of support for the NCR (and thus, one might extrapolate, for evangelicalism). Unfortunately, Wilcox's data were mostly collected in the 1970s, before the public resurgence of politically active evangelicals (the constituents of the NCR) under the auspices of the Moral Majority. As well, Wilcox claims that there is no evidence that NCR supporters understand the world as a struggle between good and evil. This assertion contradicts not only Ammerman's findings (1987:63) but also my own observations and interviews with IVCF members.

12. During an interview in my basement office at McMaster, Frank commented, "I mean look at that [Baptist] dedication upstairs about what this university used to be about. Since then we've floundered." The dedication is carved in stone on the main wall of the foyer in University Hall, the building which presently houses the Philosophy and Religious Studies departments. It reads:

"This university, named after its founder and first benefactor, the Honourable William McMaster . . . , was incorporated . . . in the year of our Lord, eighteen hundred and eighty-seven. Responsibility for the conduct of the foundation was assumed in the following year by the Convention of the Baptist Churches of Ontario and Quebec. . . . The privileges of the university are offered to all without restriction, in order that youth may receive a liberal education in a Christian atmosphere and be duly qualified for the service of God and mankind."

Although the privileges of the university were supposedly offered without restriction, readers may remember the senate's 1909 restrictions (cf. chapter 1) on classroom content. The senate wrote: "While complete freedom should be accorded in the investigation and discussion of facts, no theory should be taught which fails to give its proper place to supernatural revelation or which would impair in any way the supreme authority of the Lord Jesus Christ" (Rawlyk 1992:287).

13. John 6:69 records Peter saying to Jesus, "We have come to believe and know that you are the Holy One of God."

14. This is a good example of what Peter Berger described as "cognitive bargaining" (1992:41).

15. As an engineering student, Kirk may never actually have to face the challenges of evolutionary theory directly during his academic career. Nevertheless, his approach represents an example of fortress-maintaining "cognitive retrenchment" (Berger 1992:43).

16. Just as most atheist students have not read Feuerbach, Freud, Nietzsche, or Marx, most evangelical students are not conversant with the theological and philosophical ideas which would help to convey their beliefs or religious experiences credibly to their non-Christian peers and professors. This observation correlates with similar tendencies noted by Ammerman in her ethnography of conservative Protestantism in the United States. She writes that "the notion that everything (painful or not) can be explained by reference to God's will is more important to [the participants] than a logically consistent theory" (1987:65).

17. As I explained in chapter 1, "cognitive contamination" refers to the pollution and relativization of one's worldview resulting from interactions with plausible "other" or non-Christian perspectives (Berger 1992).

18. Another strategy for dealing with the challenges of evolutionary theory is to postpone deciding how to fit evolutionary evidence into one's creationist framework. As I explain in chapter 5, IVCF women employ an analogous strategy to deal with the challenges of the feminist critique of patriarchal traditions such as evangelicalism.

19. See, for example, his contentious recent position on the possible inclusivity of salvation, articulated in *More Than One Way?* (1995). Pinnock has been involved with the IVCF since the 1950s and since the mid-1980s has been Buff Cox's academic and personal advisor.

20. Thanks to Pinnock's interest in my project, I also had the good fortune to be able to extensively discuss the group and my thesis with him at the retreat.

21. The following is a brief summary of Pinnock's four arguments against metaphysical naturalism, which the scope of this chapter does not permit me to analyze. First, metaphysical naturalism narrows truth by limiting students' speculation to the empirical realm. Second, it discriminates against nonnaturalistic voices and thus forsakes the pluralism on which liberal academic inquiry is supposedly based. Third, it weakens society, in that a culture such as ours without transcendence and faith is likely to decline. Fourth, metaphysical naturalism is a hindrance to evangelism.

22. For example, Pinnock mentioned the following arguments in favor of Christianity and against metaphysical naturalism: that human experience is better explained by

Christianity, that religion is basic to all humans, that metaphysical naturalism cannot explain human imagination, the historicity of Jesus' resurrection, and the transformative effect that salvation has on individuals' lives.

23. In this regard, Pinnock suggested similar campaign tactics to the picketing, letter writing, boycotts, and petitioning employed by gays and lesbians, ethnic minorities, and the disabled. The IVCF students were noticeably surprised by and resistant to his suggestions that they should make public their opposition to the secular biases of the university.

24. George Marsden (1982:163) and George Grant (1986:68) observe that evangelicalism and fundamentalism are perfectly suited to the technological impetus so central to North American culture. This strand of our culture does not present evangelicals with significant problems because it does not require individuals engaging in it to explore the presuppositions of a particular technology. In Mark Noll's (1994) study of the role of evangelicals in contemporary intellectual life, he demonstrates that evangelical academics often avoid more abstract theoretical work, opting instead for more discrete pragmatic studies.

25. During interviews, I asked participants to estimate the approximate percentage of their McMaster friends associated with the IVCF. Participants were also asked to estimate the percentage of all their (McMaster-related and non-McMaster-related) friends who are Christians. Hope answered "70%" to the first question and "80%" to the second. Another Canadian Reformed participant answered these questions with "80%" and "90%," respectively; a woman with a Brethren background answered "95%" and "95%," respectively. The reluctance to maintain large numbers of non-Christian friendships is typical of fundamentalist members of the IVCF.

26. Full dinners cost approximately six Canadian dollars.

27. The money required for this trip (approximately $3,000) was raised individually and then pooled before we left Canada. This system allowed one person in the team to manage all of the expenses for the entire team.

28. See Government of Canada (1994) and also Carroll (1995).

29. See Government of Canada (1990) and also Carroll (1995), Salts (1994), and Woodruff (1986).

30. The tendency for IVCF students to seek "refuge" in the chapter is not, however, without its critics within the group. During an interview, Harriet, one of the few liberal evangelicals in the chapter, commented, "A lot of people use IV as a hideout from the real world of conflict and challenge and pain." Similarly, Ron, the most politically and theologically liberal member I met during fieldwork, commented that he was irritated because "a lot of people who are conservatives or fundamentalists use IV as a refuge to hide their conservative ideas instead of going out into the world where these ideas can be challenged. That really bugs me."

31. These prayer meetings are held in a university lounge and include singing, directed Bible reading, and prayer exercises.

32. Friendship evangelism refers to the nonconfrontational approach to witnessing in which the gospel is shared only in the context of a healthy friendship, but conversion is not the sole purpose of this relationship.

33. Moreover, Berger and Luckmann contend that ritual may play a general role in maintaining the plausibility of a worldview or symbolic universe which is perceived as being under siege: "In crisis situations the procedures are essentially the same as in routine maintenance, except that the reality confirmations have to be explicit and intensive. Frequently, ritual techniques are brought into play. While the individual may improvise reality-maintaining procedures in the face of crisis, the society itself sets up

specific procedures for situations recognized as involving the risk of a breakdown in reality" (1966:175).

34. Although Turner is vague about the potential duration of liminal periods, sociologist Bernice Martin (1979) argues plausibly that youths may be considered to be moving through a liminal stage that extends over a period of several years. Extending her argument to the university environment, undergraduates may be considered liminal during their entire three or four years at university.

35. See Grimes (1990) and Turner (1974) for a discussion of the dramatic nature of rituals.

36. Turner defines *communitas* as an unstructured or loosely structured model for human living in which interaction between individuals is not hierarchically ordered and often leads to some form of egalitarian "communion" (1969:96).

37. Mellonee Burnim refers to the saying of prayers as a means by which one can transform an explicitly secular setting into a "consecrated milieu" (1989:58).

38. During one small group meeting, we discussed non-Christians' opinions of evangelicals. Barbara, a science student, admitted that she:

> used to be called 'church girl' in high school. But in the Bible, it says 'Blessed are you who are persecuted in my name.' This makes me feel better, for sure. . . . And in university I feel different than other people because I try to do what the Bible says—especially about drinking and sex and bars and all that. This sometimes pulls me away from people. But this [alienation] is okay, because I know I'm going the right way and that in the end I will get a huge reward—eternal life and the chance to meet God and be with him forever.

39. Note the difference between this assertion and the suggestion that they maintain this belief in God's plan because it helps them to cope.

NOTES TO CHAPTER FIVE

1. Since many evangelical churches operate with a fair degree of autonomy from their denominational organizations, there may be some exceptions to these generalizations.

2. See Bibby (1993:216), Brinkerhoff and Mackie (1985), Bruland (1989), Brown (1994), and Patterson (1988:62).

3. For interpretations of the voluntary involvement of women in religious traditions that exclude women from official avenues of power, see Bendroth (1993), Bruland (1989), Davidman (1991), Ozorak (1996), and Patterson (1980).

4. See Harvey Cox's (1995:125) discussion of Aimee Semple McPherson, a Pentecostal preacher who represents one such exception.

5. As Epstein (1981) and Hardesty (1984) observe, the changes in the gender definitions built into North American Protestantism and the surrounding culture are not confined to the present century.

6. See Finson (1995) for a historical account of the development of feminist liberation theology. See Backhouse and Flaherty (1992) for a history of the women's movement in Canada and the United States. For an account of the challenges women face in the academic world, see Caplan (1993).

7. See also Barron (1990); Ehrenreich, Hess, and Jacobs (1986); Kersten (1994); and Spretnak (1982).

8. Karen McCarthy Brown argues that the marginalization of women within evan-

gelicalism is an extreme manifestation of a continuous pattern of male dominance evidenced in all other Christian denominations (1994:175). According to McCarthy Brown, evangelicals are determined to maintain control over women as a means of defending traditional Christian beliefs and values. See Balmer (1994:49) and Byle Bruland (1989: 140–144) for discussions of the transformation of the depiction of women within Protestantism (and elsewhere): from temptresses before the eighteenth century to delicate personifications of virtue by the nineteenth century.

9. I distinguish between the ordination and leadership of women because the former is beginning to be accepted by certain congregations and denominations but acceptance of the latter does not necessarily follow. For example, Convention Baptist congregations may choose to exclude women from senior leadership positions, even though their governing body permits female leadership (Anderson and Clarke 1990:94). As well, Bibby observes that Canadian Pentecostals permit the ordination of women but that potential female pastors have difficulty finding employment (1993:217; cf. Anderson and Clarke 1990:95).

10. Martina, a science student, was the only IVCF participant to describe herself as a feminist. "Yeah, and I'm a Christian feminist. Most IVers think this is an oxymoron. I've had some very *serious* conversations with IV people about this whole issue. I feel tolerated by them, even though some of them do try to prove I'm wrong."

11. Bellous, a respected member of the evangelical intellectual community, is also the mother of one of the most influential members of the chapter. During the meeting in question, Bellous argued that there is an apparent contradiction in the Bible between the universality implied in the Galatians passage and the strict hierarchy implied in the excerpt from Timothy. The IVCF fundamentalists tend to favor and quote the latter text, while more liberal evangelicals embrace the former. According to Bellous, the Galatians text is applicable to modern life because it appears to be a radical principle aimed at undoing the structure of first-century society (and would be thus typical of Jesus' radicalism on other issues). The Timothy passage, Bellous argued, is aimed at a specific problem within a specific church and is thus not applicable to modern Christians.

12. One male participant at this meeting contended that since woman was derived from Adam's rib, Paul's comments in Timothy should be obeyed. In response, Professor Bellous offered an alternative interpretation of the creation story and followed it with an almost cursory observation that the questioner was obviously predisposed toward his interpretation because he is a man, and she toward hers because she is a woman. The student seemed stunned. "That's a cultural interpretation of the Bible," he said. "I've never thought of that before. Wow."

13. See Stacey and Gerard (1990) for an account of the interpenetration of evangelicalism and feminism. See Fowler (1986) and Bendroth (1993) for discussions of the role of feminism and women within evangelicalism and fundamentalism.

14. See also Gilligan (1982), Hubbard (1988), Keller (1985), and Spanier (1984).

15. Evangelical men, however, are not as affected by these components because these elements of the modern university presuppose men's rights and moral autonomy, beliefs already entrenched in male evangelical gender roles.

16. See Wagner (1990:84–89) for a discussion of other metaphors used in Christian schools to "describe (and bring about) the desired relationship with God."

17. See Government of Canada (1990), Carroll (1995), Salts (1994), and Woodruff (1986).

18. See Patterson (1980); Stacey and Gerard (1990), and Shapiro Davie (1995); cf. Davidman (1991).

19. Since the interviews I conducted were completely confidential and students often told me quite intimate stories, I have no reason to believe that men would have withheld this motivation from me.

20. Two closely related minor controversies that arose during the academic year when I conducted fieldwork revolved around whether communion should be performed at IVCF events (as it was at the winter retreat and the final large group meeting) and whether it should be performed by a woman (as it was, in both cases, by Buff Cox, an ordained Baptist clergy member). The IVCF fundamentalists were opposed both to communion outside a formal church setting and to a woman presiding over the ritual but nevertheless participated in both communions.

21. I presented a version of this chapter during a public lecture at the University of Winnipeg, more than two thousand kilometers from McMaster. Just moments before I began speaking, Mary unexpectedly entered the room and sat in a desk in the middle of the audience of twenty-five people. Given that this lecture was the pivotal part of an interview for a tenure-track job at the university, I was more than a little worried about how she might react when she heard her own words read in public. At the beginning of the question period, she raised her hand. With some trepidation I invited her to speak. "Hi. I'm Mary in his lecture," she said, addressing the audience, "and I've left the group because of some of the things he talked about." We continued to talk about this issue in this public forum, but soon I determined that we would need to continue the conversation after the lecture. During the ensuing conversation, I learned that Mary had left not only the IVCF but also McMaster and Ontario. She told me she had transferred to the University of Winnipeg. I asked her if she had joined the IVCF group at her new university, and she replied that she had not. Since her comments during the question period suggested she had experienced a crisis of faith as a function of her own theological liberalization, I asked her if she had considered joining the university's liberal Student Christian Movement chapter (cf. chapter 1). Mary shrugged her shoulders and replied, "No, that doesn't work for me either. I've either got to be totally in or totally out, you know?"

22. For a discussion of a "vernacular community" in which women can consider complex and ambiguous experiences in a safe (yet controlled) setting, see Jody Shapiro Davie's (1995) ethnography on a women's discussion group in a suburban Presbyterian community.

23. It is difficult to hypothesize with which "side" of the issue the women I interviewed will eventually sympathize after they leave McMaster. Sometimes an IVCF member would seem to be using her four years at McMaster as an opportunity for a symbolic rebellion against her family, which will likely be followed by a prodigal daughter's return to her original tradition. However, for other women, the IVCF appeared to represent an experimental atmosphere for the egalitarian ideals these women intend to adopt in the future. Only a longitudinal study could determine which "side" these women will eventually embrace.

NOTES TO CHAPTER SIX

1. See Snow and Machalek (1982) for a discussion of the possible social-scientific fallacies underlying the sort of experience I had when discussing Satan and his demons. Specifically, Snow and Machalek suggest that scholars are surprised by some of the beliefs they encounter because they presuppose not only that doubt is natural whereas belief is unnatural but also that the maintenance of certain supposedly unconventional beliefs requires more cognitive effort than the maintenance of

conventional beliefs or disbelief. On the contrary, Snow and Machalek argue, "in daily existence, however, it is doubt, not belief that is typically suspended" (1982:24).

2. See Pagels (1995:xviii, 180); 2 Cor 11:15. For a historical and philosophical account of Satan and his demons throughout Western history, see Nugent (1983). For a discussion of the pre-Christian era and the first several centuries of the Christian period, see Forsyth (1987).

3. "Spiritual warfare" is used to denote both the war between angels and demons for influence over humans and the human contribution to this ongoing battle. According to evangelical novelist Frank Peretti, whose major novel I discuss in this chapter, one of the main human contributions to this ongoing war is prayer. In *This Present Darkness*, the final confrontation between angels and demons cannot commence until humans, or praying "saints" (1986:328) and "the remnant" (1986:349) provide sufficient "prayer cover" (1986:328; cf. Guelich 1991:56). For a scholarly evangelical account of the relationship between "spiritual warfare" and the New Testament, see Guelich (1991). For a popular evangelical discussion of this phenomenon, see Robb (1993).

4. Harvey Cox admits that while reading contemporary evangelical books on Satan, he had the "sinking feeling" that evangelicals are turning Lewis's subtle metaphor into a stiff metaphysic, and that "a story had been turned into an ideology" (1995:285). For a discussion of (and incitement to) spiritual warfare that closely resembles what Lewis seems to have had in mind when he described the spiritual realm, see Andrew Walker (1987).

5. In social science, the New Age movement may be defined as "a broad cultural ideology, a development of the countercultural sixties, which privileges holistic medicine, 'intuitive sciences' like astrology and tarot, ecological and anti-nuclear political issues, and alternative therapies, medicines and philosophers" (Luhrmann 1989:30). Anthropologist Loring Danforth comments that "the ultimate goal of New Age healing is self-realization" (1989:255). According to many of the evangelicals I met, New Age movements are inspired or even directly controlled by Satan.

6. Harvey Cox argues that *This Present Darkness* is not propelled by its plot. Rather, the novel is "about cosmology; it is a gazetteer of the angelic and demonic domains" (1995:283).

7. Peretti's novels are often ridiculed by evangelical intellectuals. During a recent discussion about *This Present Darkness*, an evangelical colleague rolled his eyes and said, "Man, sometimes I think that book is more popular than the Bible. I'm not kidding. It's bizarre."

8. Popular culture scholar Jay Howard observes that *This Present Darkness* inaugurated the beginning of a massive shift in the Christian retailing industry. In 1980, not a single novel ranked in the top ten titles listed by the Christian Booksellers Association's trade magazine. By 1990, however, half the titles on this list were popular novels, largely as a result of the success of Peretti's books and other novels portraying a similar cosmology (1994:193). On the evangelical relationship with North American popular culture, see Wagner (1990:131).

9. Demons of complacency and despair cling to human legs and clasp human organs, making the person feel weighed down or anxiety-stricken (Peretti 1986:42); angels reach over and physically touch a human conspirator, causing him to drop hidden ballots (1986:103); a demon of sickness slashes at an artery in an old woman's brain to cause a stroke (1986:104); an angel suggests that a person look behind a particular building (1986:10); demons speak "sweet words of comfort to [the] mind" of a misguided woman (1986:119) and cover the ears of a man, preventing him from hearing the

preacher (1986:231); demons take possession of and speak through humans (1986:319) and stall car engines by piercing the hoods with their swords (1986:139); and perhaps most insidiously, demons gently coax and manipulate humans to embrace ideas and values that would broaden Satan's dominion in the world. In his discussion of Peretti's novel, Wayne Booth notes that "though angelic and demonic forces can and do affect material events directly, their power is curiously and inconsistently limited" (1995:382).

10. By clinical depression, I mean to denote more than the short periods of lethargy commonly associated with the term "depression." The symptoms of clinical depression (fatigue, insomnia, loss of appetite, loss of interest in pleasure, agitation, guilt, low self-esteem) are similar to those of common depression, but in the former condition, the symptoms often do not abate when one's life conditions improve. For the sake of brevity, the term "depression" will be employed here instead of "clinical depression." The authors of the *Diagnostic and Statistical Manual of Mental Disorders* IV report studies that indicate between 10 and 25% of the population suffer from depression (American Psychiatric Association 1992:341; cf. Hagarty 1995). According to the authors of the *Merck Manual of Diagnosis and Therapy*, "The higher vulnerability of women to depression is customarily traced to their presumed greater affiliative nature, passive-dependence, and helplessness in controlling their destiny in male-oriented societies. However, biological vulnerabilities are at least as relevant. . . . Once depressed, women would have a greater difficulty recovering from their episodes" (Beers, Berkow, and Fletcher 1992: 1596).

11. It is even more difficult to determine the significance of the fact that none of the IVCF men I interviewed described themselves as depressed.

12. Similarly, when I asked Gabrielle whether she believed in angels and demons, she replied, "You sure don't ask easy questions. Yeah, I definitely do. And Peretti helped me to see how they work. I just fall on my knees and ask God for help and say I can't do this alone and then—I know this sounds cheesy—angels come to my aid. Both Satan and God have their angels. Satan is like the general who says to his demons, you go here, you go there."

13. Anxiety is another affective state that IVCF members sometimes (though less commonly) perceive to be an "attack of Satan." This sort of demonic effort has the opposite effects of spiritual attacks resulting in depression. In the case of anxiety attacks, students become frantic and are driven to study and work more than they normally would, without their usual focus, and without taking any breaks. Sometimes this anxiety lacks a specific academic theme. For example, in response to my question about the ways Satan affects his life, Howard commented, "Like sometimes, for example, I'll wake up in the middle of the night, sweating, and worried, overcome by anxiety. When this happens, I just pray that Satan will leave me alone and then almost immediately the fear vanishes and I can get back to sleep. I know that might sound strange to you, but it happens that quickly." A few minutes later, Howard noted, "A lot of my ideas on this come from Peretti."

14. In an apparent (and successful) attempt to heal any rift that might have developed between us during this conversation, Carrie added: "But there are lots of good people who are New Agers. I don't think we have to hold them totally responsible for their actions, since there is so much more going on there."

15. After this interchange, I felt completely deflated. The issue of the possible inclusivity of God is an issue of considerable personal as well as academic interest to me, and at that moment I believed Oliver and I stood on opposite sides of an untraversable chasm. Moreover, I felt—and deeply resented—the weight of his and Cindy's harsh judgment on nonevangelical religiosity. Throughout my fieldwork with the IVCF, I felt

as if I was attached to one end of an elastic band and the group to the other. At times, I would feel very strongly affiliated with and protective of the group; at other times after conversations such as the one I have just described, I could feel myself hurtling out from the group's core at a ninety-degree angle.

16. In fact, by this time in the mission, two members of the team had told me that they had experienced significant conflicts with Janice over her leadership style.

17. Peter Berger writes, "The sacred cosmos, which transcends and includes man in its ordering of reality, thus provides man's ultimate shield against the terror of anomy. To be in a 'right' relationship with the sacred cosmos is to be protected against the nightmare threats of chaos" (1967:26, 32; cf. Berger and Luckmann 1966:116).

18. See also Berger and Luckmann (1966:123). Among several IVCF students, I found a more complex form of the attitude Ammerman describes. After attributing self-doubt and lust to Satan, Janice, for example, admitted, "Not every bad thing that happens in life is from Satan, though. Like cancer and falling off my bike—that's just life." Janice's comments were typical of several of the minority of more liberal IVCF students I interviewed. These liberal participants distinguish between three sorts of events: (1) good occurrences that happen because God, angels, or humans act in harmony with God's plan; (2) negative phenomena that happen because Satan, demons, or humans ignore God's plan; and (3) negative or neutral experiences that happen as a result of accidents or human weaknesses. In other words, some IVCF students recognize a category of day-to-day experience for which nonhuman actors are not significantly responsible. Nevertheless, even events in this third category are the ultimate consequences of the original sin committed by Adam and Eve. Simon's comment reflects this more fundamental involvement of Satan in human life: "The world is Satan's domain, so therefore, the things we see around us are often from him. All thoughts are either from God or Satan. Even the so-called natural lustful thoughts are from the Devil. There is no lukewarm between the Devil and God."

19. During a conversation about demons, Sheryl, a second-year science student, told me the following story:

> When I was fifteen, I found a lump in my breast. There is a long history of breast cancer in my family. When I found this lump I felt a lot of anger and fear, and I think because I dwelt on these feelings for so long, I opened myself up to demonic influences from Fear and Anger. Then I went to a conference and asked my mother and another woman to pray over me, and they said they felt themselves going up against the spirits of Fear and Anger. Then I went to the washroom and checked myself, and just like that the lump was gone. I was so happy I went on stage at the conference and gave a testimonial right there and then. And then the next morning I woke up and discovered that the lump had returned. But that was okay because I knew that God loved me and that he had a plan for me, so I had a real sense of peace about the lump.

Later in the conversation, Sheryl observed, "I had found out that the tumor was benign before mom and the other lady prayed over me, but obviously I had a lot of anger and fear I had not dealt with by the then." In Sheryl's recounting of her story, perhaps to underscore God's potency, she does not mention the benign status of the lump until she has told her story of how God appeared to have removed the lump altogether. Even when she rediscovered the benign lump the next day, she still believed that the prayers against the demonic spirits of Fear and Anger were effective because she "had a real sense of peace about the lump." She also said, "On the day I had the benign lump removed, I remember being terrified. But then I remembered that my mom had told me that whenever I am scared I should just pray for God's help. So, as I was going into surgery, I just asked Jesus for help and immediately, the fear was gone."

20. See Bibby (1993), Finke (1992), Rawlyk (1996), and Wuthnow (1988).

21. See chapter 1 for a discussion of "differentiation" as an alternative to this secularization argument. I argue that even though religion continues to exist in "clubs" at McMaster, it exists on the merely tolerated periphery of the university system as a whole.

22. Describing the "disenchantment of the world," Weber writes: "Precisely the ultimate and most sublime values have retreated from public life either into the transcendental realm of mystic life or into the brotherliness of direct and personal human relations" (1948:155). According to Weber, the "prophetic *pneuma*, which in former times swept through the great communities like a firebrand," is evident only "in personal human situations, in *pianissimo*" (1948:155).

23. See Ammerman (1990), Cox (1995), Hammond (1983), and Wilcox (1992).

24. The scholars cited in this paragraph study religion in the United States. However, although the relationship between evangelicalism and Canadian culture has generally been less antagonistic than that between evangelicalism and American culture (Gauvreau 1991; Stackhouse 1993), the evangelicals with whom I have spoken about "contemporary culture" often describe it in polemical terms.

25. Explaining the rise of Protestant fundamentalism in the United States, Nancy Ammerman writes: "Threatened by secular humanism — not just as a deceiver stealing individual souls but as an aggressive institutional opponent encroaching on the territory they had created — they were ready to fight back" (1991:55).

26. See Martin Luther's hymn "A Mighty Fortress is Our God," quoted in Russell (1988:172):

> A mighty fortress is our God,
> A good weapon and defense;
> He helps us in every need
> That we encounter. . . .
> The Prince of this world,
> However fierce he claims to be,
> Can do us no harm;
> His power is under judgement;
> One little word can fell him.

27. There is a range of IVCF opinion about the role of the demonic realm in the lives of non-Christians. Some consider that demons of complacency, atheism, and pride have directly encouraged students to be non-Christians; others argue that demons have more generally contributed to a culture that leads individuals to choose to be non-Christians. Most students do not have a precise opinion on this issue but tend to alternate between these two positions.

28. For example, some IVCF participants engage in "intercessory prayers," in which one person prays to defend a second person from Satan's attacks.

29. Again, salvation is always available to all people, even those who are being demonically tormented. Peretti describes several cases of this divine accessibility. (In *This Present Darkness*, Marshall Hogan, Bobby Corsi, and Carmen Fraser are all demonically afflicted and then saved.)

30. I found myself interpreting other aspects of my experience according to this dimension of the evangelical worldview. For example, I normally experience one migraine headache approximately every three months. However, during the five weeks I spent writing the present chapter, I suffered six migraines. When I told an evangelical

friend about this increase, he raised his eyebrows, smiled, and said, "Maybe it's not a coincidence, Paul."

31. In fact, Guelich argues that Peretti's version of spiritual warfare "risks turning the 'Prince of Peace' into the 'Commander-in-Chief,' a role that fits the messianic expectation of Jewish apocalyptic eschatology more than the Christology of the Gospels and the Pauline corpus" (1991:63).

NOTES TO CHAPTER SEVEN

1. Thus, they have in mind a fairly clear conception of what Melinda Wagner (borrowing from Wallace[1966]) calls the conservative Christian "goal culture" and the precise ways in which this differs from the "existing culture" (1990:20).

2. For a description of the impact of foreign missions on social change, see Jon Miller (1993). For a discussion of some of the common stereotypes of Christian missionaries, see Burridge (1991:25). In defense of these foreign witnesses, anthropologist and missionary A. R. Tippett writes:

> Missiology has come through a devastating period of criticism. Missiologists have been brutally maligned. Dedicated people who believed they were responding to a divine call have been pictured as egotistical morons by novelists and other critics who never did or could stand in their shoes. And in response to these attacks, missionaries have been made to feel so guilty that they have often responded with self-flagellation far beyond what has been called for. (1983:127)

3. For an example of the former, see Malinowski (1922). For an example of the latter, see Clifford (1986), Crapanzano (1980), and Marcus and Fischer (1986).

4. For a discussion of the ambiguous relationship between anthropologists and missionaries, see Luzbetak (1983) and Sutlive (1983).

5. On the former, see Rawlyk (1988) and Stackhouse (1993). On the latter, see Marsden (1991), Noll (1992), and Rawlyk, Bebbington, and Noll (1994).

6. Rawlyk attributes this disintegration to contemporary consumerism, "the insidious antithesis to essential Christianity. . . . Consumerism, in a profound sense, cut the essential heart out of the evangelical consensus and out of revivalism" (1988:136).

7. See Hefner (1993:6) for a discussion of the origin of this impulse in nineteenth-century enlightenment sensibilities.

8. For a discussion of the biblical basis for witnessing, see Adams (1993).

9. Four of the thirteen small groups studied popular evangelical books on topics such as witnessing, prayer during busy periods of life, elements of Christian belief, and miracles. The other nine small groups had the following titles: Conflicts, Priorities, and Fine Lines; Sex and the Christian Relationship; Difficult Christian Issues; Young Life — Meeting Teens Where They're at; The Book of Romans; What Did HE Say?; Understanding Our Position in Christ ("Just for Girls"); Running the RACE in Real Life; and A Study of John 15:5.

10. On the cover of the book is a quotation from Billy Graham: "A tremendous help in witnessing." At the beginning of our first small group, one of the members said, "Well, I don't know about you, but if Billy Graham likes it, it must be good enough for us." At the top right-hand corner of the book is a graphical insert: "One million copies in print!"

11. See Musteikas (1988) and Gerutis (1969) for a history of this and the following Reformation periods. See Senn (1959) for an account of the more recent history. All

information on Lithuania in this chapter is derived from these texts, the country's official Internet Website (neris.mii.lt/serveriai/bendra/servers.html) and my own experience. Also invaluable was an unpublished essay about the history of Christianity in Lithuania, written for a class in McMaster's Divinity College by Reverend Steve Cox, a former IVCF missionary in Lithuania.

12. One of the reasons Roman Catholicism may be so popular is that the church resisted the Soviet Union's dominance.

13. According to Shawn, a Canadian missionary, because Lithuanians now have access to numerous sources of information about Western ideas and ideologies, their previously wholesale embrace of the West has waned somewhat since the country's independence. This Canadian missionary commented, "It used to be that I could walk into a university, set up a [Christian information] table and wave a few Canadian flags, and I'd have fifty people crowded all around me, wanting to hear all about North America. Now I'm lucky if I talk to ten people in a whole afternoon. By now they've seen it all already, or at least they think they have, and they aren't as interested."

14. See Ammerman (1987, 1990), Balmer (1989), and Marty (1987).

15. One night while the team waited at the bus stop after a Lithuanian folk music and dancing evening, we were approached by a group of about ten very inebriated Lithuanian men in their late twenties. When they noticed us (which did not require great perspicacity since three of the ten of us are not white), one of them stumbled around us menacingly, alternately leering at the women in the group, singing, and making comic faces. Suddenly his countenance was transformed as he began to address the team. "Why are you come here?" he asked. "To get to know Lithuanians," Steve replied, trying to avert a potentially violent situation. "But why here? Why don't you go to Germany or Italy or Greece? Lithuania is shit now. Look around—we haven't money or jobs or anything," he said as he motioned toward the main city square, picturesque by North American standards. He continued, "We are on our knees now after the Russians leave. Why don't you come back in ten or twenty years once we are better country? Now there is nothing here to see."

16. For a discussion of the resilience of minority groups in the allegedly totalizing hegemonic discourse of Western capitalist culture, see Simpson (1996).

17. Jongeneel and Van Engelen write: "This theology has become one of the most significant missiological currents, one that has found a firm place of acceptance not only in the [The World Council of Churches—a relatively liberal ecumenical assembly of Christian churches] (which established, along with a Division for World Mission and Evangelism, a Division for Dialogue), but also in the Roman Catholic Church" (1995: 453).

18. However, Jongeneel and Van Engelen comment, "In the evangelical movement, protests have been registered against the theology of 'dialogue' just as against the theology of 'presence.' There is no objection to these words as such. The problem is, rather, that they often serve as replacements for key words of Scripture" (1995:454).

19. See Hunter (1985) for a discussion of the ways evangelicalism has been made more palatable to non-Christians.

20. Fortunately, we were able to take the occasional shower at Shawn's apartment.

21. The team read and discussed the Gospel according to Luke.

22. During a "prayer walk," students walk in groups around the campus, praying for the contacts they will make that day and, as they told me, "binding Satan" so he cannot interfere with their witnessing efforts. In so doing, prayer walkers "claim the campus for Christ." Thus for many students prayer walks amount to ambulatory "spiritual warfare," while for others they are times to prepare themselves psychospiritually for the day's

events. I was invited to participate in only one of these walks, with Oliver and Denise, whose prayers on that occasion were hopeful and not explicitly oriented toward spiritual warfare.

23. They scheduled their activities to coincide with the class change times and the locations of highest traffic.

24. I was also assigned to set up the sound system the team used to amplify the music that accompanied these dramas. Specifically, I started, stopped, cued up the music, and adjusted the volume.

25. "The boys" and I eventually began calling these "delonging" sessions.

26. As well, all meals and witnessing events were preceded by prayer, and all morning devotions were concluded with prayer sessions.

27. The previous habits are enumerated in chapters 3, 4, and 5 of *How to Give Away Your Faith*. These suggestions are mostly self-explanatory, but some elaboration might be in order in some cases. A witness ought to be informed about the world and the Christian faith so that neither the individual nor the faith appears simplistic. Cox tells IVCF members to witness "with the Bible in one hand and the newspaper in the other." Witnesses should try not to suggest that the non-Christian's life has been futile or baneful even though the witness believes non-Christians are bound for hell. Missionaries should refrain from using evangelical rhetoric that is incomprehensible to non-Christians. Finally, Little (1988:91) encourages people to discuss the issue of sin experientially rather than propositionally because people are more likely to understand accounts of actual sins rather than the abstract idea of original sin.

28. These last seven recommendations are derived from a text compiled in 1996 by former Lithuania missionary, Steve Cox. Being "led by the spirit" is elaborated by Cox in the following way: "Learn to listen to the voice of the Holy Spirit. He will guide you. Learn to be looking for what God is already doing in people's lives. . . . The Spirit can give insight, direction and special sensitivity for the moment. The Holy Spirit can inspire you in what you say—He knows the heart of the one you are speaking to. The Spirit *is* speaking and guiding all the time—learn to listen—you're not on your own!" Cox provides the following two scriptural references: "Do not worry about what to say or how to say it. At that time you will be given what to say, for it will not be you speaking, but the Spirit of your Father speaking through you" (Mt 10:19–20). Also: "The Spirit guides us into all truth" (Jn 14:26).

29. During a conversation we had at the winter retreat, Pinnock compared the contemporary IVCF to the IVCF of his own formative years in the 1950s and 1960s.

> Back in the "50s and 60s," it was really a fundamentalist and doctrinally driven group. This group is not really like that, though. It's a more charismatic style of worship here. I mean, not as charismatic a style as the Vineyard, but it seems to me that the worship here is not emphasizing the doctrines of fundamentalism, but the emotional worship of God. . . . Their experience here is about relationships—with God and each other. It's not about apologetics."

30. I was beset at this moment by what might be called "ethnographic overload." Across the aisle from the seats in which Oliver and I and two Lithuanians were sitting sat Denise and two Lithuanian women. Denise was drawing a popular evangelical depiction of the human separation from God: two cliffs facing each other with a deep divide between them. "You see, on this side of the cliff is man, us. And over here is God," she said, writing "God" and "man" over their respective cliffs. "And what separates us from God is sin," she explained, writing "sin" vertically in the chasm. "The

only way we can get over this separation is through Jesus Christ. See what I mean?" At this point, she drew the cross horizontally, spanning the two cliffs.

31. Noll observes that "evangelicals are not exemplary for their thinking and they have not been so for several generations" (1994:3). Describing the portentous nature of this tendency, he writes, "If evangelicals do not take seriously the larger world of the intellect. . . . we are saying that we want our lives to be shaped by cultural forces— including intellectual forces—that contradict the heart of our religion" (1994:34).

32. See Cucchiari (1988:418), Harding (1987), Hefner (1993:17), and Snow and Machalek (1982).

33. Ozorak (1996) argues that religious women recognize the theologically and ecclesiologically derived inequalities in their faith communities but continue to be more observant or devout than men because women appreciate the emotional satisfactions of their relationships with God and other believers.

34. During one of the evening Bible studies and praise events in Panavegys, I met John, a retired fundamentalist schoolteacher from Nova Scotia who now teaches at Kaunus Technical University. The Lithuanian government pays John to teach courses on literature, economics, and English, all of which he bases on the Bible. At one point during the Bible study, referring to witnessing, John said, "In times of grief, a person is really ripe for the harvesting, and more likely to be willing to talk about transcendent explanations of life and the hereafter. We have to make sure we take the initiative then."

35. There was considerable debate about this. Some people said two people had "come to Christ," whereas others considered these to be examples of recommitments. I could not establish these figures with certainty because team members were unsure themselves and because the team had asked me not to problematize new Christians' faiths by interviewing them (even informally) about their religious investigations.

36. Several team members admitted to feeling pressure to "produce" converts. This pressure came from their churches (which were funding these students) and from the lore surrounding the previous McMaster IVCF teams, all of which attracted more converts than the 1996 team.

37. See Goffman for a discussion of these "territorial violations" (1971:28–41).

38. In fact, within the McMaster IVCF there is a tension between a minority of members who consider all their relationships with non-Christians to be opportunities to witness and a majority of members who believe that witnessing is more or less compulsory for Christians but should be understood as a part (and for some, not even a large part) of a Christian's relationship with a non-Christian.

39. Highly involved IVCF participants would tend to disagree with this characterization or definition of witnessing. These relatively exceptional evangelicals would argue that Christian should always consider themselves to be witnessing, even if only by setting an example. Several students told me they understood their role on campus in this manner. However, the majority of students would maintain that there is a significant difference between direct and indirect witnessing strategies.

40. One evening as Steve, Simon, Oliver, Jocelyn, Gabrielle, and I were walking in Vilnius, we walked through a park and were immediately assailed by loud shouts of "Nigre!" and "Go home, nigre!" from several directions. As we were leaving the park, three "skinheads" lunged at us menacingly. On another occasion, Steve and Oliver were walking around the city when a photographer from the local newspaper asked permission to take their photograph. The next day the picture appeared on the front page of the newspaper with the caption: "African tourists having fun by the fountain."

41. The verses to which Oliver referred, and which he read to the group, were 2 Peter 4:14–16: "If you are reviled for the name of Christ, you are blessed, because the

spirit of glory, which is the Spirit of God, is resting in you. . . . Yet if any of you suffers as a Christian, do not consider it a disgrace, but glorify God because you bear his name." Timothy also advises that "Everyone who wants to live a Godly life in Christ Jesus will be persecuted" (2 Tim 3:12).

42. For a parallel in another ethnographic context, see Rosaldo (1989:1–21).

43. Geertz argues that one of the defining features of a religion is that it "formulates conceptions of a general order of existence," which appear to humans as sufficiently compelling and authentic to quell our otherwise unfettered fear of chaos and our own mortality (1973:98–108).

44. In *The Courage to Be* (1952), Paul Tillich argues that humans try to diminish the persistent, vague, and crushing presence of anxiety by condensing it into the fear of a particular object or (in the case of the IVCF, a spiritual) being. This, Tillich argues, makes anxiety more palpable and therefore bearable.

45. Her explanation also assumes that this new conspicuousness is a function of a positively evaluated change (team members living out their faiths all day); mine assumes that their heightened awareness of the Evil One's opposition is a symbolic construction of a negatively experienced change (team members living in uncomfortable surroundings, experiencing culture shock, illness, and interpersonal tensions).

46. Several members of the chapter have used this metaphor in our conversations.

NOTES TO CHAPTER EIGHT

1. See Ammerman (1990) for a consideration of the pivotal role played by education in entrenching the divisions within the Southern Baptist Convention.

2. By this, I am referring to both intellectual or theological secularization and a concomitant moral liberalization.

3. A word of clarification about membrane(s) is in order. On the one hand, a semipermeable membrane is evident in the broader evangelical discourse. On the other hand, the specific form this membrane assumes is determined by each individual in response to the unique situations he or she encounters. In other words, in this chapter I refer to the general *membrane* which separates evangelicals from the secular ethos, but I also discuss the deployment of personal *membranes*, which are simply more specific individual versions of the larger and more abstract membrane. For the sake of simplicity, I normally refer to both the general and specific variants as a single membrane.

4. Historian Michael Gauvreau (1991:230) suggests that nineteenth-century Canadian Methodist and Presbyterian evangelicals used their creeds as a "screen, filtering new ideas." Gauvreau also refers to these early evangelicals' tendencies "to 'capture,' or to 'tame' what to the modern mind might seem to be serious threats to their theology" (1991:229). Taming and capturing might explain IVCF participants' relations with some aspects of the secular ethos, but it would not explain their tendencies to employ the group as what IVCF members sometimes referred to as a "haven" or "comfort zone," or their evident use of the group as a vehicle for improving relations with the secular ethos.

5. See McMullin (1985) for a collection of articles discussing the possible compatibility of evolution and creationism.

6. Mark Noll observes that even evangelical scientists "have generally gone along in silence with contestable theoretical issues" (1994:178).

7. Noll notes that even when professional evangelical scientists contribute their perspectives to the scientific discourse in a nonwitnessing context, they "have usually ap-

proached their subjects as carefully segregated fields of knowledge rather than with the intent of studying scientific concerns in relation to theology or other spheres of thought" (1994:177). Noll argues that Christian scientists avoid certain spheres of research to circumvent conflict between their faith and the materialist assumptions of their peers or disciplines. Noll's insight may help explain why only two of the two hundred members of the McMaster IVCF major in religious studies and why IVCF participants in general typically evade situations in which direct contention might arise. (If one conducted an ethnography of a campus art club at a university with a thriving art department, would one expect only 1% of the club's members to be students in the department?) The minimal interest of IVCF members in religious studies may reflect a perception among evangelicals that the academic (or, in Wuthnow's sense, the "scientific") study of religion could undermine faith.

8. Gabrielle also had a literary submission rejected by the English Department's undergraduate literary journal. She commented: "I'm not into the kinds of things the other students are into, like blood and gore and sex. I write about the way people live and can be transformed and the struggles we go through. I also use the words 'Jesus' and 'God,' so they reject my writing." Nancy Ammerman writes that many North American fundamentalists such as Gabrielle behave as though references to the divine are "fully explanatory—as much in the affairs of nations as in those of persons and families and churches. It stands therefore in marked contrast to the history practiced by the academy, where there is no room for sacred activity" (1994:151).

9. Of course, for strict fundamentalists whose courses at McMaster do not require them to grapple with the theory of evolution, no such second bridging step need occur. While these students would agree that the theory is "just" a theory, since it is so obviously an erroneous one, they are not particularly interested in learning about it.

10. See Badone (1989:18, 284), Wuthnow (1989:149), and Geertz (1973) for discussions of the common Western tendency to alternate between scientific and nonscientific worldviews.

11. See Wuthnow and Lawson (1994:44) for a discussion of the ways in which a secular education can function as a resource for strengthening evangelical faith.

12. For a consideration of the power of popular culture to shape our identities, see Collins (1989), Schultze (1991), and Fiske (1987, 1989).

13. For example, in chapter 2 when Simon said, "that's just *so* not true" (referring to his erroneous belief that God needed time to cool off to forgive him), he was echoing the intonation of several of the characters on *Friends*. Further study would be required to determine if these television programs are models of or models for undergraduate discourse (cf. Geertz 1973:93).

14. For example, I have never heard IVCF students replay any parts of *Seinfeld's* famous "masturbation episode," in which the characters wager to determine which of them could resist masturbating the longest. Many loyal fans of the show can and do quote dialogue from this episode.

15. Non-Christian students may also filter out elements of these programs. However, I would argue that evangelicals would be especially troubled by some of the moral assumptions implicit in these situation comedies.

16. See Fiske (1989) for a discussion of the way marginalized groups can appropriate and reinterpret elements from popular culture as means of resisting the hegemony of the dominant culture.

17. However, an ominous and (literally) exceptional example of fundamentalist discontent is evident in Oscar's speculations about the future of the IVCF. He commented:

The growth of IV has produced a chapter that's pretty wishy-washy in their faith. People in IV don't want to talk about doctrine or hell at large group meetings. On the whole, the group has been too influenced by humanism and not enough by the Bible. There is a big emphasis on a loving God rather than a just God. God has obviously blessed this chapter, but a lot of the ideals of the chapter are not glorifying to God. I would not be surprised if IV downsized over the next few years because a lot of people are not satisfied with it because we put all of the focus on God as he is understood in our own terms.

Since Oscar was the only member to express this kind of sentiment, I have not emphasized it in the body of this work.

18. See Ammerman (1990), Hammond and Hunter (1984), Harding (1992), Peshkin (1986), and Titon (1988).

19. Adapting the work of Daniel (1983), Kirin Narayan refers to this eclectic methodology as the " 'tool box approach,' choosing from an array of theoretical implements as different themes demanding intellectual craftsmanship emerged" (1989:7). Throughout this book, part of my toolbox has been Peter Berger's illuminating notions of "cognitive contamination," "cognitive bargaining," and "cognitive retrenchment" (1992). Berger's typology is quite helpful, but in the end I think his singular emphasis on cognition limits the kind of insight one can have into groups like the IVCF.

20. Wuthnow and Lawson continue: "But in defending the creativity of fundamentalism, its simplicity must not be neglected either, like the anthropologist who tries to turn primitives into sophisticated scientists. The reason fundamentalism often appears simpleminded is that it . . . is designed to motivate people toward taking some action" (1994:42).

21. Marty and Appleby write, "Fundamentalism appears as a strategy, or set of strategies, by which beleaguered believers attempt to preserve their distinct identity as a people or group. Feeling this identity to be at risk, fundamentalists fortify it by a selective retrieval of doctrines, beliefs, and practices from a sacred past" (1994:1). Although this definition leaves out the bridge approach I have described throughout this book, their account seems, on the surface, harmless. However, I wonder what Marty and Appleby might (unintentionally, perhaps) be suggesting by the inclusion of "selective retrieval" in their description. Does this imply that nonfundamentalist Christians are not selective (are, in other words, unbiased) in the way they approach the Christian past?

22. Wuthnow writes, "I am not at all convinced that evangelicalism, or even fundamentalism, is as rigid and intolerant, as out-of-step with the times, as most intellectuals think. It may appeal to a certain simplistic pragmatic strand in American culture, but I doubt it is really simplistic or unreflective" (1989:171).

23. For example, the equality of women in principle but the inequality of women in most evangelical churches, or the espousal of Jesus' championing of the poor but the support for conservative political parties advocating cutbacks to social programs.

24. In fact, at the end of dozens of interviews, participants told me they had never thought about these sorts of issues before. Many thanked me for giving them a forum in which to formalize these previously implicit elements of their contracts.

25. According to Luhrmann (1989), this strategy is employed by English magicians to remain simultaneously committed to magic and to the expectations of a rationalistic culture.

26. In the process of describing a given phenomenon and proposing a model for understanding an unstudied phenomenon, the following issues arose but must be de-

ferred for future consideration or the work of another researcher. First, a more elaborate examination of the McMaster chapter's prominent place in the Canadian IVCF and within North American Protestantism could situate this group in the broader context and further illustrate the theoretical arguments I have advanced. Second, a comparison between the McMaster IVCF and chapters in other regions of North America could determine the extent to which regional differences influence the interaction between evangelicals and their non-Christian surroundings. Third, it would also be interesting to apply the model I have developed to non-Christian religious or minority ethnic groups operating within contexts they perceive to be threatening or indifferent. Fourth, a longitudinal study of several IVCF members would explore these individuals' relations with the non-Christian world over time and outside the slightly artificial context of a university program.

27. It is on these emerging patterns of religious practice that we might consider focusing our attention rather than religious organizations or functions (Ammerman 1997: 214). Obviously, religious groups and organizations are still of vital importance, but the "new paradigm" (Warner 1997b:203) emerging for the study of contemporary religion encourages us to view these groups as dynamic facilitators and mediators of selfhood, otherness, solidarity, dissension, and the like.

28. For example, like the vast majority of IVCF members, she believes the Bible is literally true and that one should not have sex before marriage.

Bibliography

Adams, Daniel. 1993. "The Biblical Basis for Mission, 1930–1980." In *Missions and Ecumenical Expressions*. Martin Marty, ed. Modern American Protestantism and Its World, vol. 13, pp. 82–101. New York: K. G. Saur.

Almond, Gabriel A., Emmanuel Sivan, and R. Scott Appleby. 1995. "Politics, Ethnicity, and Fundamentalism." In *Fundamentalisms Comprehended*. Martin Marty and R. Scott Appleby, eds. The Fundamentalisms Project, vol. 5, pp. 483–504. Chicago: University of Chicago Press.

American Psychiatric Association. 1992. *Diagnostic and Statistical Manual of Mental Disorders*. Fourth Edition. Washington, D.C.: American Psychiatric Association.

Ammerman, Nancy. 1997. "Organized Religion in a Voluntaristic Society." *Sociology of Religion* 58:203–216.

———. 1994. "Accounting for Christian Fundamentalisms: Social Dynamics and Rhetorical Strategies." In *Accounting for Fundamentalisms*. Martin Marty and R. Scott Appleby, eds. The Fundamentalisms Project, vol. 4, pp. 149–170. Chicago: University of Chicago Press.

———. 1991. "North American Protestant Fundamentalism." In *Fundamentalisms Observed*. Martin Marty and R. Scott Appleby, eds. The Fundamentalisms Project, vol. 1, pp. 1–65. Chicago: University of Chicago Press.

———. 1990. *Baptist Battles: Social Change and Religious Conflict in the Southern Baptist Convention*. New Brunswick, N.J.: Rutgers University Press.

———. 1987. *Bible Believers: Fundamentalists in the Modern World*. New Brunswick, N.J.: Rutgers University Press.

Anderson, Grace, and Juanne Clarke. 1990. *God Calls, Man Chooses: A Study of Women in Ministry*. Burlington, Ont.: Trinity Press.

Backhouse, Constance, and David Flaherty, eds. 1992. *The Women's Movement in Canada and the United States*. Montreal: McGill Queens Press.

Badone, Ellen. 1989. *The Appointed Hour: Death, Worldview, and Social Change in Brittany*. Berkeley: University of California Press.

Bakhurst, David, and Christine Sypnowich, eds. 1995. *The Social Self*. London: Sage.

Balmer, Randall. 1994. "American Fundamentalism: The Ideal of Femininity." In *Fundamentalism and Gender*, John Stratton Hawley, ed., pp. 47–62. Oxford: Oxford University Press.

———. 1989. *Mine Eyes Have Seen the Glory: A Journey into the Evangelical Subculture in America*. New York: Oxford University Press.

Barber, Benjamin. 1996. *Jihad vs. McWorld*. New York: Ballantine.

Barron, Bruce. 1990. "Putting Women in Their Place: 1 Timothy 2 and Evangelical Views of Women in Church Leadership." *Journal of the Evangelical Theological Society* 33:451–459.

Barth, Fredrik. 1994. "A Personal View of the Present Tasks and Priorities in Cultural and Social Anthropology." In *Assessing Cultural Anthropology*, Robert Borofsky, ed., pp. 349–360. New York: McGraw-Hill.

Baum, Gregory. 1975. *Religion and Alienation*. New York: Paulist Press.

Bauman, Richard, ed. 1992. *Folklore, Cultural Performances, and Popular Entertainments*. New York: Oxford University Press.

Baxter, Brian. 1982. *Alienation and Authenticity*. London: Tavistock.

de Beauvoir, Simone. 1989. *The Second Sex*. New York: Vintage.

Becker, Gay. 1997 *Disrupted Lives: How People Create Meaning in a Chaotic World*. Berkeley: University of California Press.

Becker, Lee. 1977. "Predictors of Change in Religious Beliefs and Behaviors during College." *Sociological Analysis* 38:65–74.

Beers, M., R. Berkow, and A. Fletcher. 1992. *The Merck Manual of Diagnosis and Therapy*. Sixteenth Edition. Rahway, N.J.: Merck Research Laboratories, 1992.

Behar, Ruth. 1993. *Translated Woman: Crossing the Border with Esperanza's Story*. Boston: Beacon.

Bendroth, Margaret Lamberts. 1993. *Fundamentalism and Gender: 1875 to the Present*. New Haven: Yale University Press.

Berger, Peter. 1992. *A Far Glory: The Quest for Faith in an Age of Credulity*. New York: Free Press.

———. 1989. *American Apostasy: The Triumph of the "Other" Gospels*. Grand Rapids: Eerdmans.

———. 1977. *Facing Up to Modernity: Excursions in Society, Politics, and Religion*. New York: Basic Books.

———. 1967. *The Sacred Canopy: Elements of a Sociological Theory of Religion*. New York: Doubleday.

Berger, Peter, and Thomas Luckmann. 1966. *The Social Construction of Reality: A Treatise in the Sociology of Knowledge*. New York: Penguin.

Berryman, Phillip. 1987. *Liberation Theology: The Essential Facts about the Revolutionary Movement in Latin America and Beyond*. New York: Pantheon.

Beutel, Ann, and Margaret Marini. 1995. "Gender and Values." *American Sociological Review* 60:436–448.

Bibby, Reginald. 1993. *Unknown Gods: The Ongoing Story of Religion in Canada*. Don Mills, Ont.: Stoddart.

———. 1990. *Mosaic Madness: Pluralism without a Cause*. Toronto: Stoddart.

———. 1987. *Fragmented Gods: The Poverty and Potential of Religion in Canada*. Toronto: Stoddart.

———. 1982.*Religionless Christianity: A Profile of Religion in the Canadian 1980s*. Lethbridge: University of Lethbridge.

Bibby, Reginald, and Merlin Brinkerhoff. 1994. "Circulation of the Saints 1966–1990: New Data, New Reflections." *Journal for the Scientific Study of Religion* 33:273–280.

———. 1973. "The Circulation of the Saints." *Journal for the Scientific Study of Religion* 12:273–293.

Bibby, Reginald, and Donald Posterski. 1985. *The Emerging Generation: An Inside Look at Canada's Teenagers*. Toronto: Unwin.

Bloch, Maurice. 1989. *Ritual, History and Power: Selected Papers in Anthropology*. London: Athlone.

Boone, Kathleen. 1989. *The Bible Tells Them So: The Discourse of Protestant Fundamentalism*. Albany: State University of New York Press.

Booth, Wayne C. 1995. "The Rhetoric of Fundamentalist Conversion Narratives." In *Fundamentalisms Comprehended*. Martin Marty and R. Scott Appleby, eds. The Fundamentalisms Project, vol. 5., pp. 367–395. Chicago: University of Chicago Press.

Borofsky, Robert, ed. 1994. *Assessing Cultural Anthropology*. New York: McGraw-Hill.

Boverie, Patricia, Sherri Huffman, Marge Philbin, and Eliza Meier. 1995. "A Survey of Gender and Learning Styles." *Sex Roles* 32:485–494.

Bridges, William. 1994. *Jobshift: How To Prosper in a Workplace without Jobs*. New York: Addison-Wesley.

Brinkerhoff, Merlin and Marlene Mackie. 1985. "Religion and Gender: A Comparison of Canadian and American Student Attitudes." *Journal of Marriage and the Family* 47:415–429.

Brouwer, Steve, Paul Gifford, and Susan D. Rose. 1996. *Exporting the American Gospel: Global Christian Fundamentalism*. New York: Routledge.

Brown McCarthy, Karen. 1994. "Fundamentalism and the Control of Women." In *Fundamentalism and Gender*. John Stratton Hawley, ed., pp. 175–202. Oxford: Oxford University Press.

Bruce, Steve. 1994. "The Inevitable Failure of the New Christian Right." *Sociology of Religion* 55:229–242.

———. 1988. *The Rise and Fall of the New Christian Right*. New York: Oxford University Press.

———. 1982. "The Student Christian Movement: A Nineteenth Century Movement and Its Vicissitudes." *International Journal of Sociology and Social Policy* 2:67–82.

Bruce, Steve, ed. 1992. *Religion and Modernization: Sociologists and Historians Debate the Secularization Thesis*. Oxford: Clarendon.

Bruland Byle, Esther. 1989. "Evangelical and Feminist Ethics: Complex Solidarities." *Journal of Religious Ethics* 17:139–160.

Buehrens, John, and Forrester Church. 1989. *Our Chosen Faith: An Introduction to Unitarian Universalism*. Boston: Beacon.

Burnim, Mellonee. 1989. "The Performance of Black Gospel Music as Transformation." *Concilium* 202:52–61.

Burridge, Kenelm. 1991. *In the Way: A Study of Christian Missionary Endeavours*. Vancouver: University of British Columbia Press.

———. 1983. "Missionaries and the Perception of Evil." In *Missionaries, Anthropolo-*

gists, and Cultural Change. D. Whiteman, ed. Studies in Third World Societies, 25, pp. 153–170. Williamsburg: Department of Anthropology, College of William and Mary.

Cahill, Lisa Sowle. 1985. *Between the Sexes: Foundations for a Christian Ethics of Sexuality.* Philadelphia: Fortress.

Caplan, Lionel. 1987. "Fundamentalism as Counter-Culture: Protestants in Urban South India." In *Studies in Religious Fundamentalism.* Lionel Caplan, ed., pp. 156–176. Albany: State University of New York Press.

Caplan, Paula. 1993. *Lifting a Ton of Feathers: A Woman's Guide for Surviving in the Academic World.* Toronto: University of Toronto Press.

Capps, Walter. 1990. *The New Religious Right: Piety, Patriotism, and Politics.* Columbia: University of South Carolina Press.

Carpenter, Joel. 1980. "Fundamentalist Institutions and the Rise of Evangelical Protestantism." *Church History* 49:62–75.

Carroll, James. 1995. "Alcohol Use and Risky Sex among College Students." *Psychological Reports* 76:723–726.

Carter, Stephen L. 1994. *The Culture of Disbelief: How American Law and Politics Trivialize Religious Devotion.* New York: Basic Books.

Chaves, Mark. 1989. "Secularization and Religious Revival: Evidence from U.S. Church Attendance Rates." *Journal for the Scientific Study of Religion* 28:464–477.

Church, F. Forrester, and John A. Buehrens. 1989. *Our Chosen Faith: An Introduction to Unitarian Universalism.* Boston: Beacon.

Clifford, James. 1986. "Introduction: Partial Truths." In *Writing Culture: The Poetics and Politics of Ethnography.* James Clifford and George Marcus, eds., pp. 1–26. Berkeley: University of California Press.

Code, Lorraine. 1991. *What Can She Know? Feminist Theory and the Construction of Knowledge.* Ithaca: Cornell University Press.

Cohen, Edmund. 1986. *The Mind of the Bible Believer.* Buffalo: Prometheus.

Collins, Jim 1989. *Uncommon Cultures: Popular Culture and Post-Modernism.* New York: Routledge.

Collins, Mary, and Elisabeth Schüssler-Fiorenza, eds. 1985. *Concilium: Women: Invisible in Theology and Church.* Edinburgh: T. and T. Clark.

Comaroff, Jean. 1985. *Body of Power, Spirit of Resistance: The Culture and History of a South African People.* Chicago: University of Chicago Press.

Conway, Flo, and Jim Siegelman. 1984. *Holy Terror: The Fundamentalist War on America's Freedoms in Religion, Politics, and Our Private Lives.* New York: Dell.

Coupland, Douglas. 1994. *Life after God.* New York: Pocket Books.

———. 1993. *Shampoo Planet.* New York: Pocket Books.

———. 1991. *Generation X.* New York: St. Martin's Press.

Cox, Harvey. 1995. *Fire from Heaven: The Rise of Pentecostal Spirituality and the Reshaping of Religion in the Twenty-First Century.* Reading: Addison-Wesley.

———. 1990. *The Secular City.* Twenty-fifth Anniversary Edition. New York: Macmillan.

———. 1987. "Fundamentalism as an Ideology." In *Piety and Politics: Evangelicals and Fundamentalists Confront the World.* Richard John Neuhaus and Michael Cromartie, eds., pp. 287–302. Washington, D.C.: Ethics and Public Policy Center.

Crapanzano, Vincent. 1980. *Tuhami: Portrait of a Moroccan.* Chicago: University of Chicago Press.

Cromartie, Michael. 1993. *No Longer Exiles: The Religious New Right in American Politics.* Washington, D.C.: Ethics and Public Policy Center.

Cucchiari, Salvatore. 1988. " 'Adapted for Heaven': Conversion and Culture in Western Sicily." *American Ethnologist* 15:417–441.

Daly, Mary. 1973. *Beyond God the Father: Toward a Philosophy of Women's Liberation.* Boston: Beacon.

DaMatta, Roberto. 1994. "Some Biased Remarks on Interpretivism: A View From Brazil." In *Assessing Cultural Anthropology.* Robert Borofsky, ed., pp. 119–131. New York: McGraw-Hill.

Danforth, Loring M. 1989. *Firewalking and Religious Healing: The Anastenaria of Greece and the American Firewalking Movement.* Princeton: Princeton University Press.

———. 1982. *Death Rituals of Rural Greece.* Princeton: Princeton University Press.

Daniel, Sheryl. 1983 "The Tool Box Approach of the Tamil to the Issues of Moral Responsibility and Human Destiny." In *Karma: An Anthropological Inquiry.* C. Keyes and E. V. Daniel, eds., pp. 27–62. Berkeley: University of California at Berkeley.

Davidman, Lynn. 1991. *Tradition in a Rootless World: Women Turn to Orthodox Judaism.* Berkeley: University of California Press.

Davie Shapiro, Jody. 1995. *Women in the Presence: Constructing Community and Seeking Spirituality in Mainline Protestantism.* Philadelphia: University of Pennsylvania Press.

Deaner, Stephanie, Eileen Lightner, and Jasmin McConatha. 1994. "Culture, Age, and Gender as Variables in the Expression of Emotions." *Journal of Social Behaviour and Personality* 9:481–488.

Derrida, Jacques. 1978. *Writing and Difference.* Alan Bass, trans. London: Routledge.

Diamond, Sara. 1989. *Spiritual Warfare: The Politics of the New Christian Right.* Boston: South End Publishers.

Dobbelaere, Karel. 1985. "Secularization and Sociological Paradigms: A Reformulation of the Private-Public Dichotomy and the Problem of Social Integration." *Sociological Analysis* 46:377–387.

———. 1984. "Secularization Theories and Sociological Paradigms: Convergences and Divergences." *Social Compass* 31:199–219.

———. 1981. "Secularization: A Multi-Dimensional Model." *Current Sociology* 29:1–216.

Dobson, James. 1995. *Life from the Edge: A Young Adults' Guide to a Meaningful Future.* Dallas: Word.

Dollar, George. 1973. *A History of Fundamentalism in America.* Greensville, S.C.: Bob Jones University Publishing.

Donald, Melvin. 1991. *A Spreading Tree: A History of Inter-Varsity Christian Fellowship, 1928–1989.* Richmond Hill, Ont.: Inter-Varsity Christian Fellowship of Canada.

D'Souza, Dinesh. 1991. *Illiberal Education.* New York: Free Press.

Durkheim, Émile. 1973. *On Morality and Society.* Robert Bellah, ed. Chicago: University of Chicago Press.

Eddie, David. 1996. *Chump Change.* Toronto: Random House.

Ehrenreich, Barbara, Elizabeth Hess, and Gloria Jacobs. 1986. *Remaking Love: The Feminization of Love.* New York: Anchor.

Ellul, Jacques. 1964. *The Technological Society.* John Wilkinson, trans. New York: Vintage.

Epstein, Barbara Leslie. 1981. *The Politics of Domesticity: Women, Evangelicalism, and Temperance in Nineteenth Century America.* Middletown, Conn.: Wesleyan University Press.

Erickson, Millard. 1968. *The New Evangelical Theology.* Westwood, N.J.: Revell.

Escobar, Samuel, and Mary Fisher. 1991. "IVCF's Urbana '90: A Student Missionary Convention and Missiological Event." *Missiology* 19:333–346.

Evans-Pritchard, E. E. 1937. *Witchcraft, Magic, and Oracles among the Azande.* London: Oxford University Press.

Fabian, Johannes. 1983. *Time and the Other: How Anthropology Makes Its Object.* New York: Columbia University Press.

Fea, John. 1993. "American Fundamentalism and Neo-Evangelicalism: A Bibliographical Survey." *Evangelical Journal* 11:21–30.

Fernandez, James. 1974. "The Mission of Metaphor in Expressive Culture." *Current Anthropology* 15:119–133.

Festinger, Leon. 1962. *A Theory of Cognitive Dissonance.* Stanford, Calif.: Stanford University Press.

Fields, Echo. 1991. "Understanding Activist Fundamentalism: Capitalist Crisis and the Colonization of the Lifeworld." *Sociological Analysis* 52:175–190.

Finke, Roger. 1992. "An Unsecular America." In *Religion and Modernization: Sociologists and Historians Debate the Secularization Thesis.* Steve Bruce, ed., pp. 145–169. Oxford: Clarendon.

Finke, Roger, and Rodney Stark. 1992. *The Churching of America: 1760–1990.* New Brunswick, N.J.: Rutgers University Press.

Finley, Bob. 1991. "Lead Us Not into Colonialism, But Deliver Us from Tourists." *Christian Mission*, p. 2. October.

Finson, Shelley Davis. 1995. *A Historical Review of the Development of Feminist Liberation Theology.* Ottawa: The Canadian Research Institute for the Advancement of Women.

Fishwick, Marshall, and Ray Browne, eds. 1987. *The God Pumpers: Religion in the Electronic Age.* Bowling Green, Ohio: Bowling Green University Press.

Fiske, John. 1989. *Reading the Popular.* Boston: Unwin Hyman.

———. 1987. *Understanding Popular Culture.* London: Methuen.

Foot, David, and Daniel Stoffman. 1996. *Boom, Bust and Echo.* Toronto: Macfarlane, Walter, and Ross.

Forsyth, Neil. 1987. *The Old Enemy: Satan and the Combat Myth.* Princeton: Princeton University Press.

Fortosis, Steve, and Ken Garland. 1991. "Historical Origins of Professional Evangelical Youth Work in the Church." *Religious Education* 86:275–284.

Foucault, Michel. 1990. *A History of Sexuality: An Introduction.* New York: Vintage.

Fowler, R. B. 1986. "The Feminist and Anti-Feminist Debate within Evangelical Protestantism." *Women and Politics* 5:7–39.

Frame, Randall. 1990. "IVCF President Clarifies View on Homosexuality." *Christianity Today* 34:47–48.

Frank, D. W. 1986. *Less Than Conquerors: How Evangelicals Entered the 20th Century.* Grand Rapids: Eerdmans.

Frankel, Gail, and W. E. Hewitt. 1994. "Religion and Well-Being among Canadian University Students: The Role of Faith Groups on Campus." *Journal for the Scientific Study of Religion* 33:62–73.

Freud, Sigmund. 1961. *The Future of an Illusion.* James Strachey, trans. New York: W. W. Norton.

Fuller, David. 1961. *Valiant for the Truth: A Treasury of Evangelical Writings.* New York: Lippincott.

Fuller, Robert. 1985. *Naming the Anti-Christ: An American Obsession.* New York: Oxford University Press.

Galbraith, John Kenneth. 1992. *The Culture of Contentment.* Boston: Houghton Mifflin.

Gallup, George Jr., and Jim Castelli. 1989. *The People's Religion: American Faith in the 90's.* New York: Macmillan.

Gauvreau, Michael. 1994. "The Empire of Evangelicalism." In *Evangelicalism: Comparative Studies of Popular Protestantism in North America, the British Isles, and Beyond, 1700–1990.* George Rawlyk, David Bebbington, and Mark Noll, eds., pp. 219–252. New York: Oxford University Press.

———. 1991. *The Evangelical Century: Church and Creed in Canada between the Great Awakening and the Great Depression.* Montreal: McGill-Queen's Press.

Gay, Craig. 1990. "The Uneasy Intellect of Modern Evangelism." *Crux* 26:8–11.

Geertz, Clifford. 1994. "The Uses of Diversity." In *Assessing Cultural Anthropology.* Robert Borofsky, ed., pp. 454–465. New York: McGraw-Hill.

———. 1983. *Local Knowledge.* New York: Basic Books.

———. 1973. *The Interpretation of Cultures.* New York: Basic Books.

Gerutis, Albertas, ed. 1969. *Lithuania: 700 Years.* New York: Manyland Books.

Gilligan, Carol. 1982. *In a Different Voice: Psychological Theory and Women's Development.* Cambridge: Harvard University Press.

Goffman, Erving. 1974. *Frame Analysis.* Cambridge: Harvard University Press.

———. 1971. *Relations in Public.* New York: Harper Torchbooks.

———. 1961. *Asylums: Essays on the Social Situation of Mental Patients and Other Inmates.* Garden City, N.J.: Anchor.

Government of Canada. 1997. "Labour Characteristics of Youths, by Age and Sex, Selected Years." *Statistics Canada Labour Force Update.* vol. 1, no. 1. (Spring). Catalogue no. 71-005-XPB.

———. 1994. *Canada's Alcohol and Other Drugs Survey: A Discussion of the Findings.* Ottawa: Health Canada Office of Alcohol, Drugs and Dependency Issues.

———. 1990. *Canada's Health Promotion Survey, 1990: Technical Report.* Ottawa: Health and Welfare Canada.

Grant, George. 1986. *Technology and Justice.* Concord: Anansi Press.

Grant, John W. 1988. *The Church in the Canadian Era.* Burlington, Ont.: Welch.

Grimes, Ronald. 1990. *Ritual Criticism.* Columbia: University of South Carolina.

———. 1982. *Beginnings in Ritual Studies.* Lanham, Md.: University Press of America.

Guelich, Robert. 1991. "Spiritual Warfare: Jesus, Paul, and Peretti." *The Journal of the Society for Pentecostal Studies* 13:33–64.

Guinness, H. 1978. *Journey among Students.* Sydney: Anglican Information Office.

Hadden, Jeffrey. 1987. "Broadcasting and the Mobilization of the New Christian Right." *Journal for the Scientific Study of Religion* 26:1–24.

Hadden, Jeffrey, and Anson Shupe, eds. 1989. *Secularization and Fundamentalism Reconsidered.* New York: Paragon.

Hagarty, Bonnie. 1995. "Advances in Understanding Major Depressive Disorder." *Journal of Psychosocial Nursing* 33:27–33.

Haiven, Judith. 1984. *Faith, Hope, No Charity: An Inside Look at the Born Again Movement in Canada and the United States.* Vancouver: New Star.

Hallen, G. C. 1983. "Towards Developing a Theory of Alienation." *Eastern Anthropologist* 36:167–177.

Hammersley, Martyn. 1992. *What's Wrong with Ethnography? Methodological Explorations.* London: Routledge.

Hammond, Phillip, ed. 1985. *The Sacred in a Secular Age.* Berkeley: University of California Press.

———. 1983. "Another Great Awakening?" In *The New Christian Right: Mobilization and Legitimation.* Robert Wuthnow and Robert Liebman, eds., pp. 208–228. Hawthorne, N.Y.: Aldine.

Hammond, Phillip, and James D. Hunter. 1984. "On Maintaining Plausibility: The Worldview of Evangelical College Students." *Journal for the Scientific Study of Religion* 23:221–238.

Hanks, William F. 1987. "Discourse Genres in a Theory of Practice." *American Ethnologist* 14:668–692.

Hardesty, Nancy. 1984. *Women Called to Witness: Evangelical Feminism in the Nineteenth Century.* Nashville: Abingdon.

Harding, Susan. 1994. "Imagining the Last Days: the Politics of Apocalyptic Language." In *Accounting for Fundamentalisms.* Martin Marty and R. Scott Appleby, eds. The Fundamentalisms Project, vol. 4, pp. 57–78. Chicago: University of Chicago Press.

———. 1992. "The Afterlife of Stories: Genesis of a Man of God." In *Storied Lives: The Cultural Politics of Self-Understanding.* George Rosenwald and Richard Ochberg, eds., pp. 60–75. London: Yale University Press.

———. 1991. "Representing Fundamentalism: The Problem of the Repugnant Cultural Other." *Social Research* 58:373–93.

———. 1990. "If I Should Die before I Wake: Jerry Falwell's Pro-Life Gospel." In *Uncertain Terms: Negotiating Gender in American Culture.* Faye Ginsburg and Anna Lowenhaupt Tsing, eds., pp. 76–97. Boston: Beacon.

———. 1987. "Convicted by the Holy Spirit: The Rhetoric of Fundamental Baptist Conversion." *American Ethnologist* 14:167–181.

Hayes, Kathleen. 1994. "Opening Up the Club: Are Evangelicals Finally Ready to Bring Women in from the Fringes?" *Other Side* 30:44–47.

Hayner, Stephen. 1988. "Challenges Face New IVCF President." *Christianity Today* 32: 55–56.

Heaton, Timothy. 1986. "Sociodemographic Characteristics of Religious Groups in Canada." *Sociological Analysis* 47:54–65.

Hedges, Larry, and Amy Nowell. 1995. "Sex Differences in Mental Test Scores: Variability of Numbers of High-Scoring Individuals." *Science* 269:41–45.

Hefner, Robert W., ed. 1993. *Conversion to Christianity: Historical and Anthropological Perspectives on a Great Transformation.* Berkeley: University of California Press.

Heinz, Donald. 1983. "The Struggle to Define America." In *The New Christian Right: Mobilization and Legitimation.* Robert Liebman and Robert Wuthnow, eds., pp. 136–146. New York: Aldine.

Hewitt, W. E., ed. 1993. *The Sociology of Religion: A Canadian Focus.* Toronto: Butterworths.

Hexham, Irving. 1993. "Canadian Evangelicals: Facing the Critics." In *The Sociology of Religion.* W. E. Hewitt, ed., pp. 289–302. Toronto: Butterworths.

Hofstadter, Richard, and Walter Metzger. 1955. *The Development of Academic Freedom in the United States.* New York: Columbia University Press.

Howard, Jay. 1994. "Vilifying the Enemy: The Christian Right and the Novels of Frank Peretti." *Journal of Popular Culture* 28:193–206.

Hubbard, Ruth. 1988. "Some Thoughts about the Masculinity of the Natural Sciences." In *Feminist Thought and the Structure of Knowledge.* M. Gergen, ed., pp. 1–15. New York: New York University Press.

Hunter, James D. 1985. "Conservative Protestantism." In *The Sacred in a Secular Age.* Phillip Hammond, ed., pp. 150–166. Berkeley: University of California Press.

———. 1983. *American Evangelicalism.* New Brunswick, N.J.: Rutgers University Press.

————. 1982. "Subjectivization and the New Evangelical Theodicy." *Journal for the Scientific Study of Religion* 21:39–47.

Iannaccone, Laurence R. 1993. "Heirs to the Protestant Ethic? The Economics of American Fundamentalists." In *Fundamentalisms and the State*. Martin Marty and R. Scott Appleby, eds. The Fundamentalisms Project, vol. 3, pp. 342–366. Chicago: University of Chicago Press.

Ingram, Jay. 1989. "Evangelism as Frame Intrusion: Observations on Witnessing in Public Places." *Journal for the Scientific Study of Religion* 28:17–26.

————. 1986. "Testimony and Religious Cohesion." *Religious Education* 81:295–309.

Inter-Varsity Christian Fellowship Websites (September 1999) McMaster University
IVCF: www.mcmaster.ca/ivcf
IVCF Canada: www.ivcf.ca/index.shtml and www.ivcf.ca
IVCF USA: www.gospelcom.net/iv/

Jackson, Anthony, ed. 1987. *Anthropology at Home*. London: Tavistock.

Janz, Harold. 1991. "Evangelicals in the Canada of the 90's." *Ecumenism* 101:15–16.

Johnston, Charles. 1976. *McMaster University: The Toronto Years*, vol. 1. Toronto: University of Toronto Press.

Johnston, Charles, and John Weaver. 1986. *Student Days: A Study of Life at McMaster University from the 1890s to the 1980s*. Hamilton: McMaster University Alumni Association.

Jongeneel, J. A. B., and J. M. Van Engelen. 1995. "Contemporary Currents in Missiology." In *Missiology: An Ecumenical Introduction: Texts and Contexts of Global Christianity*. A. Camps, A. Hoedemaker, and M. R. Spindler, eds., pp. 438–457. Grand Rapids: Eerdmans.

Jorstad, Erling. 1993. *Popular Religion in America: The Evangelical Voice*. Westport, Conn.: Greenwood.

Kapchan, Deborah A. 1995. "Performance." *Journal of American Folklore* 108:479–508.

Kaplan, Lawrence, ed. 1992. *Fundamentalism in Contemporary Perspective*. Amherst: University of Massachusetts Press.

Keller, Evelyn Fox. 1985. *Reflections on Gender and Science*. New Haven: Yale University Press.

Kersten, Katherine. 1994. "How the Feminist Establishment Hurts Women: A Christian Critique of a Movement Gone Wrong." *Christianity Today* 38:20, 22–25.

Kingwell, Mark. 1996. *Dreams of Millennium: Report from a Culture on the Brink*. Toronto: Viking.

Kirkley, Robert, and Christopher Madden. 1995. "Gender Differences in Competitive Stress." *Perceptual Motor Skills* 80:848–850.

Kirshenblatt-Gimblett, Barbara. 1989. "Authoring Lives." *Journal of Folklore Research* 26: 123–149.

Klassen, Pamela. 1994. *Going by the Moon and the Stars: Stories of Two Russian Mennonite Women*. Waterloo: Wilfrid Laurier Press.

Kuran, Timur. 1993. "Fundamentalisms and the Economy." In *Fundamentalisms and the State*. Martin Marty and R. Scott Appleby, eds. The Fundamentalisms Project, vol. 3, pp. 289–301. Chicago: University of Chicago Press.

Kwabena, Nketia. 1989. "Musical Interaction in Ritual Events." *Concilium* 202:111–126.

Labouvie-Vief, Gisela, Lucinda Orwell, and Marianna Manion. 1995. "Narratives of Mind, Gender, and the Life Course." *Human Development* 38:239–257.

Langness, L. L., and Gelya Frank. 1985. *Lives: An Anthropological Approach to Biography*. Novato, Calif.: Chandler and Sharp.

Lawless, Elaine. 1988. " 'The Night I Got the Holy Ghost . . . ': Holy Ghost Narratives and the Pentecostal Conversion Process." *Western Folklore* 47:1–20.

Lawrence, Bruce B. 1989. *Defenders of God: The Fundamentalist Revolt against the Modern Age*. San Francisco: Harper and Row.

Leonard, Bill. 1990. *God's Last and Only Hope: The Fragmentation of the Southern Baptist Convention*. Grand Rapids: Eerdmans.

Lerner, Michael, ed. 1991. "PC in Our Time: A Symposium [on political correctness]." *Tikkun* 6:35–57.

Levinas, Emmanuel. 1969. *Totality and Infinity: An Essay on Exteriority*. Pittsburgh: Duquesne University Press.

Lévi-Strauss, Claude. 1966. *The Savage Mind*. Chicago: University of Chicago Press.

Lévy-Bruhl, Lucien. 1925. *How Natives Think*. New York: Knopf.

Lewis, C. S. 1945. *The Screwtape Letters*. Toronto: S. J. Reginald Saunders.

Liemensch, Michael. 1993. *Redeeming America: Piety and Politics in the New Christian Right*. Chapel Hill: University of North Carolina Press.

Linde, Charlotte. 1993. *Life Stories: The Creation of Coherence*. New York: Oxford University Press.

Lithuanian Federal Government Website (September 1999) neris.mii.lt/serveriai/bendra/servers.html

Little, Paul. 1988. *How to Give Away Your Faith*. Downer's Grove, Ill.: InterVarsity Press.

Luckmann, Thomas. 1990. "Shrinking Transcendence, Expanding Religion?" *Sociological Analysis* 51:127–138.

———. 1967. *Invisible Religion: The Problem of Religion in Modern Society*. New York: Macmillan.

Luhmann, Niklas. 1984. *Religious Dogmatics and the Evolution of Societies*. Peter Beyer, trans. New York: Edwin Mellen.

———. 1982. *The Differentiation of Society*. S. Holmes and C. Larmore, trans. New York: Columbia University Press.

Luhrmann, T. M. 1989. *Persuasions of the Witch's Craft: Ritual Magic and Witchcraft in Present-day England*. Oxford: Basil Blackwell.

Luzbetak, Louis J. 1983. "Prospects for a Better Understanding and Closer Cooperation between Anthropologists and Missionaries." In *Missionaries, Anthropologists, and Cultural Change*. D. Whiteman, ed. Studies in Third World Societies 25, pp. 1–54. Williamsburg: Department of Anthropology, College of William and Mary.

MacDonald, Gordon. 1986. "Surviving Leadership in Fast Forward." *Christianity Today*. 30:22–26.

Madsen, Gary E., and Glenn Vernon. 1983. "Maintaining the Faith during College: A Study of Campus Religious Group Participation." *Review of Religious Research* 25: 127–141.

Magnuson, Norris, and William Travis. 1990. *American Evangelicalism: An Annotated Bibliography*. West Cornwall, Conn.: Locust Hill.

Malinowski, Bronislaw. 1922. *Argonauts of the Western Pacific*. London: Routledge.

Mandelbaum, David G. 1973. "The Study of Life History: Gandhi." *Current Anthropology* 14:177–206.

Marcus, George E. 1994. "After the Critique of Ethnography: Faith, Hope, and Charity, but the Greatest of These Is Charity." In *Assessing Cultural Anthropology*. Robert Borofsky, ed., pp. 40–52. New York: McGraw-Hill.

Marcus, George E., and Michael M. Fischer. 1986. *Anthropology as Cultural Critique: An Experimental Moment in the Human Sciences*. Chicago: University of Chicago Press.

Marsden, George. 1991. *Understanding Fundamentalism and Evangelicalism*. Grand Rapids: Eerdmans.

———. 1988. *The Fundamentals: A Testimony to Truth*. New York: Garland.

———. 1982. "Preachers of Paradox: The Religious Right in Historical Perspective." In *Religion and America*. Mary Douglas and Steven Tipton, eds., pp. 150–168. Boston: Beacon.

———. 1980. *Fundamentalism and American Culture: The Shaping of 20th Century Evangelicalism 1870–1925*. New York: Oxford University Press.

Marsden, George, and Bradley Longfield, eds. 1992. *The Secularization of the Academy*. New York: Oxford University Press.

Marshall, Howard. 1992. "Are Evangelicals Fundamentalists?" *Vox Evangelica* 11:7–24.

Martin, Bernice. 1979. "The Sacralization of Disoder: Symbolism in Rock Music." *Sociological Analysis* 40:87–124.

Marty, Martin. 1988. "Morality, Ethics, and the New Christian Right." In *Border Regions of Faith*. Kenneth Aman, ed., pp. 269–275. New York: Orbis.

———. 1987. "Fundamentalism as a Social Phenomenon." In *Piety and Politics: Evangelicals and Fundamentalists Confront the World*. Richard John Neuhaus and Michael Cromartie, eds., pp. 303–320. Washington: Ethics and Public Policy Center.

Marty, Martin, and R. Scott Appleby, eds. 1995 *Fundamentalisms Comprehended*. The Fundamentalisms Project, vol. 5. Chicago: University of Chicago Press.

———. 1994 *Accounting for Fundamentalisms: The Dynamic Character of Movements*. The Fundamentalisms Project, vol. 4. Chicago: University of Chicago Press.

———. 1994. "Introduction." In *Accounting for Fundamentalisms*. Martin Marty and R. Scott Appleby, eds. The Fundamentalisms Project vol. 4, pp. 1–9. Chicago: University of Chicago Press.

———. 1993 *Fundamentalisms and the State: Remaking Polities, Economics, and Militance*. The Fundamentalisms Project, vol. 3. Chicago: University of Chicago Press.

———. 1993 *Fundamentalisms and Society: Reclaiming the Sciences, the Family, and Education*. The Fundamentalisms Project, vol. 3. Chicago: University of Chicago Press.

———. 1991 *Fundamentalisms Observed*. The Fundamentalisms Project, vol. 1. Chicago: University of Chicago Press.

———. 1991. "The Fundamentalisms Project: A User's Guide." In *Fundamentalisms Observed*. Martin Marty and R. Scott Appleby, eds. The Fundamentalisms Project, vol. 1, pp. vii–xiii. Chicago: University of Chicago Press.

Marty, Martin, and Frederick Greenspan, eds. 1988. *Pushing the Faith: Proselytism and Civility in a Pluralist World*. Denver: University of Denver.

Marx, Karl. 1956. *Selected Writings in Sociology and Social Philosophy*. T. B. Bottomore, trans. and ed. New York: McGraw-Hill.

Mathisen, Gerald, and James Mathisen. 1988. "The New Fundamentalism: A Sociorhetorical Approach to Understanding Theoretical Change." *Review of Religious Research* 30:18–32.

Matthews, Robin, and James Steele, eds. 1969. *The Struggle for Canadian Universities*. Toronto: New Press.

Maudlin, Michael G. 1989. "Holy Smoke! The Darkness Is Back: *Christianity Today* Speaks with Frank Peretti." *Christianity Today* 15:58–59.

McAfee Brown, Robert. 1988. "The Religious Right and Political/Economic Conservatism." In *Border Regions of Faith*. K. Aman, ed., pp. 258–263. New York: Orbis.

McCoy, Charles, and Neely McCarter. 1959. *The Gospel on Campus: Rediscovering Evangelism in the Academic Community*. Richmond, Va.: John Knox.

McIntyre, John. 1992. "It's Time to Rejoin the Scientific Establishment: The Need for an Evangelical Presence in Universities." *Perspectives on Science and Christian Faith* 44:124–127.

McKillop, A. B. 1994. *Matters of Mind: The University in Ontario, 1791–1951.* Toronto: University of Toronto Press.

———. 1979. *A Disciplined Intelligence: Critical Inquiry and Canadian Thought in the Victorian Era.* Montreal: McGill-Queens University Press.

McMaster University. 1995. "McMaster University Anti-Discrimination Policy." Approved by McMaster University Senate, 11 October.

McMullin, Ernan, ed. 1985. *Evolution and Creation.* Notre Dame, Ind.: Notre Dame Press.

Miller, Alexander. 1960. *Faith and Learning: Christian Faith and Higher Education in 20th Century America.* New York: N. P.

Miller, Jon. 1993. "Missionaries, Social Change and Resistance to Authority: Notes toward an Understanding of the Relative Autonomy of Religion." *Journal for the Scientific Study of Religion* 32:29–50.

Minneman, Charles, ed. 1970. *Students, Religion, and the Contemporary University.* Ypsilanti: East Michigan University Press.

Mintz, Sidney. 1960. *Worker in the Cane: A Puerto Rican Life History.* New Haven: Yale University Press.

Mirowsky, John, and Catherine Ross. 1995. "Sex Differences in Distress: Real or Artificial?" *American Sociological Review* 60: 449–468.

Morris, Brian. 1987. *Anthropological Studies of Religion: An Introductory Text.* Cambridge: Cambridge University Press.

Morris, Henry and Gary E. Parker. 1982. *What Is Creation Science?* San Diego: Master Book Publishers.

Motz, Arnell, ed. 1990. *Reclaiming a Nation: The Challenge of Re-Evangelizing Canada by the Year 2000.* Richmond, B.C.: Church Leadership Library.

Moulton, Janice. 1983. "A Paradigm of Philosophy: The Adversarial Method." In *Discovering Reality: Feminist Perspectives on Epistemology, Methodology, and the Philosophy of Science.* Sandra Harding and Merrill Hintikka, eds., pp. 49–164. Dordrecht: Reidel.

Musteikas, Antanas. 1988. *The Reformation in Lithuania.* East European Monographs. New York: Columbia University Press.

Myerhoff, Barbara, and Jay Ruby, eds. 1982. *A Crack in the Mirror: Reflexive Perspectives in Anthropology.* Philadelphia: University of Pennsylvania Press.

Narayan, Kirin. 1989. *Saints, Storytellers and Scoundrels: Folk Narrative in Hindu Religious Teaching.* Philadelphia: University of Philadelphia Press.

Nash, Ronald. 1987. *Evangelicals in America: Who They Are, What They Believe.* Nashville: Abingdon.

Neitz, Mary Jo. 1987. *Charisma and Community.* New Brunswick, N.J.: Transaction.

Neuhaus, Richard John, and Michael Cromartie, eds. 1987. *Piety and Politics: Evangelicals and Fundamentalists Confront the World.* Washington, D.C.: Ethics and Public Policy Center.

Nock, David. 1993. "The Organization of Religious Life in Canada." In *The Sociology of Religion.* W. E. Hewitt, ed., pp. 41–64. Toronto: Butterworths.

Noll, Mark A. 1994. *The Scandal of the Evangelical Mind.* Grand Rapids: Eerdmans.

———. 1992. *A History of Christianity in the United States and Canada.* Grand Rapids: Eerdmans.

Norton, H. Wilbert. 1993. "The Student Foreign Missions Fellowship over 55 Years." *International Bulletin of Missionary Research* 17:17–18, 20–21.

Nugent, Christopher. 1983. *Masks of Satan: The Demonic in History.* London: Sheed and Ward.

Okely, Judith. 1992. "Anthropology and Autobiography." In *Anthropology and Autobiography.* J. Okely and H. Callaway, eds., pp. 1–28. London: Routledge.

Osberg, Lars, Fred Wien, and Jan Grude. 1995. *Vanishing Jobs: Canada's Changing Workplaces.* Toronto: James Lorimer.

O'Toole, Roger. 1985. "Society, the Sacred and the Secular: Sociological Observations on the Changing Role of Religion in Canadian Culture." *Canadian Issues* 7:99–117.

Ozorak, Elizabeth Weiss. 1996. "The Power but Not the Glory: How Women Empower Themselves through Religion." *Journal for the Scientific Study of Religion* 35:17–29.

Pagels, Elaine. 1995. *The Origin of Satan.* New York: Random House.

———. 1991. "The Social History of Satan, the 'Intimate Enemy': A Preliminary Sketch." *Harvard Theological Review* 84:105–128.

Patterson, Beverly. 1980. "Finding a Home in the Church: Primitive Baptist Women." In *Diversities of Gifts: Field Studies in Southern Religion.* James Peacock and Ruel Tyson, eds., pp. 61–78. Chicago: University of Illinois Press.

Peacock, James, and Ruel Tyson. 1989. *Pilgrims of Paradox: Calvinism and Experience among the Primitive Baptists of the Blue Ridge.* Washington, D.C.: Smithsonian Institute Press.

Peacock, James, and Ruel Tyson, eds., 1980. *Diversities of Gifts: Field Studies in Southern Religion.* Chicago: University of Illinois Press.

Peek, Charles, George Lowe, and Susan Williams. 1991. "Gender and God's Word: Another Look at Religious Fundamentalism and Sexism." *Social Forces* 69:1205–1221.

Peretti, Frank E. 1986. *This Present Darkness.* Wheaton: Ill.: Crossway Books.

Personal Narratives Group. 1989. "Truths." In *Interpreting Women's Lives: Feminist Theory and Personal Narratives,* Personal Narratives Group, eds., pp. 261–264. Indianapolis: Indiana University Press.

Peshkin, Alan. 1986. *God's Choice: The Total World of a Fundamentalist School.* Chicago: University of Chicago Press.

Pierard, Richard. 1970. *The Unequal Yoke: Evangelical Christianity and Political Conservatism.* Philadelphia: Lippincott.

Pierce, Roland. 1993. "Evangelicals and Gender Roles in the 1990s: 1 Timothy 2:8–15: A Test Case." *Journal of the Evangelical Theological Society* 36:343–355.

Pinnock, Clark, John Hick, Alister E. McGath, R. Douglas Geirett and W. Cary Phillips. 1995. *More Than One Way? Four Views on Salvation in a Pluralistic World.* Grand Rapids: Zondervan.

Placher, William. 1992. "Preaching the Gospel in the Academy and Society." *Theology Today* 49:5–20.

Pohli, Carol Virginia. 1983. "Church Closets and Back Doors: A Feminist View of Moral Majority Women." *Feminist Studies* 9:529–558.

Pool, Robert. 1991. "Postmodern Ethnography?" *Critique of Anthropology* 11:309–331.

Rabinow, Paul. 1977. *Reflections on Fieldwork in Morocco.* Berkeley: University of California Press.

Rambo, Lewis R. 1993. *Understanding Religious Conversion.* New Haven: Yale University Press.

Rawlyk, George. 1996. *Is Jesus Your Personal Saviour? In Search of Canadian Evangel-icalism in Canada in the 1990s.* Kingston: McGill-Queen's University Press.

————. 1992. "Protestant Colleges in Canada: Past and Present." In *The Secularization of the Academy.* George Marsden and Bradley Longfield, eds., pp. 278–302. New York: Oxford University Press.

————. 1988 "A. L. McCrimmon, H. O. Whidden, T. T. Shields, Christian Higher Learning at McMaster University." In *Canadian Baptists and Christian Higher Education.* G. Rawlyk, ed., pp. 31–62. Kingston: McGill-Queen's Press.

Rawlyk, George, ed. 1990. *The Canadian Protestant Experience: 1760–1990.* Burlington, Ont.: Welch.

Rawlyk, George, David Bebbington, and Mark Noll, eds. 1994. *Evangelicalism: Comparative Studies of Popular Protestantism in North America, the British Isles, and Beyond, 1700–1900.* New York: Oxford University Press.

Reimer, Jeffrey, and Deborah Willsie. 1980. "The Campus Bar as a 'Bastard Institution.' " *Mid-American Review of Sociology* 5:61–89.

Robb, John. 1993. "Satan's Tactics in Building and Maintaining His Kingdom of Darkness." *International Journal of Frontier Missions* 10:173–184.

Roof, Wade Clark. 1996. "God Is in the Details: Reflections on Religion's Public Presence in the United States in the Mid-1990s." *Sociology of Religion* 57:149–162.

————. 1993. *A Generation of Seekers.* San Francisco: Harper San Francisco.

Rosaldo, Renato. 1989. *Culture and Truth: The Remaking of Social Analysis.* Boston: Beacon.

Rosenwald, George. 1992. "Conclusion: Reflections on Narrative Self-Understanding." In *Storied Lives: The Cultural Politics of Self-Understanding.* George Rosenwald and Richard Ochberg, eds. pp. 265–290. London: Yale University Press.

Russell, Jeffrey Burton. 1988. *The Prince of Darkness: Radical Evil and the Power of Good in History.* Ithaca: Cornell University Press.

Sahgal, Gita, and Nira Yuval-Davis, eds. 1992. *Refusing Holy Orders: Women and Fundamentalism in Britain.* London: Virago.

Said, Edward. 1978. *Orientalism.* New York: Vintage.

Salts, Connie. 1994. "Attitudes toward Marriage and Premarital Sexual Activity of College Freshmen." *Adolescence* 29:775–779.

Schofthaler, Traugot. 1980. "Systems Theory in the Study of Religion in German-Speaking Countries: The Religious Paradoxes of Niklas Luhmann." *Social Compass* 27:63–74.

Schultze, Quentin, ed. 1991. *Dancing in the Dark: Youth, Popular Culture and the Electronic Media.* Grand Rapids: Eerdmans.

Senn, Alfred. 1959. *The Emergence of Modern Lithuania.* New York: Columbia University Press.

Shelley, Bruce. 1986. "The Rise of Evangelical Youth Movements." *Fides et Historia* 18: 45–63.

Sidey, Kenneth. 1991. "Twentysomething Missionaries: IVCF's Urbana Missions Conference." *Christianity Today* 35:52–55.

Simpson, John H. 1996. " 'The Great Reversal': Selves, Communities, and the Global System." *Sociology of Religion* 57:115–125.

————. 1994. "The Mood of America in the 1980s: Some Further Observations on Sociomoral Issues." *Sociology of Religion* 55:291–305.

————. 1986. "Globalization, the New Religious Right, and the Politics of the Body." *Psychohistory Review* 15:59–75.

————. 1983. "Moral Issues and Status Politics." In *The New Christian Right: Mobili-*

zation and Legitimation. Robert Wuthnow and Robert Liebman, eds., pp. 188–207. Hawthorne, NY: Aldine.

Smith, Harry. 1968. *Secularization and the University.* Richmond, Va: John Knox.

Smith, Page. 1990. *Killing the Spirit: Higher Education in America.* New York: Viking.

Snow, David, and Richard Machalek. 1984. "The Sociology of Conversion." *Annual Review of Sociology* 10:167–190.

———. 1982. "On the Presumed Fragility of Unconventional Beliefs." *Journal for the Scientific Study of Religion* 21:15–26.

Spanier, Bonnie. 1984. "The Natural Sciences: Casting a Critical Eye on 'Objectivity.' " In *Toward a Balanced Curriculum: A Sourcebook for Initiating Gender Integration Projects.* Alexander Bloom, Darlene Boroviak, and Bonnie Spanier, eds., pp. 49–56. Cambridge: Schenkman.

Spretnak, Charlene. 1982. "The Christian Right's 'Holy War' against Feminism." In *The Politics of Women's Spirituality.* C. Spretnak, ed., pp. xi–xxx. Garden City, N.Y.: Anchor.

Stacey, Judith, and Susan E. Gerard. 1990. " 'We are not doormats': The Influence of Feminism on Contemporary Evangelicals in the United States." In *Uncertain Terms: Negotiating Gender in American Culture.* Faye Ginsburg and Anna Lowenhaupt Tsing, eds., pp. 98–117. Boston: Beacon.

Stackhouse, John. 1993. *Canadian Evangelicalism in the 20th Century: An Introduction to Its Character.* Toronto: University of Toronto Press.

———. 1991. "The Emergence of a Fellowship: Canadian Evangelism in the 20th Century." *Church History* 60:247–262.

———. 1988. "Canadian Evangelicalism since World War I." Ph.D. dissertation, University of Chicago.

Stafford, Tim. 1992. "Campus Christians and the New Thought Police." *Christianity Today* 36:15–20.

Staples, Clifford, and Armand Mauss. 1987. "Conversion or Commitment? A Reassessment of the Snow and Machalek Approach to the Study of Conversion." *Journal for the Scientific Study of Religion* 26:133–147.

Stark, Rodney, and William Bainbridge. 1985. *The Future of Religion.* Berkeley: University of California Press.

Steel, Brent, Rebecca Warner, and Blair Strieber. 1992. "Post-Materialist Values and Support for Feminism among Canadian and American Men and Women." *Western Political Quarterly* 45:339–353.

Stoller, Paul. 1989. *The Fusion of the Worlds: An Ethnography of Possession among the Songhay of Niger.* Chicago: University of Chicago Press.

Stout, Jeffrey. 1988. *Ethics after Babel: The Languages of Morals and Their Discontents.* Boston: Beacon.

Straub, Gerard Thomas. 1988. *Salvation for Sale: An Insider's View of Pat Robertson,* Buffalo: Prometheus.

Strozier, Charles B. 1994. *Apocalypse: On the Psychology of Fundamentalism in America.* Boston: Beacon.

Sutlive, Vinson. 1983. "Anthropologists and Missionaries: Eternal Enemies or Colleagues in Disguise." In *Missionaries, Anthropologists, and Cultural Change.* D. Whiteman, ed. Studies in Third World Societies, 25, pp. 55–90. Williamsburg: Department of Anthropology, College of William and Mary.

Sutton, Brett. 1980. "Speech, Chant, and Song: Patterns of Language and Activity in a Southern Church." In *Diversities of Gifts: Field Studies in Southern Religion.* James Peacock and Ruel Tyson, eds., pp. 157–176. Chicago: University of Illinois Press.

Swatos, William. 1983. "Enchantment and Disenchantment in Modernity: The Significance of 'Religion' as a Sociological Category." *Sociological Analysis* 44:321–337.

Swidler, Leonard. 1987. "Jesus Was a Feminist." In *Border Regions of Faith: An Anthology of Religion and Social Change*. Kenneth Aman, ed., pp. 30–38. New York: Orbis.

Tapper, Richard, and Nancy Tapper. 1987. "Thank God We're Secular: Aspects of Fundamentalism in a Turkish Town." In *Studies in Religious Fundamentalism*. Lionel Caplan, ed., pp. 51–78. Albany: State University of New York Press.

Taylor, Charles. 1991. *The Malaise of Modernity*. Concord, Ont.: Anansi.

Tedlock, Dennis. 1983. *The Spoken Word and the Work of Interpretation*. Philadelphia: University of Pennsylvania Press.

Thomas, William I., and Florian Znaniecki. 1918. *The Polish Peasant in Europe and America*. Chicago: University of Chicago Press.

Thorogood, Bernard. 1993. "Say Goodbye to the Empire Model." *International Review of Missions* 82:297–304.

Tidball, Derek. 1994. *Who Are the Evangelicals? Tracing the Root of the Modern Movement*. London: Marshall Pickering.

Tillich, Paul. 1952. *The Courage to Be*. New Haven: Yale University Press.

Tippett, A. R. 1983. "Parallaxis in Missiology: To Use or Abuse." In *Missionaries, Anthropologists, and Cultural Change*. D. Whiteman, ed. Studies in Third World Societies, 25, pp. 91–152. Williamsburg: Department of Anthropology, College of William and Mary.

Tipton, Steven, and Mary Douglas, eds. 1983. *Religion and American Spiritual Life in a Secular Age*. Boston: Beacon.

Titon, Jeff Todd. 1988. *Powerhouse for God: Speech, Chant, and Song in an Appalachian Baptist Church*. Austin, Tex.: University of Austin Press.

Toelken, Barre. 1979. *The Dynamics of Folklore*. Boston: Houghton Mifflin.

Turner, Victor. 1974. *Dramas, Fields, and Metaphors: Symbolic Action in Human Society*. Ithaca: Cornell University Press.

———. 1969. *The Ritual Process*. Ithaca: Cornell University Press.

Tyler, Stephen A. 1986. "Post-Modern Ethnography: From Document of the Occult to Occult Document." In *Writing Culture: The Poetics and Politics of Ethnography*. James Clifford and George Marcus, eds., pp. 122–140. Berkeley: University of California Press.

United States Department of Health and Human Services. 1993. "Depression in Primary Care: Detection, Diagnosis, and Treatment." *Journal of Psychosocial Nursing* 31: 19–28.

Van Leeuwan, Mary Stewart. 1988. "North American Evangelicalism and the Social Sciences: A Historical and Critical Appraisal." *Perspectives on Science and Christian Faith*. 40:194–203.

Vowles, Andrew. 1996. "Say Good-Bye to the Old World." *McMaster Times* 12:3.

Wagner, Melinda Bollar. 1990. *God's Schools: Choice and Compromise in American Schools*. New Brunswick, N.J.: Rutgers University Press.

Walker, Andrew. 1987. *Enemy Territory: The Christian Struggle for the Modern World*. Grand Rapids: Zondervan.

Wallace, Anthony. 1966. *Religion: An Anthropological View*. New York: Random House.

Warner, R. Stephen. 1997a. "Religion, Boundaries, and Bridges." *Sociology of Religion* 58:217–238.

———. 1997b. "Approaching Religious Diversity." *Sociology of Religion* 59:193–216.

———. 1988. *New Wine in Old Wineskins: Evangelicals and Liberals in a Small Town Church*. Berkeley: University of California Press.

Watson, Lawrence C., and Maria-Barbara Watson-Franke. 1985. *Interpreting Life Histories: An Anthropological Inquiry*. New Brunswick, N.J.: Rutgers University Press.

Weber, Max. 1948. *From Max Weber: Essays in Sociology*. H. H. Gerth and C. W. Mills, trans. and eds. London: Routledge and Kegan.

Weiss Ozarak, Elizabeth. 1996. "The Power but Not the Glory: How Women Empower Themselves through Religion." *Journal for the Scientific Study of Religion* 35:17–29.

Whitehead, Harriet. 1987. *Renunciation and Reformulation: A Study of Conversion in an American Sect*. Ithaca: Cornell University Press.

Wilcox, Clyde. 1994. "Premillennialists at the Millennium: Some Reflections on the Christian Right in the Twenty-first Century." *Sociology of Religion* 55:243–261.

———. 1992. *God's Warriors: The Christian Right in Twentieth Century America*. Baltimore: Johns Hopkins University Press.

———. 1989. "Feminism and Anti-Feminism among Evangelical Women." *Western Political Quarterly* 42:147–160.

Wilmsen, Edwin, and Patrick McAllister. 1996. *The Politics of Difference: Ethnic Premises in a World of Power*. Chicago: University of Chicago Press.

Wilson, Bryan. 1992. "Reflections on a Many-Sided Controversy." In *Religion and Modernization: Sociologists and Historians Debate the Secularization Thesis*. Steve Bruce, ed., pp. 198–209. New York: Macmillan.

———. 1985. "Secularization: The Inherited Model." In *The Sacred in a Secular Age*. Phillip E. Hammond, ed., pp. 9–20. Berkeley: University of California Press.

Wolf, Margery. 1992. *A Thrice-Told Tale: Feminism, Postmodernism, and Ethnographic Responsibility*. Stanford, Calif.: Stanford University Press.

Woodruff, J. Timothy. 1986. "Reference Groups, Religiosity, and Premarital Sexual Behaviour." *Journal for the Scientific Study of Religion* 25:436–60.

Wulf, Jean, David Prentice, Donna Hansum, Archie Ferrar, and Bernard Spilka. 1984. "Religiosity and Sexual Attitudes and Behaviour among Evangelical Christian Singles." *Review of Religious Research* 26:119–131.

Wuthnow, Robert. 1989. *The Struggle for America's Soul: Evangelicals, Liberals, and Secularism*. Grand Rapids: Eerdmans.

———. 1988. *The Restructuring of American Religion: Society and Faith since World War II*. Princeton: Princeton University Press.

Wuthnow, Robert, and C. Y. Glock. 1973. "Religious Loyalty, Defection and Experimentation among College Youth." *Journal for the Scientific Study of Religion* 12:157–180.

Wuthnow, Robert, and Matthew P. Lawson. 1994. "Sources of Christian Fundamentalism in the United States." In *Accounting for Fundamentalisms*. Martin Marty and R. Scott Appleby, eds. The Fundamentalisms Project, vol. 4, pp. 18–56. Chicago: University of Chicago Press.

Wuthnow, Robert, and Robert Liebman, eds. 1983. *The New Christian Right: Mobilization and Legitimation*. Hawthorne, N.Y.: Aldine.

Index

abstinence, 84

adversarialism, in university teaching, 94

alcohol, 23, 31, 45, 46, 82, 85, 87, 140, 142, 144, 148

alienation, definition of, 163 n.1
    self-imposed, 88

Almond, Gabriel, 149

ambivalence, strategy of, 99, 100, 145, 148

Ammerman, Nancy T., 112, 113, 137, 138, 178 n.1, 179 n.8, 146, 165 n.16,173 n.25, 175 n.14, 181 n.27

angels, 59
    influence on human realm, 106, 107, 108, 170 n.9
    as mediators of God's will, 113
    stereotypical depictions of, 105

apostolic self-understanding, 49, 133, 135, 141

Appleby, R. Scott, 149

Badone, Ellen, 80, 179 n.10

Balmer, Randall, 25, 92, 175 n.14

Beavis and Butthead, 73

Behar, Ruth, 159 n.23

Bellous, Joyce, 93

Bendroth, Margaret L., 92

Berger, Peter, 18, 112, 123, 135, 143, 154 n.39, 155 n.47, 172 n.17, 180 n.19

bias against God, 19, 77, 80, 81, 118, 128, 142

Bibby, Reginald, 18–19, 61, 71, 155 n.40, 155 n.41, 155 n.42., 155 n.43

Booth, Wayne, 55, 171 n.9

boundary maintenance, 88, 132

bricoleurs, IVCF students as, 147

bridge and fortress strategies, in conjunction, 143, 145

bridge rhetoric, 64–68

bridge strategy, 22, 64, 89, 101, 116, 137, 138, 141, 143, 145

Brown, Karen McCarthy, 92

Buff. *See* Cox, Elizabeth "Buff"

Byle Bruland, Esther, 92

capitalism and evangelicalism, 123
Carole, 44–48
Children of God, 66, 67
Christian, as a limited description, 47,
    49, 59, 61–64, 88
Christianese, 56, 61, 67
Church at the John, 3–5, 41, 87, 96, 151
    n.4
Churchianity vs. Christianity, 57, 99
Clifford, James, 7
Code, Lorraine, 94
cognitive bargaining, 18, 22, 82, 140, 145,
    165 n.14, 180 n.19
cognitive contamination, 141, 143, 154
    n.39, 21, 165 n.17, 180 n.19
cognitive dissonance, 4, 21, 39, 83
cognitive retrenchment, 22
collective effervescence, 4, 57
communitas, 87, 88
contracts, negotiation of, 21, 22, 77, 79,
    82, 86, 88, 89, 93, 100, 135, 137, 139–
    150, 155 n.47,
conversion, 34, 40, 44, 46, 50, 138, 159
    n.20
  as a goal of witnessing, 122, 124, 126,
    127, 130, 132, 138, 144, 177 n.36, 177
    n.38, 177 n.39
  second, 34, 40, 50
coping strategy, evangelical belief as a,
    76, 167 n.39, 147
Coupland, Douglas, 70, 73, 89
Cox, Elizabeth "Buff" (IVCF staff
    worker), 5, 9, 21, 31, 32, 41, 57, 91,
    98, 99, 107, 123, 128, 149, 154 n.26,
    165 n.19
Cox, Harvey, 115, 170 n.4, 170 n.6
creationism, 78–82, 141, 143, 150

damnation, Satan's role in, 117
demons
  influence on human realm, 106, 107,
    108, 170 n.9
  as mediators of Satan's efforts, 113
  stereotypical depictions of, 106
depression, clinical, 108, 171 n.10
devotions, 108, 126
dialogue theology, 124, 128, 175 n.17, 175
    n.18
difference, definition of, 163 n.1
difference, in a positive sense, 72

differentiation, theory of, 17
discipling, 33, 59
disenchantment of world, 114, 115, 121
dispensationalism, 116
Dobson, James, 16
dramatic performances, 54, 59, 66, 118,
    160 n.8, 176
  Church at the John, 87
  in Lithuania, 126, 131, 132, 136
drunkenness. *See* alcohol
dualism, 49, 58, 59, 64, 81, 113, 116
Durkheim, Émile, 4, 17, 57

economic climate facing IVCF students,
    72–74
economy, Lithuanian, 123
education and religiosity, correlation, 139
elective parochial, 88, 150
environmentalism, 130
estrangement, definition of, 163 n.1
ethnography, as a methodology, 7–9, 26,
    27
evangelical, definition of, 10–12, 92
evolutionary theory, challenges of, 23, 32,
    78, 111, 140–144, 148 , 156 n.48
executive committee, 41, 151 n.4
existence of God, 76

Fathergod, 66, 67, 110
feminism, 11, 49, 78, 91–95, 98, 114, 140
Fernandez, James, 54, 56, 63
filters, as the means to negotiate
    contracts, 79, 82, 140, 141, 144
fortress rhetoric, 59–64, 81
fortress strategy, definition of, 22, 59, 68,
    88, 89, 115, 116, 137, 141, 145, 165 n.15
fragmentation, theory of, 18–19
frame intrusion, 20, 137
Frankel, Gail, 108
Freud, Sigmund, 50, 112, 115, 141
Friday lunch, 119
Friends, 144
friendship evangelism, 87, 124, 128, 130,
    138, 166 n.32
Fundamentalisms Project, 149, 153 n.20
fundamentalist, definition of, 10–12, 92,
    154 n.26
fundamentalist economics, 123

Gabrielle, 28–33, 41, 109, 112, 125, 129, 142, 177 n.40

gatekeepers, 5, 32, 124

Gauvreau, Michael, 121, 143

Geertz, Clifford, 7

gender differences and learning styles, 94

general undergraduate estrangement, 72–74, 77

generation X, 73, 74, 89, 164 n.8

ghetto, Christian, 22, 23, 139

globalization, 123, 148

glossolalia (speaking in tongues), 161 n.13

God Scale, 9

God's plan for IVCF students' lives, 74, 113, 131, 172 n.19

God's will. *See* God's plan

Graham, Billy, 174 n.10

Great Commission (mt 28:19), 119, 122, 133, 136, 138

Guelich, Robert, 118

Hammond, Phillip, 22, 23, 137, 138, 139

Harding, Susan, 34, 53, 58, 68, 116, 117, 146, 159 n.18, 160 n.3

Holy Spirit, 38, 39, 41, 130, 176 n.28

homosexuality, 23, 79, 140, 142

How to Give Away Your Faith, small group, 64, 122, 127, 131

human responsibility, 117

Hunter, James, 14, 22, 23

Iannaccone, Laurence, 148

Ingram, Jay, 20, 128, 130,133, 137

intellectual otherness/alienation, 78–82, 140

intercessory prayers, 173 n.28

International Fellowship of Evangelical Students (IFES), 123, 125

IVCF, history of, 10, 17

IVCF, Statement of Purpose, 12

Jesus, as judge, father, teacher (for men), 97

Jesus, as lover (for women), 96, 97, 100, 168, n.16

"just" as a rhetorical strategy, 67

Kapchan, Deborah, 54, 160 n.3

Kingdom of God, 66, 67, 162 n.28

Kuran, Timur, 123

Laws, Curtis Lee, 11

learning styles, gender differences in, 94

Lévi-Strauss, Claude, 147

Lewis, C. S., 103

Lietuvos, Krikščionių Studentų Bendrija (LKSB), 124, 128

life history, as a methodology, 27, 52, 156 n.1, 156 n.2, 157 n.3, 157 n.5, 159 n.23

liminality, 87, 149, 167 n.34

Linde, Charlotte, 39

Lithuania mission 1996, 32–33, 43, 49, 58, 83, 108, 161 n.13

  details of country and mission field, 122–124, 174 n.11

  dramatic performances in, 58

Little, Paul, 63, 65, 122, 127

logical consistency, 148

Luhmann, Niklas, 17

Luhrmann, T. M., 148

lust, 85, 102, 106, 108

male dominance in evangelicalism, 98

Mandelbaum, David, 27

Marsden, George, 10–12, 76, 154 n.35

Marty, Martin, 116, 175 n.14

Marx, Karl, 115, 163 n.1

McMaster University, history of, 15–17

membership, characteristics of, 4, 6, 90, 94, 151 n.1, 162 n.23, 166 n. 25

missionary work. *See* witnessing

moral permissivism, 78, 95, 115, 137, 140

Moulton, Janice, 94

Narayan, Kirin, 180 n.19

negotiation, between individuals and groups, 72, 77, 82, 86, 147

new Christians, 36, 48

new age movement, 104, 110, 114, 170 n.5

Noll, Mark, 81, 130, 178 n.6, 178 n.7

non-Christian, 59, 61–64, 67

NSLC (National Student Leadership Conference), 35, 36, 41

objectivism, in university teaching, 94, 100

occasional apostles, 133, 144

paganism, 120

parallel institution, IVCF as a, 85, 86, 149

patriarchy, 92, 99

Patterson, Beverly, 98

Pentecostalism, influence of, 6, 114, 152
n.8, 161 n.13
roots of, 161 n.13

Peretti, Frank E. 104, 105, 170 n.6, 170
n.7, 170 n.8
popularity of, 104, 170 n.7, 170 n8, 171,
n.12

personal relationship with God, 10–12, 49,
61–63, 79, 112, 120, 123, 124, 131, 148

Pinnock, Clark, 19, 62, 77, 80, 81, 88, 118,
128, 142, 165 n.21

plausibility maintenance, 112, 135

pluralism, 71, 78, 80, 81, 110, 137, 139, 165
n.21

political affiliations of members, 11, 154
n.25

prayer, 86, 88, 99, 67, 105, 108, 110, 125,
129, 133, 137, 142, 170 n.3 172 n.19,
176 n.26
as means of fighting Satan, 105, 107,
109–111, 117, 118, 126, 134, 135, 170
n.3, 171 n.13, 172, n.19, 173 n.28

principalities and powers, 102

profanity, 64, 65, 162 n.27

Rawlyk, George, 13, 15, 19, 20, 61, 77, 121,
174 n.5, 174 n.6

reductionism, as a tendency in social
scientific research, 51, 76, 111, 164
n.9

reenchantment of the world, 118

relativism, 23, 71, 78, 110, 140

remnant, the, 116, 145

residence life at McMaster, 40, 72, 84,
85, 87–89, 140

rhetoric 49, 53–69
as essentially uniform, 56–57, 118, 128,
160 n.10, 161 n.12, 161 n.13
and the insinuation into the
subliminal mind, 58, 162 n.26
pitfalls in interpretation of, 57
as representation of beliefs, 56, 142, 160
n.9
strategy of substitution, 64–66

ritualized events, Church at the John as
a, 87, 88, 166 n.33

rituals of status reversal, 87

Roman Catholics, 62–63, 124, 154 n.28,
162 n.23

Russell, Jeffrey Burton, 103, 112, 115

sacred canopy, 112, 123

Said, Edward, 7

saints, 116

salvation, 60, 56, 84, 116, 137

Satan, interpretations of his prominence
in IVCF discourse, 111–117
as afflicting all people, 117, 144
and anxiety, 171 n.13
in biblical studies, 103, 112, 170 n.2
and the challenge to common
understandings of autonomy, 115
and the challenge to common
understandings of causality, 115
and clinical depression, 108, 171 n.10
and the control of public education,
114
and deception, 109–111, 172 n.16
as metaphor, 103, 104, 115, 170 n.4
in new age movement, 104, 110, 114,
115, 170 n.5
and other religions, 110
as part of explanation of suffering, 112,
146
as part of response to secularization,
113, 118
in rhetoric, 57, 135
and temptation, 107, 108

saved. *See* salvation

scientific method, challenges of, 156
n.48, 78

Scottish common-sense philosophy, 153
n.23

secularization, 12–20, 77, 80, 86, 92, 113,
114, 121, 139, 146, 150, 164 n.12, 178n.2

Seinfeld, 73, 144, 179 n.14

selectively permeable membrane, 23, 59,
79, 87, 88, 115, 140–145

self-sufficiency, as a danger, 79, 110

semi-permeable membrane. *See*
selectively permeable membrane

semiotics, 56

sexuality, 21, 23, 45–46, 48, 82, 84–85, 79,
87, 96, 140, 144, , 158 n.17, 167 n.38,
181 n.28

Simon, 33–37, 78, 85, 105, 125, 172 n.18,
177 n.40, 179 n.13

Simpson, John H., 11, 175 n.16
Sivan, Emmanuel, 149
slain in the spirit, 161 n.13
small group, 64, 61, 100, 110, 122, 131
social alienation/otherness, 82–88, 140
social work students in IVCF, 79
songs, lyrics in, 61, 58, 66, 97, 116, 126, 129
songs, ways of interpreting, 58
speaking in tongues. *See* glossolalia.
specific evangelical estrangement, 77
specific female alienation, 94
spiritual realm
  influence on human realm, 106, 107, 170 n.9
  See also angels, demons, Satan and God
spiritual walk, 36, 49, 108, 146
spiritual warfare, 103, 104, 107, 109–111, 134, 170 n.4, 175 n.22
splitting, 112
St. Petersburg, 125
Stacey, Judith, 93, 96
Stackhouse, John, 11, 57, 154 n.27, 162 n.23, 174 n.5
Steve, 37–44, 50, 51, 74, 83, 85, 125, 130, 134, 159 n.21,162 n.24, 175 n.15, 177 n.40
Stout, Jeffrey, 154 n.38
Stow, Anthony, 61
Strozier, Charles, 50, 96, 159 n.19
Sutton, Brett, 57
swearing, 64, 65, 162 n.27

Tedlock, Dennis, 55
temptation, 107, 108
testimonials, 60, 61, 126, 136, 159 n.21, 172 n.19
The Simpsons, 73
The Screwtape Letters, 103
theodicy, 112, 129, 172 n.17
This Present Darkness, 104–118
threats, cognitive, 47, 140–143
threats, moral, 140–145, 147
Titan, Jeff Todd, 57, 147, 160 n.8
total institution, 21
transdenominational evangelicalism, 57
tribalism, 148, vii

turf, 23, 87, 88, 101, 135, 145
Turner, Victor, 54, 87, 149, 161 n.13

Unitarian Universalism, 9–10, 117, 127, 153 n.14
United Church of Canada, 152 n.5, 44, 48
Urbana conference, Urbana, Illinois, 43

values crisis in North America, 114

Wagner, Melinda, 146, 160 n.5, 146
Warner, Stephen, 88, 149, 150, 181 n.27
Weber, Max, 112, 114
well-being and its relationship to religious involvement, 71, 75, 108
Whidden, Chancellor, 16
Wilcox, Clyde, 164 n.11
witnessing, 65 120, 126
  dramatic performances in, 126, 131, 132
  emphasis on emotional content, 39, 128–130, 135, 176 n.29
  God's plan in, 123, 131, 132
  in Hamilton, 120, 122
  history and critique of , 121, 124, 129, 174 n.2
  and mission work, 122
  to professions and peers, 122
  Satan and, 134
  self-understanding during, 132–135
  strategies for, 127, 176 n.27
  testimonials in, 126
women's roles, 31, 32, 36, 47, 49
  as alternative means of exerting influence, 98
  in Bible, 90, 93, 98, 99
  in communion, 169 n.20
  in evangelicalism in general, 90, 167 n.2, 167 n.3, 168 n.9
  in IVCF, male acceptance of, 98, 99
  IVCF as a means of allowing temporary ambiguity in, 99, 100, 145, 148
  as ministers, 91, 99, 148
  as subversive, 97, 100
world's turf, 23, 87, 88, 101
Wuthnow, Robert, 23, 80, 139, 146, 147

X Files, 73

young earth hypothesis, 32